Albrecht Behmel, Kelly Neudorfer

The Foreigner's Guide to German Universities

Origin, Meaning, and Use of Terms and Expressions in Everyday University Life

Albrecht Behmel, Kelly Neudorfer

THE FOREIGNER'S GUIDE TO GERMAN UNIVERSITIES

Origin, Meaning, and Use of Terms and Expressions
in Everyday University Life

ibidem-Verlag
Stuttgart

Bibliografische Information der Deutschen Nationalbibliothek
Die Deutsche Nationalbibliothek verzeichnet diese Publikation in der
Deutschen Nationalbibliografie; detaillierte bibliografische Daten sind
im Internet über http://dnb.d-nb.de abrufbar.

Bibliographic information published by the Deutsche Nationalbibliothek
Die Deutsche Nationalbibliothek lists this publication in the Deutsche
Nationalbibliografie; detailed bibliographic data are available in the Internet at
http://dnb.d-nb.de.

Coverabbildung: Die „Kommode" in Berlin am Bebelplatz. Foto: Christian Thiele.
Quelle: http://commons.wikimedia.org/wiki/File:Berlin_kommode.jpg?uselang=de.
Lizenziert unter Creative Commons-Lizenz Namensnennung 2.5
(s. http://creativecommons.org/licenses/by/2.5/deed.de).

Gedruckt auf alterungsbeständigem, säurefreien Papier
Printed on acid-free paper

ISBN-13: 978-3-8382-0832-9

© *ibidem*-Verlag

Stuttgart 2016

Alle Rechte vorbehalten

Das Werk einschließlich aller seiner Teile ist urheberrechtlich geschützt. Jede Verwertung
außerhalb der engen Grenzen des Urheberrechtsgesetzes ist ohne Zustimmung des Verlages
unzulässig und strafbar. Dies gilt insbesondere für Vervielfältigungen,
Übersetzungen, Mikroverfilmungen und elektronische Speicherformen sowie die
Einspeicherung und Verarbeitung in elektronischen Systemen.

All rights reserved. No part of this publication may be reproduced, stored in or introduced into a
retrieval system, or transmitted, in any form, or by any means (electronical, mechanical,
photocopying, recording or otherwise) without the prior written permission of the publisher. Any
person who does any unauthorized act in relation to this publication may be liable to criminal
prosecution and civil claims for damages.

Printed in Germany

For Lilo and Martin

Foreword

Everyday life at German universities is characterized by a particular jargon that does not always make it easy for newcomers to quickly and reliably find their way around. This language has developed over time and is primarily a mix of Greek-Latin words such as *Dekan, Doktor,* or *Seminar*, of German bureaucratic words such as *Hochschulrektorenkonferenz* and, finally, of vocabulary drawn from European educational policies with terms like *Kredit, Master, Bologna,* or *Modul*.

This dictionary is designed to aid foreign students in orienting themselves at German universities; it is meant to provide practical assistance in completing academic tasks and give insights into academic terms and ways of thinking. Both those who are familiar with the German academic world and those who are looking back can also draw nearer to the time they spent abroad.

The entries in this lexicon have been collected such that they mostly fall into one of the following six main areas:

1. **Studying and learning** (e.g. *Bibliographie, Hausarbeit, Prüfungsangst, Recherche*)
2. **Institutions** (e.g. *CHE, DFG, DSW, Erasmus-Programm, Kölner Runde*)
3. **University politics** (e.g. *Bund-Länder-Kommission, ECTS, Präsidialverfassung*)
4. **Academic operations and administration** (e.g. *Drittmittel, Ranking, Sokal-Affäre, Venia Legendi*)
5. **University history** (e.g. *Augenwischerei, Pedell, Rektorkette, Siegel*)
6. **Academic ways of thinking** (e.g. *Falsifikation, Versuch und Irrtum, Weltbild*)

Because academic abbreviations are so prevalent, special lists of abbreviations have been included in the annexes (one for those found in academic publications and one for those related to matters of university life such as university institutions or the search for accommodations).

Since a collection of general university terms does not allow for a clear separation of terminology in individual subject jargons or in the various regions or universities, or in the German-language countries of Austria, Switzerland, and Germany, it is unfortunately next to impossible to avoid omissions and ambivalences in the catalog.

Suggestions and comments from readers about entries that should be taken into consideration in the future are therefore always most welcome.

The authors,

Freudenstadt im Schwarzwald, 2012

Kirchentellinsfurt, 2016

Tips for readers

Because this reference work is intended for foreign students to better understand the German university terms, all entries are given first in German. All words are in alphabetical order, whereby umlauts are not split in the word. Possible English translations are given in parentheses directly after the German entry. There is often not an exact corresponding term in English, and in these cases several English terms giving similar meanings may be listed or simply a literal translation of the German word (e.g. Abendstudium (evening studies)). If there is no equivalent in English for the term in English, then "no direct translation" is written in place of the translation. In these cases, the entry describes the term. Multiple meanings of a term are marked and separated by Arabic numerals.

In order to understand the context, important references to additional articles are marked with an arrow if the content will give more information. The references with arrows noted in parentheses at the end of some entries usually do not mark synonyms but related areas. Synonyms are marked with a preceding "Also:". They have been left in German so that the reader knows what alternative terms might be used.

The tilde (~) stands for the entry word in all of its forms.

Entries from languages other than German are put in italics, especially when their pronunciation is different from the German or if it is a relatively new term, for example *Paper*. The following abbreviations are used depending on the language of origin: Lat. = Latin, Greek = Greek, French = French, Ital. = Italian. A brief etymological explanation is given for terms with Latin or Greek origin if these are of interest (e.g. Gremium. Lat. *gremium* = lap, bosom). If the German pronunciation differs from English or French (e.g. Senat) or in the case of uncommon words (e.g. Rara), the emphasized syllable is underlined to assist pronunciation. When listing contents of legal documents, if the section is missing, then that part of the law has since been removed.

Terminological differences in Germany, Austria, and Switzerland are taken into account. In some cases notes are also made on American words or Anglicisms, e.g. "senior," if the German word has an entirely different meaning. Some entries are supported with current figures from the German Federal Statistics Office (www.destatis.de) or an internet address is given.

Table of Contents

Foreword VII

Tips for readers IX

Alphabetic part 1

Annex 181

Lists of Universities 191

Universities in Germany 193

Universities in Austria 201

Universities in Switzerland 203

List of common subjects 205

Further Literature 215

A

Abbildungsnachweis (picture credits) →Bildnachweis

Abendstudium (evening studies, evening classes) Continuing education offer from universities, usually for professionals to obtain an academic degree while continuing their career (→Studium Generale).

Abgabetermin (deadline, submission deadline) The latest point in time by which the manuscript (→Manuskript) of an academic work must be delivered to the examiner, examinations office, editor, or publisher (→Prüfer, →Prüfungsamt, →Korrektor, or Verlagslektor). The ~ for a seminar paper or final thesis is relevant for obtaining a degree and is either set individually by the instructor (→Dozent) or in general by the examination regulations.

Abitur (German upper-level secondary school diploma) Lat. *abire* = depart. Highest possible secondary school leaving certificate in Germany. The ~ is the same as a higher education entrance qualification, which allows a person to study at a higher education institution. In earlier times, in all German-speaking areas the ~ was called the Matura, but today this is only the case in Austria, Liechtenstein, and Switzerland, where it is called the Maturität. Due to the cultural sovereignty of the Bundesländer, there are certain regional differences in terms of how the individual ~ examinations are carried out and their quality. Originally, the universities could decide on their own whether the applicants were eligible for admission, but in 1788, university entrance qualification was regulated by the Abitur – first in Prussia – and the competency for making this decision was thus transferred from the universities to the upper-level secondary schools (Gymnasien).

Abiturient (person with an Abitur) Person who has passed the →Abitur and is therefore qualified to start studying at a university (→Hochschule), usually used as a term for a graduate from an upper-level secondary school (Gymnasium) before starting university, vocational training, or military service.

Abkürzungsverzeichnis (List of abbreviations) Part of the annex (→Anhang) of academic works in which all abbreviations used are listed. Typically, works differentiate between abbreviations for academic journals as sources and the linguistic-terminological abbreviations within texts.

Abschluss (degree) Successful completion of studies in contrast to dropping out (→Studienabbruch). The following types of degrees exist: (University) →Bachelor's, →Master's, →Diplom, and →Magister, doctorate (→Promotion), teaching degree (→Lehramt), artistic degrees, degrees from universities of applied science, and religious degrees. Students who have passed their final examinations are called graduates (→Absolventen).

Each year at German universities, more than 200,000 successful degree examinations are completed. Most are completed in the subjects of social sciences, law, business, and economics (34% total), while only around 9% of degrees are in medicine.

Abschlussarbeit (final thesis, dissertation) State examination (→Examen), →Diplom, →Magister, →Bachelor's, or →Master's thesis. A longer academic text of up to 100 pages. Its submission to the examinations office typically also marks the end of studies. In combination with an oral examination, the academic degree can then be awarded. In terms of content, and in contrast to a →dissertation, a ~ must not present unique research but must satisfy scientific requirements. The ~ are thus more challenging and longer than seminar papers (→Hausarbeiten).

Abschlussprüfung (literally: final examination) The accumulation of all examinations that a degree candidate must complete to obtain his academic degree. This term is often used to describe only the final oral examination, as it is often the last examination completed (→Prüfungsordnung). Depending on the type of university (→Hochschulart), the ~ can be cumulative, that is, it is not a separate examination but is considered passed when all requirements for the degree have been met, or it can be a specific examination held once at the end of the studies.

Abschlussprüfung, kommissionelle (final examination before a committee) The typical Austrian term for the oral defense (→Disputation).

Absolvent (graduate) Lat. *absolvere* = set free, acquit. Candidates are called ~ after they have successfully obtained their degree (→Abschlussprüfung). A part of the ~ stay at the university to start a second, consecutive, or complementary course of studies or to start a doctorate (→Nachwuchswissenschaftler).

Absolventenalter (age of graduates) Between 1993 and 2002, the ~ in Germany slowly increased and graduates were almost 29 years old after an average study time of 12 semesters. In the debate on higher education reform, various approaches for lowering the ~ were suggested. The main points are: demands for shorter standard periods of study, tuition fees for long-time students, re-structuring of the curriculum and examination regulations, teaching evaluations, introduction of new degree programs (→Bachelor's), and the shortening of the time at primary and secondary school to 12 years (instead of the 13 years typical in many Bundesländer). Since 2003, the average

age of graduates decreased to just over 26 years in 2013. This development is attributed to several factors, including the shortening of time in primary and secondary school in some Bundesländer, the introduction of the Bachelor's/Master's system, the repeal of the requirement for males to perform military service for one year, and more strict regulations on maximum periods of study in examination regulations.

Absolventenverbleib (literally: where graduates remain) Study to evaluate the professional paths of university graduates, their career choices, continuing education, or whether they stayed in the university system for an academic career.

Absolventenzahlen (number of graduates) The ~ does not develop at the same rate as the enrollment numbers. In 2013, 408,713 students completed their degrees (not including doctorates (→Promotion)) in Germany. 41,349 of these were foreign students.

A̲bstract (abstract) Lat. *abstractus* = drawn away. Short, summary text at the beginning of a monograph or article in which the most important ideas of an academic argument are clearly described. The word ~ can be pronounced as in German or English.

***Academic record* (academic record)** Complete overview of the course of a student's progress in a study program and all credits obtained in connection with the modules as foreseen by the Bologna Process (→Bologna-Prozess). In particular, all credits are shown whether they count toward the degree program or not.

***Academy* (academy)** In the English-speaking regions, a term used very broadly and inconsistently for all types of private and public educational institutions from sports schools to academic societies (→Akademie).

Achtundsechziger-Revolte (Revolt of 1968) Term for the student movement (→Studentenbewegung) in Western Europe towards the end of the 1960s. It was inspired by Californian universities then those in Paris, primarily in May 1968. It first had the goal of comprehensive university reform but then developed into a fundamental opposition (→SDS) calling for social reforms. The hot spots in Germany were Frankfurt am Main and Berlin. The key points were: the demand for more participation at universities; anti-Vietnam War; pacifism; the call for free love; critique of their parents' generation, that is, of traditional structures; legalized drug use; a general attitude of resistance; and anti-authoritarian upbringing. While a large part of the so-called "68ers" went on a "march through the institutions," a much smaller group went underground as terrorists, for example the Red Army Faction. At the same time, but with a completely different character, in China and Czechoslovakia protests and mass movements took place that had fundamental effects on the university structures there.

Achtundsechziger-Revolte, Diskussion (Discussion of the Revolt of 1968) The effects of the year 1968 on the modern university are controversial. The following are considered problematic: the general loss of traditions, manners, and values; a lack of respect for the rooms and property of the universities; graffiti and an excess of posters on the bulletin boards and walls; reduction of work discipline and worsening of student's orientation on achievement; too much tolerance of poor student and instructor performance; discrimination of the terms "excellence" and "elite"; lack of significance of grades; the ideologization and trivialization of academic contents by the political scientific-psychological jargon of the 68ers; uncritical perspective of dictators such as Mao or Pol Pot; and the introduction of supposedly proletarian manners or actions at the university (→Busenattacke).

The emancipatory consequences that were at the time seen as progress against the traditional roles and authoritarian behavior of instructors seem rather minimal from today's perspective and in light of the later careers of many former 68ers.

Addenda (addenda) Lat. *addenda* = additional contents. List of new entries that are to be taken into consideration for planned new editions of reference works.

Admission (admission) Also: →Zulassung

Adress-Reader studentischer Adressen (student address database) An online database of e-mail and web addresses for university members, student representatives, student organizations, unions, political organizations, and university and study-relevant institutions. www.adressreader.de

Aeskulapstab (staff of Asclepius) Symbol of pharmacists, named after Asclepius, one of the demi-gods instructed in healing by the centaur Chiron and capable of healing all illnesses so that the gods of the underworld began to complain about him. Zeus then killed Asclepius so that balance was restored to nature and normal mortality resumed.

Affirmative Action **(affirmative action)** In German also called "positive Diskriminierung." Controversial measure to select applicants by giving preferential treatment to minorities or otherwise discriminated groups in order to create equal opportunity. One speaks of ~ in the context of university spots (→Studienplätzen), jobs, or scholarships (→Stipendien); those affected are primarily women, ethnic and religious minorities, the disabled, immigrants, and members of other groups that are often discriminated against.

AG Abbreviation for working group (→Arbeitsgruppe)

Ägide (aegis) Greek *aigis* = goatskin. Traditional term for a patronage, including of a non-academic organization or person for an academic initiative. In classical symbolism, the goatskin is an attribute of the Greek goddess Athena (→Athene), protector of scholars.

Ahnengalerie (ancestral portrait gallery) Representatively displayed or presented paintings or photographs of famous university members or →alumni occupying a prominent place in a building, often in a stairway or hallway.

AIESEC Abbreviation for: *Association Internationale des Etudiants en Sciences Economiques et Commerciales*; an international student organization founded in 1948 for internships abroad. The focus lies primarily on business and economics (→Wirtschaftswissenschaften) and computer science, and secondarily on the humanities (→Geisteswissenschaften) and social sciences (→Gesellschaftswissenschaften).
www.aiesec.org

AiP Abbreviation for a doctor in the first year of residency (→Arzt im Praktikum)

Akademie (academy) Greek *akademia* = Grove of Akademos. From the temple dedicated to the Greek hero of Troy, Akademos. The students of the philosopher Plato, who had purchased the property after a trip to Sicily in 387 BCE, gathered here and were thus called academics. The ~ has thereafter been considered the term for schools of philosophy.

Today the term is sometimes used as a synonym for university (→Hochschule) or as a description of an association of researchers such as the Academy of Sciences and the Humanities (→Akademie der Wissenschaften) or for private institutions offering any form of teaching, even if they are non-scientific. In the area of sports, for example, there are golf academies. There are also independent professional academies, art academies, and academies for continuing education for teachers (especially in Austria). ~ can be state-funded, recognized by the state, religious, or private.

Akademie der Wissenschaften (Academy of the Sciences and Humanities) National institution to promote academic research either in private or state form. In contrast to universities, no teaching is offered. In Germany, there are seven such institutions: Berlin, Dusseldorf, Göttingen, Heidelberg, Leipzig, Mainz, and Munich, joined together in the Union of the German ~.

Akademiker (academic (noun)) In Germany, usually a general term for holders of a university degree, more seldom used like in France or Russia as a term for a member of an Academy of the Sciences and Humanities (→Akademie der Wissenschaften), and thus a much smaller, more elite group.

Akademikerarbeitslosigkeit (unemployment for academics) In 2002, 223,600 academics (→Akademiker) with a degree from a university or university of applied sciences were unemployed, 25,600 more than in 1993.

Akademikermangel (lack of academics) Economic location disadvantage due to too few university graduates in a region or an economic area, in Germany primarily in engineering subjects. The disproportion of the ~ to the academic unemployment rate (→Akademikerarbeitslosigkeit) can be explained by the choice of subjects (→Studentenzahlen).

Akademisch (academic (adjective)) Besides the meaning of "belonging to the university," this term can also describe a certain way of thinking and working, for example consistently giving evidence from the expert literature (→Fachliteratur) and a certain kind of factual, scientific argumentation (→wissenschaftlichen Argumentation). A so-called "~ question" is one without any practical relevance in reality (ivory tower, →Elfenbeinturm).

Akademischer Kalender (academic calendar) Timetable in which all relevant data and dates for the ongoing semester are set down, in particular this includes: module periods, registration periods for modules, length of the lecture period, length of the academic year, and the academic holidays.

Akademische Ferien (academic holidays) See semester holidays (→Semesterferien)

Akademische Freiheit (academic freedom) See research and teaching (→Forschung und Lehre)

Akademische Gerichtsbarkeit (academic jurisdiction) Privilege of the early universities to regulate internal matters without interference from outside (churches, rulers). This included legal and penal jurisdiction, →Rechts- und Strafgewalt. In the baroque period, this privilege was continually restricted in favor of the sovereign power. In the 17th century, the ~ developed into an expression of state authority. External symbols of ~ were: the university scepter, the keeping of a seal (→Siegelführung), the privilege of the sword, and the right to wear robes (→Talarrecht) as well as other insignia (→Insignien). In administration: setting of its own budget, self-determination according to the basic order, privilege of admission, and disciplinary rights. Today, it only exists to a relatively small degree, for example in cases of plagiarism (→Betrugsfällen) that can lead to a revocation of an academic degree.

Akademisches Jahr (academic year) Also: Studienjahr. The entirety of both semesters in a year, whereby the lecture-free period is included. An ~ is not identical with the calendar year (→dies academicus) because it starts with the start of the semester.

Akademische Karriere (academic career) The career path of an academic at a university. The typical stations are called degrees (→Grad):

Abitur/Matura/Secondary school diploma; Pre-Diplom/Bachelor's; Diplom/Master's or comparable degrees; Doctorate or more than one doctoral degree; and the Habilitation (post-doctoral lecturing qualification); appointment to a professorship; offices and honors; and finally the emeritus status. It also includes various functions at a university, tasks in committees (→Gremien) and meetings, etc. Key aspects of an ~ are also publications and appearances in professional circles.

Akademische Laufbahn (academic career) See →akademische Karriere

Akademisches Bürgerrecht (academic rights) Traditional expression for the status of enrolled students and university members at the university. The term is related to the special social status of students and instructors and earlier universities that led to certain privileges vis-à-vis non-academics.

Akademisches Auslandsamt (Office of International Affairs) Abbreviation also: AA or AAA. An organization at nearly all universities and higher education institutions that deal with students or instructors going abroad. At most universities, it is also responsible for organizing many of the programs for incoming international students. Important topics are often: scholarships (→Stipendium), the recognition of credits obtained at foreign universities, and advising for foreign students. (→DAAD)

akademisches Fehlverhalten (academic misconduct) Violation of the principles of scientific integrity (→Redlichkeit) as set down by the German Research Foundation (→Deutschen Forschungsgesellschaft) in the form of guidelines. They primarily relate to dealing with intellectual property of third parties and to violations of customs of correct publication (→Recherche). Financially, this often pertains to the procurement of external funding (→Drittmitteln), research funding, or subsidies (→junkscience).

akademischer Grad (academic degree) A title obtained by completing several examinations at a university, or a name affix such as Doctor (→Doktor, see also →Magister, →Diplom). In contrast to Austria, in Germany it is not typical to include a Master's degree title on business cards or when introducing someone in person.

akademisches Jahr (academic year) Separation of a year into a summer semester (→Sommersemester) and a winter semester (→Wintersemester) with the semester holidays (→Semesterferien) in between. The start of an ~ is often celebrated with a ceremonial act.

akademisches Viertel (academic quarter-hour) The start of university courses with a 15-minute delay *cum tempore* (abbreviated c.t.). There are doubts as to how this practice began. One explanation is that until the Early Modern era, courses started with the ringing of the church bells. A quarter-hour delay was allowed to give the students time to get to the lecture hall. Another explanation states that the ~ is related to the church tradition: The courses were not to begin until after the (short) hourly prayer. The German expression ~ is relatively new and likely arose in the first decade of the 1900s.

At technical universities, this tradition is not common. There, the courses start →*sine tempore* (abbreviated s.t.), that is, on time. Only very seldom used today is *magna cum tempore*, with a 30-minute delay.

Akkreditierung (accreditation) This refers to the evaluation process for quality assurance that ends with the acceptance of a degree program at a university by state authorities as well as by a committee of the affected university. This is often linked to the evaluation (→Evaluation), which looks at existing degree programs and the instructors.

Akkreditierungsrat (Accreditation Council) Committee with eight members to accredit degree programs or private universities in Austria.

Akklamation (acclamation) Lat. *acclamatio* = approval, applause. Approval or recognition of a contribution, e.g. a presentation, by knocking on the table with a closed fist (→auf den Tisch). The ~ can replace a vote if there is unanimity and a counting of the votes thus seems unnecessary. The ~ was originally an important element of coronation ceremonies in the Middle Ages.

Alexander von Humboldt-Stiftung (Alexander von Humboldt Foundation) The ~ promotes scientists with outstanding achievements or potential who come to Germany from abroad and thus make a contribution to the internationalization of the sciences and to cultural exchange. Primarily financed by tax money, the budget of the Foreign Office, and the Federal Ministry of Education and Research. www.avh.de

ALFA-Programm (ALFA program) Abbreviation for: *América Latina Formación Académica*. Cooperation among universities in the EU and Latin America. The focus is on projects in the areas of social, business, economic, and engineering sciences as well as medicine, natural sciences, and technical subjects.

Allgemeinbildung (general knowledge, general education) The entirety of educational contents that belong to a canon of cultural heritage and are relatively accessible. At universities, these contents are usually conveyed in the framework of the →Studium Generale. For daily scientific work, the ~ is constantly relevant, as all information that goes beyond ~ must be cited with footnotes (→Fußnoten). Example: The information that Johann Gregor Mendel is considered one of the "fathers of genetics" is a matter of general knowledge, but not the specialized knowledge that his physics teacher, upon whose recommendation Mendel became a monk in 1843 with the Augustinians in Brünn, was called Dr. Friedrich Franz. The boundaries between specialized and general knowledge are blurry. (→Weltbild)

Allgemeiner Deutscher Hochschulsport (General German University Sports) Umbrella organization for German university sports since 1948, today with over 150 member universities and around 1.5 million student members. The ~ concentrates primarily on popular sports. www.adh.de

A̱lma Ma̱ter (alma mater) Lat. *alma mater* = nourishing mother. A now slightly antiquated term in existence since the 13th century for universities (→Hochschule, →Universität), originally it was the nickname of the Roman fertility goddesses. The university was metaphorically equated with the goddesses' life-giving functions.

Alter Herr (old man) Term from the jargon of fraternity students (→Philister). A member of a fraternity after completing his studies or after his active time in the fraternity (→Studentenverbindung).

Aḻumni (alumni) Lat. *alumnus* = foster son, the nourished. Association of former university members. Depending on the university, the ~ can be more or less organized, serve as a network, and offer continuing education, cultural events, and contacts (→Nachkontakte). The extent to which they are organized varies greatly among different countries. The ~ culture is particularly intensive in the United States (→Alma Mater).

Amt (agency, office) Official position at a university that is linked to certain rights and obligations. Institutions can also be called ~, for example the Enrollment Office (Immatrikulationsamt) or the Office of International Affairs (→Akademische Auslandsamt).

Anerkennung (recognition) Brought about by the Bologna Process (→Bologna-Prozess), achievements can be more easily recognized with points that can be completed at various universities and be counted toward the requirements for admission for another university (→Nostrifizierung).

Anfangssemester (beginning semester(s)) The first one or two semesters within a degree program before the first preliminary examination and thus the initial part of the basic study period (→Grundstudium). Typical problems in the ~ include: general orientation at the university, understanding the differences between school and academic studying, and the change in the social environment (→Erstsemester).

Angewandte Wissenschaften (applied sciences) Sciences related to concrete and practical application. In contrast to results of basic research (→Grundlagenforschung), the results of ~ can often be more or less directly used by businesses or other third parties, e.g. in the case of scientific reports for a technology company in which direct recommendations or instructions for actions are given.

Anhang (annex) The part of academic literature that serves to make the work reproducible and transparent (→Wissenschaftlichkeit). Depending on the requirements, it can include: Index of names (→Namensregister), subject index (→Sachregister), index of locations (→Ortsregister), list of abbreviations, bibliography (→Literaturangaben), maps, list of maps, tables, glossary (→Glossar), index, historical context, list of illustrations, picture credits, author bibliography.

An-Institute (associated institutes) Legally independent institutes for research or continuing education that complement the offers of a university, usually under the leadership of a professor. The ~ have an obligation to report to the university management.

Ankreiden (count it against s.o., blame s.t. on s.o., literally: chalk s.t. up) An expression in older student jargon (→Studentensprache): To put drinks on a tab. The open tab was written on the wall of a bar with chalk so that it was obvious who owed money because he couldn't pay. Today, it has become idiomatic for "blame." It is closely connected to the expression also rooted in student jargon "ein X für ein U vormachen" (making a U into an X) that goes back to the Roman numerals for X = ten and V or U = five. It was not difficult to change a V written with chalk into an X, thus doubling the tab.

Ankündigungsbogen (notification form) Form with which instructors give notification of new courses or series of courses.

Anmerkung (comment, note) Also: Kommentar. A description usually in short form or an addition to another's thoughts orally or in writing. If it is in writing, then usually in the form of footnotes (→Fußnoten) or endnotes (→Endnoten) on a text. Comments are part of the good scientific practice not to adopt others' ideas uncritically but to evaluate them, critique them, and then to mark them with ~ (→Wissenschaftlichkeit).

Anrede, Besonderheiten (particularities in forms of address) Those with doctorates don't use "Doctor" when addressing one another. In written forms of address, "Doctor" is rarely abbreviated, "Professor" is never abbreviated. Professors speak to each other with "Colleague" (Herr Kollege) if they do not know each other. The following list shows the typical forms of address in their masculine forms. Female forms of address are made analog to this. See the annex for tables on oral and written forms of address.

Anschaulichkeit (clarity) A key problem of all sciences is the need to describe phenomenon or abstractions in words and numbers. It is controversial whether language and numbers are able to give correct depictions of non-linguistic concepts. There is also the difficulty that especially figures are not always completely clear. That is why, regardless of the subject area, one didactic task is to present results clearly and to visualize them. Particular problems are: finding or developing correct terms, exact descriptions, and good explanations; using clear language; the correct use of pictures and symbols; and the right balance between simplification and complexity. One primary way to achieve greater ~ is to use graphics and other ways of showing numbers or words (→Statistik). A key method is the development of scientific models (→Modelle).

Anthologie (anthology) Greek *anthologia* = collection of flowers. A collection of texts from one or more genres and possibly of varying lengths on a more or less narrowly defined topic (→Thema) usually used in connection with poetic texts. One of the most famous ~ in Germany is the so-called Freiburger ~, a collection of German-language poems from 1720 to 1900.
www.freiburger-anthologie.de

Antrittsvorlesung (first lecture) An instructor's first lecture at a new university or at a new position at the same university, for example after the →Habilitation or receiving a professorship (→Berufung), often followed with great attention by university members.

Anwesenheitspflicht (attendance requirement) In some subjects, students are required to attend the course sessions to obtain credit. The more school-like (→verschult) a degree program is, the more probable it is that there is an ~. Also: Requirement for foreign students to participate in the lectures of a preparatory course (→Studienkolleg).

Apollon (Apollo) Greek god of music, poetry, and fine arts, but also of medicine and sudden death. The principle embodied by ~ is that of a clear spirit: analytical, passionless rationality in contrast to emotions as well as a personified model (→Leitbild) of scientific character (→Wissenschaftlichkeit).

Aporie (aporia) Greek *aporia* = perplexity. Term from philosophical history to describe a researcher's motivation. Based on puzzlement about a connection or observation, a logical discussion of a topic begins. Finding an ~ and thus a worthwhile research topic requires basic knowledge of the field (→Logik).

Apparat Lat. *parare* = set up.
1. (annex) The ~ of a scientific text in which the sources, literature (→Literaturverzeichnis), timelines, and other supplementary texts are printed.
2. (seminar collection) A seminar ~ is the main collection of information sources provided to participants in a

course, usually in a separate section of the library. There it can be found as a binder with copies of bibliographies, sources, articles, and other relevant texts.

Appendix (appendix) Lat. *adpendere* = attach (→Anhang).

Applikationsverantwortlicher (application manager) Staff member in an institute, department, or university who is the contact person for computer-supported aids, for example SAP applications within the university administration or also technical and research-related tasks: support, training sessions, contact to manufacturers and operators.

Approbation (license) Lat. *approbatio* = permission. Official permission for vocational training, mostly in medical professions, comparable with a license. The details are described in the license regulations for the profession (→Approbationsordnungen).

Approbationsordnungen (license regulations, medical practice regulations) Regulations on access to the following professions: doctor, dentist, veterinarian, psychologist, child and adolescent psychologist, and pharmacist. The ~ regulate the contents of degree programs and the examination parameters of the individual subjects. ~ are valid nationwide.

Arbeitsgruppe (working group) Abbreviation: AG. Usually an interdisciplinary, research-related, and project-like cooperation of instructors and students with a clear timeframe and content goals, often supported by sponsor funds. ~ do not have to have scientific goals but can also be related to PR measures such as the unification of university websites in terms of graphics and structure.

Arbeitsroutine (work routine) Individual working habits developed over a longer period of time for studying, writing, and publishing, whereby certain stages are selected so that the least amount of effort is necessary for the greatest effect. There are no generally valid instructions for ~, each individual must develop them personally. Aspects of ~ include: working hours, workstation, workload, organization of working conditions, definition of goals, variation between challenging and less challenging working phases, quieter periods, and breaks as well as rewards.

Arboretum (arboretum) Lat. *arbor* = tree. Part of a botanical garden or an entire botanical garden with a focus on trees, forests, or tree-like plants. The term was coined in 1838 by John Claudius Loudon in its current meaning.

Archaeoraptor liaoningensis-Affäre (Archaeoraptor liaoningensis hoax) →Hoax with a very skillful fossil forgery in Liaoning, China, in 1999 that was supposed to "prove" the relationship between birds and dinosaurs. After extensive tests, the find was shown to have been constructed from various fossils of differing ages.

Arch̲iv (archive) A topical or otherwise conceptualized collection of media (→Medien) documents, books, journals, or other types of media funded by a state authority (such as the ~ of the Federal Republic of Germany) or a private institution such as a newspaper, a foundation, or a private person, usually under the supervision of an archivist, who typically has an academic education. Entire libraries (→Bibliotheken) and museums can be part of an archive and be represented at multiple locations.
www.bundesarchiv.de

Archiv-Benutzungsantrag (request for use of archive) Before the first use of archival and finding aids, archive visitors must submit this ~ to the archive and enter their name, address, and purpose of use. The length of time until the request is granted for using the archive must be calculated into a research plan.

Archiv-Benutzungsordnung (archive user regulations) Public legal ordinance passed on the basis of the archive laws that regulates the use of an archive. The ~ are accepted when the user signs the request for use.

Archivsprengel (archival area) Geographic range of an archive's or an archive consortium's area of responsibility. A ~ is a historical area that has an important influence on the organization and collection of the archive.

Archivar (archivist) →Archiv

Argumentation (line of argument) The link between claims and theses (→Thesen) and facts to support the claims. A factual or objective ~ is a basic element of scientific discussion, whereby one typically differentiates between inductive (→induktive) and deductive (→deduktive) arguments.

Ars legendi – Preis für exzellente Hochschullehre (Ars legendi – prize for excellent university teaching) An annual prize awarded alternately to various teams or instructors of different disciplines, in 2014 for an interdisciplinary project on "research-oriented learning." "The prize is to make the particular importance for the education of young academics visible and create a career-relevant incentive to work on university teaching and promote teaching beyond one's own area of influence. At the same time, the quality of teaching is to be established as a key criterion of excellence (→Exzellenzkriterium) for top universities and as a strategic goal of quality management at universities."

a̲rtes liber̲ales (liberal arts) Lat. *artes liberales* = liberal arts. Classical division of sciences at Middle Age universities. The ~ was divided into the so-called *trivium* (grammar, rhetoric, and dialectics), and the *quadrivium* (mathematics, geometry, music, and astronomy). Knowledge of the first three disciplines was considered a basic prerequisite for studying all other subjects, which is where the term "triviality" arises. This type of general basic education is no longer typical at modern universities. After completing the artistic faculty (→Artistenfakultät), studies of the higher subjects could begin, that is, "theology law, and medicine," as Faust's monologue correctly states (→Universitätsgeschichte; →Wegestreit).

Artikel (article) Lat. *articulus* = element, part. Essay in a scientific journal, often as an excerpt of a longer monograph (→Monographie) or a report of current research, or another contribution to a controversy (→Kontroverse) in written form (→Paper). Articles are usually several pages in print, include a scientific annex (→Anhang) and discuss a relatively narrow topic with a title that often attracts attention but does not reveal much of the contents. The subtitle usually goes into more detail. An abstract (→Abstract) is placed before longer articles.

Artistenfakultät (artistic faculty) Old term for the lower faculty (→Fakultät, Also: Lat. *facultas inferior*), at which the liberal arts (→*artes liberales*) were taught that served as an entrance to the three higher faculties: law, medicine, and theology. The ~ was therefore not equivalent to today's basic study period (→Grundstudium) in terms of content, as all students had to go through the same basic education no matter which subject they studied later (→Philosophicum).

Arzt im Praktikum (first-year resident doctor) Abbreviated: *AiP*. With the changes to the Federal Physician's Regulations in May 2004, this was discontinued. Those who successfully complete their studies have received their license to practice medicine immediately since October 2004.

Assessment Center (assessment center) In the private sector, this method of applicant selection is done by observing group work and the evaluation of individual behavior and social competencies in a group.

Assi (no direct translation) Student slang abbreviation for assistant (→Assistant) that has a negative connotation, as it is meant to sound similar to the pejorative slang term for "asocial."

Assistent (assistant) Lat. *assistere* = aid, help. Academic personnel in departments below the level of a professor. It is therefore a very imprecise term. Usually, however, it refers to scientists with a postdoctoral lecturing qualification (→Habilitation).

AStA (student steering committee, students' union) Abbreviation for: Allgemeiner Studierenden Ausschuss. A committee not recognized everywhere that is open for all students and represents student interests within a university. AStA is often the steering committee for the larger student parliament (→Studierendenparlament, →verfasste Studentenschaft). One function is advising students about financial assistance for education (→Bafög), health insurance, or finding accommodations. The AStA costs are sometimes covered by a fee assessed to students together with the other semester fees. The ~ is the executive organ of the elected student body.

Athene (Athena) Lat. *Minerva*. The Greek goddess of wisdom and innovation, often represented as the goddess of sciences and the arts, belongs to one of the most important allegorical figures of the spirit of research and humanist education (→Bildung).

Atlas (Atlas) Greek mythological figure whose task was to carry the world on his shoulders. From this, the name for a collection of geographical maps arose, first published in the form of large books. Today they are increasingly published using multimedia. Theoretically, all material can be put into the form of an atlas. In particular, there are historical, political, medical, and geographical atlases.

Audimax (main auditorium) Lat. *auditorium maximum* = largest auditorium. Often used for conventions, large meetings, student parties (→Partys), or guest lectures by famous speakers. It may also be used for lectures (→Vorlesungen) with a large number of attendees, for example in →Studium Generale lectures.

Aufbaustudium (postgraduate studies) Short academic education that builds on another study program, usually lasting 4 semesters on a defined topic or subject area and often related to a profession.

Auf-den-Tisch-klopfen (rapping on the table) A tradition that started at German universities in the 1950s to show approval (→Akklamation). In earlier times, walking sticks were pounded on the ground or feet were scraped to show approval or disapproval. Rapping on the table with a closed fist may come from freemasonry or from the guilds in the Middle Ages.

Auflage (edition, print run) The number of copies of a medium produced at a certain time that are completely identical. If a book is being published for the first time, for example, then one speaks of a first edition.

New and improved or revised editions can follow as soon as a book is reprinted. The number of editions of a book can allow for conclusions about its commercial success. The number of the edition used must always be mentioned in a bibliography (→Bibliographie) in order to ensure clarity.

Aufsatz (article) Multiple-page scientific contribution on a clearly defined topic that can be published as an article (→Artikel) in a journal (→Zeitschrift) and must be structured according to a certain form. Key aspects are: placing the topic in a larger context, description of current research, innovative interpretation or new results, conclusion, and outlook as well as references.

Augenwischerei (eye washing, sham) A ritual at universities especially in the 17th century going back to the New Testament story of the healing of a deaf-mute. During the ritual, newly enrolled students' ears and eyes were symbolically cleaned and thus opened. Today it is used as an idiomatic expression that means exactly the opposite.

A̲ula (hall, auditorium) Greek *aule* = courtyard or other part of an antique residence that served as a gathering place. At modern universities, the ~ is also often a festively decorated gathering place for representative ceremonies or lectures, for example during →*dies academicus*. The term ~ also serves to describe academic culture as a whole.

Ausgabe (edition, issue) The specific publication type for a title (→Titel), for example as a paperback, study edition, or e-book. Individual types of publication can thus be formally differentiated from one another, also in terms of content, depending on the edition (→Auflage). For journals, the term indicates the number of the publication.

Ausgabe, kritische (critical edition) Usually in the context of old works that are printed in new form with commentary, for example novels of world literature or the Bible with explanations and cross-references, or also with publications of new sources. Commentary published on controversial passages within the manuscript (→Paginierung), often with references to other editions or contributions in academic literature. ~ take into consideration the state of research on the debate about a text and are thus always to be preferred over uncritical editions.

Aushang (posted notification) General information on a bulletin board (→schwarzen Brett) on various current topics at the university such as deadlines, office hours, exams, and events.

Ausländeranteil (proportion of foreigners) Term for the percentage of students who do not have a German education. In Germany, the total number of international students at the universities is around 250,000 with an average age of about 26 years. This corresponds to the average age of those students who have a German education (→Bildungsinländer).

Ausländerbeauftragter (representative for foreign students) Staff member at a university who is the contact person for issues, questions, and difficulties of international students. Important topics include: residency, language courses, scholarships, insurance, accommodation, integration, rights, and obligations.

Auslands-Bafög (education assistance abroad) Students eligible for financial assistance (→Bafög) can also receive assistance abroad under certain conditions after studying for one academic year. www.auslands bafoeg.de

Auslandsamt (Office of International Affairs) →Akademisches Auslandsamt

Auslandsstudium (study abroad) By taking advantage of partnership programs from universities for students or private initiatives, students can spend time at an international university for a certain amount of time, usually supported by a program and after showing proof of language proficiency. The largest program for international exchange within Europe is Erasmus+, in which 270,000 students took part in 2012-2013. The German Academic Exchange Service (→DAAD) also offers support for German students going abroad and for foreign students in Germany.

Ausleihbibliothek (lending library) Special form of library that allows media to be borrowed in contrast to a reference library (→Präsenzbibliothek). Specific lending periods and deadlines for reservations apply that are used to regulate the movement of media between readers and the location. Typical examples are: university libraries, city libraries, and state and national libraries. In order to use the library, a library card with an expiration date is needed. An application for the library card is necessary.

Austauschstudent (exchange student) A student studying at another university (host university) on the basis of international university agreements. Coursework and examinations done there are recognized at the home university based on the agreements. Problems can arise if the recognition of coursework and examinations at the other university is not regulated by an agreement (→Erasmus+).

Auswahlverfahren (selection procedure) Procedure at individual universities or the →Stiftung für Hochschulzulassung to match the number of applicants to the number of existing places, for example by using acceptance tests, interviews, calculating waiting semesters, or using minimum grade requirements. At artistic universities, there is also the possibility to require an audition.

Auszeichnungen, akademische (academic honors) Besides various scientific awards (→Wissenschaftspreisen), deserving persons can also be given ~ independent of their subject area, for example honorary academic members of the university (→*Doctor honoris causa*) or honorary senators.

Autonomie (autonomy) →Hochschulautonomie

Autor (author) Creator or writer of a work (→Werk) whose intellectual property is protected by copyright laws (→Urheberrechtsgesetz) and whose texts have been published. Scientific authors are writers of monographs (→Monographien) and articles (→Aufsätzen) or other text genres such as reviews or encyclopedia articles (→Artikeln). The modern differentiation among author, co-author, editor, copyist, commentator, and publisher were unknown or atypical until the Early Modern era.

B

BA (BA) →Bachelor

Baccalauréat (baccalauréat) Late Latin *baccalaureus* = knight, novice. It was the first degree at French universities introduced by Napoléon Bonaparte, first only for men, then starting in 1861 also for women. Etymologically, it corresponds to a Bachelor's degree (→Bachelor).

Ba**cchus (Bacchus)** Lat. *bacchus* = god of wine. In many traditional student songs, he is mentioned as the protector of student pleasures and leisure activities. Patron saint of long-term students (→Langzeitstudenten).

Ba**chelor (Bachelor, Bachelor's degree)** Late Latin *baccalaureus* = knight, novice. An academic degree according to the model of Anglo-Saxon universities that was introduced at most German universities after the decision by the conference of education ministers in 2003 declared Bachelor's degrees to be the new standard first degree. The Bachelor's degree is completed with a standard period of studying lasting at least 3 and a maximum of 4 years. Promoted by the European Bologna Process (→Bologna-Prozess), the ~ and Master's degree (→Master) are part of a newly introduced system of tiered degrees that is gradually replacing the traditional degrees such as Diplom, Magister, and state examination. These degree programs have been discontinued for the most part and replaced by the Bachelor/Master system.

*Bachelor***studiengang (Bachelor's degree program)** Study model introduced at German universities in the course of the Bologna Process (→Bologna Prozess) to shorten the period of study, create improved practical relevance of academic education, and ensure international comparability of degrees. A ~ is made up of a core scientific subject and a complementary subject (obtaining professionally relevant key qualifications) for a period of study of 6 semesters. After this, it is possible to enter a career or continue with a Master's degree program (an additional 4 semesters) or doctorate (→Promotion). Most examinations are completed as part of the courses.

*Bachelor***studiengang, Vorteile des (advantages of the Bachelor's degree programs)** Often the following points are mentioned as improvements on the old system: Students study an average of 2-4 semesters less until obtaining the degree; it includes key competencies such as media skills; studying and presentation techniques; increased practical experience with mandatory internships (→Praktika) or similar requirements; more flexibility due to interdisciplinary studies; internationality because credits completed abroad can be recognized; and, finally, easing the workload of the universities (→Massenuniversität) since not every student needs to stay until completing the Diplom or Magister but can finish studying earlier as long as he does not want to pursue a more in-depth scientific education.

BaföG (federal financial assistance for education, Federal Training Assistance Act) Bundesausbildungsförderungsgesetz. Act dealing with the financial support of students with long-term loans to socially underprivileged students to improve equal opportunities. With this term, both the law and the funds provided by the law are meant. Despite ~, around 70% of the students enrolled at German universities work for money.
www.bafoeg.bmbf.de

BAföG Betrug (BaföG fraud) The illegal receipt of benefits by fraudulently concealing the actual economic situation, especially if assets are more than the exemption limit of 7,500 euros. Damage is done because the support is given as an interest-free loan to the students. In the Federal Republic, in the spring of 2005 alone 40,000 applications from students were under suspicion of fraud. If supporting evidence is found, then the students may have to repay the amount they have received and face criminal charges.

BAföG, Inhalt (BaföG, contents) Sec. 1 Principle; Sec. 2 Education Institutions; Sec. 3 Distance Learning; Sec. 4 Education in Germany; Sec. 5 Education Abroad; Sec. 5a Education Periods Not Taken into Consideration; Sec. 6 Support of Germans Abroad; Sec. 7 First Education; Additional Education Periods; Sec. 8 Nationality; Sec. 9 Eligibility; Sec. 10 Age; Sec. 11 Scope of Educational Support; Sec. 12 Need for Secondary School Students; Sec. 13 Need for University Students; Sec. 13a Health and Long-Term Care Insurance Fee; Sec. 14 Need for Interns; Sec. 14a Additional Benefits in Hardship Cases; Sec. 15 Duration of Benefits; Sec. 15a Maximum Duration of Benefits; Sec. 15b Acceptance into and Ending Education; Sec. 16 Duration of Benefits Abroad; Sec. 17 Types of Benefits; Sec. 18 Conditions of the Loan; Sec. 18a Income-Dependent Repayment; Sec. 18b Partial Relief of the Loan; Sec. 18c Bank Loan; Sec. 18d Deutsche Ausgleichsbank; Sec. 19 Offsetting; Sec. 20 Repayment Obligation; Sec. 21 Definition of Income; Sec. 22 Period of Calculation for the Student's Income: Sec. 23 Allowances for Student's Income; Sec. 24 Period of Calculation for the Income of the Parents and Spouse; Sec. 25 Allowances for Income of Parents and Spouse; Sec. 26 Extent of Assets Taken into Account; Sec. 27 Definition of Assets; Sec. 28 Determining Value of Assets; Sec. 29 Allowances for Assets; Sec. 30 Monthly Amount Taken into Account; Sec. 35 Adjustment of the Calculation of Benefits and Allowances; Sec. 36 Advance Payment of

Benefits; Sec. 37 Transfer of Maintenance Claims; Sec. 38 Transfer of other Claims; Sec. 39 Application Management; Sec. 40 Offices for Federal Student Assistance; Sec. 40a State Offices for Federal Student Assistance; Sec. 41 Tasks of Offices for Federal Student Assistance; Sec. 42 Assistance Committees; Sec. 43 Tasks of Assistance Committees; Sec. 44 Advisory Council for Student Assistance; Sec. 45 Local Jurisdiction; Sec. 45a Change of Jurisdiction; Sec. 46 Application; Sec. 47 Disclosure Obligations; Sec. 47a Spouse and Parents' Obligation to Compensate; Sec. 48 Participation of Education Institutions; Sec. 49 Determination of Requirements for Benefits Abroad; Sec. 50 Notification; Sec. 51 Method of Payment; Sec. 53 Change of Notification; Sec. 54 Legal Remedies; Sec. 55 Statistics; Sec. 56 Obtaining the Funds; Sec. 58 Misdemeanors; Sec. 60 Victim of Political Persecution by SED Injustice; Sec. 63 Transfer of Tasks to Federal Office of Administration; Sec. 64 Assumption of Staff by the Federal Office of Administration; Sec. 65 Existing Regulations; Sec. 66 Abrogation of Regulations; Sec. 66a Transitional Regulation

Bafög-Rechner (BaföG calculator) Online service to calculate the amount of possible benefits. The results, broken down and taking special cases into account, primarily serve to orient the user and do not replace the regular application.
www.bafoeg-rechner.de

Band 1. ~, der **(band)** A term for the physical book with cover. Often it is falsely used as a synonym for title (→Titel). A book or title can be made up of multiple ~, for example most encyclopedias, although the band must be differentiated in the bibliography. This is usually done in parentheses after the title.

2. ~, das **(sash)** Sign of recognition by members of student societies (→Studentenverbindungen) that is worn over the chest and possibly dates back to the tricolored sashes from the French Revolution. Since around 1800 they have been in use in the current form. During this period in which elite fraternities were being established, wearing the ~ was first forbidden. That is likely where the tradition comes of wearing it under the coat.

Barett (barett) Lat. *bereta* = flat hat. Ancient head covering without a brim from the tradition of the Byzantine Empire's official attire. From there it went to the Catholic Church and today is part of the official ceremonial attire of academic rectors, judges, or in the military, but there they are usually much smaller.

BAT (collective agreement for the public sector) Abbreviation for: Bundesangestellten Tarif. Former collective bargaining agreement for state employees valid from 1961 until 2005, 2006, or 2010 depending on the *Land*. Replaced by the →TVöD/TV-L.

Beamter (civil servant, civil service employee) Person employed by the state or another public administrative institution in contrast to a non-civil servant employee (e.g. certificate of employment, not an employment agreement). With very few exceptions, civil servants must be German citizens or citizens of other EU member states. The status of civil servants, a public service and loyalty relationship, can differ in the various *Länder*. However, there are four general types of careers: ordinary service, mid-level service, higher-intermediate service, and higher service. The last type of service is on the basis of a completed university education. In particular, one differentiates among: civil servant candidate, civil servant in probationary period, and civil servant for life as well as among employers: federal civil servants, indirect civil servants, *Länder* civil servants, and municipal civil servants. The civil servant status of professors is the object of various discussions, including those of hierarchy (→Hierarchie), evaluation (→Evaluation), and university reform (→Hochschulreform).

www.beamten-informationen.de

Begabtenförderung (assistance for gifted students) Grants to individual students at secondary schools or universities, usually from state institutions and usually in the form of a scholarship (→Stipendiums). Numerous institutions and foundations (→Stiftungen) exist for this purpose.

Beihilfe (benefit) Legally guaranteed part of civil servants' (→Beamten) pay in the case of illness, death, or births as regulated in the benefit regulations of the individual *Länder*.

Behindertenbeauftragter (representative for the disabled) Administrative position with the task of contributing to improving the conditions for disabled or chronically ill students to study with technical, structural, logistical, or personnel support (→Dezernat).

Beisitzer (observer) A minute-taker with the right to ask questions in an oral examination (→Prüfung), usually a member of the department in which the examination is being held, and with at least one degree. Besides taking minutes, the most important task is consulting with the examiner to reach a conclusion on the grade (→Notenfindung).

Belegen (taking) University language: By regularly attending a course, it is taken. At many universities or individual departments, registration systems have been started with which students must register for the courses before attending them. This is done in particular for courses in which only a limited number of participants are permitted (due to space or equipment constraints, e.g. in a laboratory). The students receive credit for courses taken if they complete the necessary coursework and/or examination. This sometimes requires separate registration.

Belegbogen/Belegbuch (record of courses) →Studienbuch

Berufsakademie (university of cooperative education) Institution of tertiary schooling on the basis of a three-year education consisting of both theoretical and practical sections as part of the "dual system." Depending on state laws, the requirement for admission in the ~ is a general or subject-related higher education admission qualification or qualification for admission to a university of applied sciences as well as an apprenticeship agreement with a suitable training center.

Berufung (professorial appointment procedure, vocation) The procedure at a university to fill an open chair (→Lehrstuhl) with a suitable academic by means of invitation by a committee. This can be done on the basis of an application or as the result of a selection procedure. It is seen as a considerable honor to receive an appointment.

Berufungskommission (professorial appointment committee) A temporary committee put together for the sole purpose of appointing (→Berufung, Also: Ruf) persons to fill professorships (→Professorenstellen). Similar to the senate (→Senat), all groups are represented in this committee, whereby the professors make up the deciding majority, meaning that it is not possible to appoint someone against the will of this group. It should be noted, however that the professors are not necessarily always in agreement with one another.

Besoldung (pay for civil servants) The payment of civil servants (→Beamten) and professors (→Professoren) is the responsibility of the state. Civil servant instructors receive their pay in certain pay groups (Besoldungsstufen), for example professors between W1 and W3. It is possible for professors who were hired under the old "C" system before 2005 to remain in that system or to switch to the new "W" system. As of 2011 around 47% of professors at universities and 38% of professors at universities of applied sciences were in the "W" system. The pay is made up of the following components: basic pay, family supplement, other supplements, remunerations, supplement for service abroad, pre-service training pay, special payments, contributions to capital formation, and vacation supplements (→Beamte).

Besoldungsstufe (pay group) →Besoldung

Bestand (holdings, stock of books) Scope of books and other media belonging to a library (→Bibliothek). Depending on the type of library, the holdings can be very extensive and include several million volumes.

Bestandsübersicht (overview of holdings) Representation of all holdings in a library or an archive with formal and content-related comments on search words, running times, periodization, scope, degree of indexing, chronology, holdings history, and content structure.

Betriebswirtschaftslehre (Business Administration, microeconomics) →Wirtschaftswissenschaften

Betreuungsrelation (student to instructor ratio) →Betreuungsverhältnis

Betreuungsverhältnis (student to instructor ratio) Description of the quota of students per instructor for the →evaluation. In Germany, the average is 15 students per instructor, but there are extreme variations depending on the subject area and this average must be heavily qualified. For example, in 2013 in medicine and health sciences the ratio was 2.6 students per academic staff member while for legal sciences it was 25.4. For the subjects business administration and economics, no student to instructor ratio is calculated. According to the Federal Statistics Office, no clear ratio can be made out for these two subjects.

Betrug 1. (cheating) Unpermitted attempt to gain an advantage in examinations or other academic coursework, e.g. by trying to hide the true source of information from the examiner. Depending on the severity of the ~, the examination is typically graded as "failed."

2. **(fraud)** Also: Fälschung (forgery), Vetternwirtschaft (nepotism), Fehlverhalten (misconduct). Criminal act within academic operations that violates either statutory laws or common decency. This could include embezzlement, corruption, mismanagement, or falsifying research results. (→Archaeoraptor liaoningensis-Affäre; →Piltdown-Affäre, →Sokal-Affäre)

Beurlaubung (leave of absence, suspension) After completing the first semester, students can request a leave of absence. The most common reasons include: pregnancy, semester abroad, and illness. A semester leave of absence does not count as a subject-related semester (→Fachsemester), but it does count as a university semester (→Hochschulsemester), which can be relevant for insurance policies.

Beweis (proof) Term from logic (→Logik). Showing a statement or judgment is right (verification) or wrong (falsification, →Falsifikation) with empirical or logical reasons. Here one can differentiate between inductive or empirical ~ and deductive or axiomatic ~, as significantly developed by the Greek mathematician Euclid. A ~ can also be falsified, for example if it can be shown that an experimental set-up was flawed.

Bewerbermesse (applicant fair, career fair) Event for graduates (→Absolventen) and companies to make contacts that is meant to make the entry into professional life easier. ~ offer insights into professions, possibilities for development, and career opportunities.

Bibliographie (bibliography) Greek *biblos* = book and Greek *graphein* =

write. Systematically ordered, complete list of book titles on a subject or during a period according to certain parameters that can be very extensive so that a ~ can also be published as a book (→Biblio-Bibliographie). The individual elements of a correct bibliographical entry are:

Author's full name, title of the article, title of the book or journal, name of the translator, number of the edition used, volume number or series number of the work, series title, place of publication, publisher's name, year of publication, page numbers of the reference.

Bibliographie, glossierte (annotated bibliography) Also: kommentierte. A list of relevant titles for a specific subject topic with critical or summarizing comments. According to the usual representation of the bibliographic information in a bibliography (→Bibliographie), comments that are graphically separated are offered either with keywords or briefly stated evaluations in order to serve as orientation for further reading.

Biblio-Bibliographie (metabibliography, biblio-bibliography) Index of bibliographies (→Bibliographien) in the form of a list or catalog, or often in a multi-volume book.

Bibliothek (library) 1. Greek *bibliotheke* = place for storing books. Differentiated according to reference libraries (→Präsenzbibliotheken), whose holdings may not leave the premises, and lending libraries (→Ausleihbibliotheken), whose holdings may be borrowed. In addition, they can be separated according to the responsible bodies, e.g. department ~, university ~, or state ~.

www.bix-bibliotheksindex.de

2. Functional building for storing media. The essential sections of this building include: stack rooms, reading and working rooms, special departments, administrative rooms, counter for borrowing and returning books, IT area, exhibition rooms, and a visitor's cloakroom. In antiquity, special buildings were already being designed to optimally meet the requirements of a library. Modern buildings sometimes resemble high-tech institutions, especially in the stack rooms (→Magazinbereich).

Bibliothek, Aufgaben der (responsibilities of the library) The primary responsibilities of a library are collecting, conserving, cataloging, and managing media (→Medien) in order to lend them to library users, also with inter-library loans (→Fernleihe). Depending on a library's subject focus, the entire population of an area (e.g. a city) or a subject area or representatives of a subject area are provided with media. In addition, many libraries have the function of promoting the population's literacy and making educational content accessible to the public. Only a few libraries in Germany are open around the clock, for example the university library in Constance.

Bibliothek, nationale (national library) Due to historical developments, in Germany there are two – now unified – central national libraries (→Deutsche Bibliothek), and therefore in contrast to many other countries a decentral tradition that has extended beyond the time of German separation. The Library of Congress, the British Library, or the Bibliothèque Nationale de France are examples of old national collections that have often been ongoing for several centuries and whose main holdings are kept at one central location, whereby they also require numerous external branches.

Bibliothekar (librarian) Academically educated manager of a library (→Bibliothek). Primary responsibilities are: caring for, conserving, and expanding the holdings (→Bestands), continuation and updating of the catalog, supervision of the library users, supervision of the stack rooms (→Magazinaufsicht), communication with other libraries, inter-library loans (→Fernleihe), management of circulations, possible new structuring of call number systems, digital registration of new titles, management of and care for special departments, and the organization of exhibitions.

Bibliotheksführung (library tour) Informational event held by the library management, usually at regular intervals, that includes a tour in order to acquaint the users with the many possibilities in the library. The ~ is a regular part of introductory events at universities (→Tutorium).

Bibliotheksreform (library reform) Over the last twenty years, the following reforms can be mentioned: automatization of user services: →OPAC; online borrowing orders and management; library functions such as purchasing, cataloging, lending, and journal management are increasingly being integrated; commercial systems are being taken into consideration and integrated (e.g. e-journals); and libraries have joined into large, supraregional consortia (→Verbundssystemen).

Bibliotheksverbundsysteme, deutsche (German library consortia) Merging of libraries to supraregional networks. In Germany these are: Bibliotheksverbund Bayern (BVB); Gemeinsamer Bibliotheksverbund Bremen, Hamburg, Mecklenburg-Vorpommern, Sachsen-Anhalt, Schleswig-Holstein, Thüringen (GBV/"Nordverbund"); Hessisches Bibliotheks-Informations-System (HeBIS); Kooperativer Bibliotheksverbund Berlin-Brandenburg (KOBV); Online-Katalog der Zeitschriftendatenbank (ZDB); Südwestdeutscher Bibliotheksverbund (SWB); Verbunddatenbank Nordrhein-Westfalen (HBZ)

Bibliothekswesen (library sector, library sciences) The entirety of all libraries (→Bibliotheken) in a geographical area or a subject area is called a ~. This also includes the profession and the university subject of library sciences.

Bildnachweis (picture credits) Also: Abbildungsnachweis. Part of a scientific annex (→Anhang) in which the holders of rights to pictures or the reference point in the literature for illustrations, photographs, or graphics are listed. The reproduction of pictures in published texts can, in contrast to word citations, incur costs. That is why it is necessary to get permission to print from the rights holders of the respective rights (private persons or legal entities, for example archives or museums) before printing. It is also not uncommon to state thanks together with a ~.

Bildung (education) →Allgemeinbildung

Bildungsinländer (foreigner with German education) Foreign citizen who completed his schooling in Germany and thus earned a German higher education entrance qualification (→Hochschulzugangsberechtigung). Completing a preparatory course (→Studienkolleg) at a university or an acceptance test at an artistic or music university also leads to a person being considered a ~. Likewise, a foreigner applying for a Master's program who completed his Bachelor's in Germany or applying for a doctorate who completed his Master's in Germany is considered a ~. The status as a ~ has the following advantages: the person is eligible for BAföG (→BAföG), the person can receive a preferred status in selection procedures compared to foreigners without the status of a ~, and the person is eligible for scholarships from institutions. Regulations on who is considered a ~ can be found in →BAföG, section 8.

Bildungskatastrophe (education catastrophe) →Bildungsnotstand

Bildungsministerium (Ministry of Education) →Bundesministerium für Bildung und Forschung

Bildungsnotstand (education crisis) A popular term from the criticism of German education since the mid-1960s. A larger number of graduates from *Gymnasien* and improved conditions for instruction were among the demands. For the university, the term ~ refers in particular to overflowing lecture halls and the insufficient equipment at many institutes, which have also been the trigger for repeated student protests.

Bildungsweg, zweiter ("second-chance" educational path) Term for educational offers that lead to secondary school degrees outside of standard schools, traditionally a part of adult education.

Binnenzitat (paranthetical citation) Also: amerikanische →Zitierweise

Biographie (biography) Greek *biographia* = life description. Also Lat. *vita* = life. Description of the most important stations of an academic career (→akademische Karriere) or another résumé. A ~ can be published in a journal or a book as a brief author biography or as a separate book exclusively about the life of a person.

Blaue Liste (blue list) A non-university consortium supported by the federal government comprised of 82 research institutions and service providers with the task of carrying out long-term research projects that aren't covered by universities for various reasons, for example because of the equipment required or content of the project. 89 institutions, most of which are on the ~, have combined to form the Liebniz Association.
www.leibniz-gemeinschaft.de

Blockade (writer's block) Also: →Schreibhemmungen

Blockveranstaltung (blocked course) Also: Blockseminar. A course that takes place once for a longer period of time, usually on two or three days in a row for several hours in order to intensively prepare for something, for example in advance of a longer excursion (→Exkursion) or to circumvent scheduling conflicts (→Stundenplan).

Bologna-Deklaration (Bologna declaration) A declaration signed in 1999 by the European ministers of education in order to ensure improved compatibility of European degrees, for example by introducing a diploma supplement (→Diplomzusatz) and the European standardization of two study cycles, Bachelor's and Master's; starting a point system to recognize degrees in relation to the study objectives; promoting the greatest degree of mobility for students, instructors, and administrative personnel; encouraging cooperation among universities; quality assurance; curriculum development; and creating integrated education and funding programs.

Bolognaprozess (Bologna Process) Named after the oldest university in Europe in Bologna in Northeast Italy. In 1999 it was the location of a conference for European education ministers to create a unified structure for European education by: making degrees comparable, →ECTS, increasing the mobility of students, and general European standards in quality controls for research and teaching (→Forschung und Lehre).

Brain drain **(brain drain)** Loss of intellectual elites. Phenomenon describing the migration of qualified workers from less developed economic or education areas to more highly developed countries. In the case of Germany, a ~ toward the United States of America can be seen. Reasons German scientists emigrate include: better pay and research funding, career opportunities, scientific freedom, better conditions for research, less bureaucracy, and the prestige of American institutions.

Brainstorming **(brainstorming)** Discussion technique to find new solutions. Suggestions and inspirations are first collected unsystematically and without judgment or critique, and they are not sorted until later. At the end, the useful ideas are selected and refined in a second round of ~.

British Council (British Council) Organization to convey the British culture, language, and literature abroad; often in connection with language courses and events, analogous to the →Goethe Institute in Germany.
www.britishcouncil.org

Brückenkurs (bridging course) Special course offer to introduce people to a topic or subject area, usually during the lecture-free period (→Semesterferien) for better preparation for the regular program during the lecture period.

Buch (book) Still the most important medium to convey information at universities, especially in teaching. Important factors for the success of the book, especially in comparison to parchment made of animal skin, were the invention of the paper mill (in 1390 in Nuremberg for the first time), then the printing press around 1450 by Johannes Gutenberg. In a scientific context, one differentiates in terms of content primarily among: monographs, edited books, dictionaries, lexicons, bibliographies, and source editions. According to the type of production, the following categories can be named: Handwritten books, codices, printed books, and electronic books (e-books). Printed books are categorized according to the type of binding: paperback and hardcover. The majority of modern books are published in the format (→Format) DIN A 5, which considerably eases copying and lowers production costs.

Bücherverbrennung (burning of books) A conflict ritual carried out around the world since antiquity in which unpopular books are symbolically or actually burned, often in the context of religious controversies. In Germany, there were at least two historically important cases of ~, both of which were done with the participation of students and instructors: During the Wartburg Festival (→Wartburgfest) and the National-Socialist ~ in May 1933.

Budget **(budget)** Also: Haushalt or Etat. The ~of a university, institute, or department is made up of funding from the university, primary funds (→Grundmittel), external funds (→Drittmitteln), and sometimes profits from other work, and is managed collaboratively by several committees (→Gremien). The pronunciation is traditionally French, although the English form is becoming more prevalent.

Bundesbildungsministerium → Bundesministerium für Bildung und Forschung

Bundesministerium für Bildung und Forschung (Federal Ministry of Education and Research) Coordinator of university policies in cooperation with the *Länder*, which have primary competency in university policies. The highest authority for

→Bafög with around 1,000 staff members and an annual budget of approximately 15.3 billion euros (2015).
www.bmbf.de

Bundeswehr, Universität der (University of the Federal Armed Forces) Universities of the Federal Armed Forces were founded in 1973 in Hamburg and Munich to provide officers and officer candidates with an academic education. Currently there are around 3,000 students enrolled, including around 500 women, nearly 100 foreign officers, and over 30 civilian students. In terms of organization, the ~ are an exception in the German university landscape. The ~ provide an education that is in part like the education at a university and in part as at a university of applied sciences. They also have a trimester system (→Trimestersystem), they are campus universities (→Campusuniversität), and there is a very low student to faculty ratio in small groups. In addition, the standard period of study (→Regelstudienzeit) is 3.25 years.

Bund-Länder-Kommission (Federal-Länder Commission) An institution established in 1970 to unify the different university standards and the education and research policies of the *Länder* and thus a permanent discussion forum for all education and research-related questions relevant to the federal and *Länder* governments.
www.blk-bonn.de

Bursch (fraternity brother) Old term from the language of fraternity students for a full member of a student association (→Studentenverbindung) or for students in general (→Burse).

Burschenherrlichkeit (student glory) Term from an old student song from the 19th century that today is usually used to illustrate traditional student representations, often found to be cheesy:
O alte Burschenherrlichkeit, Wohin bist du verschwunden, Nie kehrst du wieder, gold'ne Zeit, So froh und ungebunden! Vergebens spähe ich umher, Ich finde deine Spur nicht mehr. O jerum, jerum, jerum, O quae mutatio rerum!

Burse (Burse, student residence hall) At first ~ was simply the name for a kind of residence hall at universities in the Middle Ages, whereby in some places there was a requirement to live in the ~ or be punished in order to live and study with the other instructors and students. The university of the Middle Ages therefore had strong characteristics of an association. It wasn't the close proximity to the university building(s) that was important but the personal aspect. Those who refused to live in the ~ lost their university privileges and were not allowed to graduate. These rules originated in Paris. However, at the oldest university in Europe, Bologna, this requirement did not exist. There the students lived throughout the city, renting rooms in citizens' houses.

The modern word "Burschenschaft" (→Studentenverbindung) is derived from ~.

Busenattacke (bosom attack) The ~ is one of the low points of German university history: On 22 April 1969, students associated with the Revolt of 1968 (→Achtundsechzigern) mobbed Professor Theodor W. Adorno. A group of female students bared their breasts, crowded Adorno into a corner, and tried to kiss him in an attempt to humiliate him. They thoroughly succeeded in doing so, as only a few weeks after the attack, Adorno, who was 65 years old, died of a heart attack. The students found themselves accused of being partially responsible for Adorno's death.

C

c.t. Abbreviation for: *cum tempore*: →akademisches Viertel

Caféteria (cafeteria) Institution from Student Services with less variety than a canteen (→Mensa).

Campus (campus) Lat. *campus* = field. The university district. German universities with a campus character, for example as in Constance, are rare since German universities are usually spread out across an entire city. At universities in the United States these types of universities are very common, as in Great Britain and those in other countries that were established according to the Anglo-Saxon model.

Campusroman (campus novel) Literary fiction genre dating back to the 1950s and primarily originating in Anglo-Saxon areas. The stories take place at a university with a focus on the particular circumstances of academics' life and work, usually written in an ironic tone with a criminal plot or as a romance (→Wissenschaftsparodie).

Cand. Abbreviation for: candidate (→Kandidat)

CBT Abbreviation for: →*Computer Based Training*

Chancengleichheit (equal opportunity) Term for just distribution of goods and opportunities in social contexts. At universities and in particular in human resource policies it refers to the prohibition against discrimination based on skin color, religion, disability, or nationality (→*affirmative action*).

Chargierter (one who is charged) Term from the language of fraternity students. An officer in the executive committee of a student association (→Studentenverbindung).

CHE Abbreviation for: *Centrum für Hochschulentwicklung*. A non-profit research institute founded in Gütersloh in 1994 by the German University Rectors' Conference (→Hochschulrektorenkonferenz) and the foundation of the media corporation Bertelsmann in order to monitor organizational and institutional reforms at German universities (→Ranking; →Evaluation). www.che.de

Civis Academicus (Civis Academicus) Lat. *civis academicus* = academic citizen. Widespread handbook of German, Austrian, and Swiss corporations and student societies at universities (→Hochschule) and schools with many references to Japanese, South American, and Central European societies but not to fraternities (→Fraternities) in the United States..

CLOZE-Test (CLOZE test) Written English language test on the basis of word completion and texts with blanks. (→Sprachenzentrum)

CO Abbreviation for: →Kolloquium

Co-Autor (co-author) →Mitverfasser

Coimbra Gruppe (Coimbra Group) A network of leading European universities. It was founded in 1985 and includes, among other universities: Oxford, Cambridge, Louvain, Montpellier, Göttingen, Heidelberg, Dublin, Bologna, Siena, Leiden, Coimbra, Barcelona, Tartu, and Granada. The tasks are: creating academic connections and contacts, exchanging ideas, internationalizing, cooperating, promoting excellence in research and teaching, and influencing the educational and science policies of individual countries.
www.coimbra-group.be

College (college) Research or teaching institution at British or American universities, whereby there can be differences among the various English-speaking countries and university systems (→Hochschulsystem). The term ~ is not precisely defined, which is why great differences in the quality of research and teaching (→Forschung und Lehre) can exist. A ~ can also be the place where its members live (→Oxbridge). As used in the United States, ~ is a term for the entire university (→Hochschule) or time at university. In the United States, a university is also often divided into several colleges that represent particular subject areas, e.g. a College of Business, College of Arts & Sciences, College of Music.

Collegium Musicum (Collegium Musicum) An expression from the 18th century for a musical society made up of students and non-academics who performed for an audience. Instrumental music was the primary focus. The Leipzig ~ was famous due to the participation of Johann Sebastian Bach and Georg Philipp Telemann.

COMETT (COMETT) The first EU (then EC) educational program to improve cooperation between universities and business by educating in the area of technology. It was started in 1987 and discontinued in 1995; the →Erasmus program can be considered its successor.

Computer-based Training **(computer-based training)** Usually multimedia learning software for offline or online self-study, also known as →e-learning. Key element of distance learning (→Fernstudium).

Convivium (no direct translation) Lat. *vivo* = life. Principle of academic living, learning, and working communities in the tradition of the Middle Age monasteries (*ora et labora*, work and pray) and monastic schools (→Klosterschulen), universities or even the ancient academies (→Akademien), or communities of scholars, for example the Pythagoreans. In modern times, this principle is closest to being achieved on campus universities (→Campus-Universität) or in some sense in fraternity houses. The goal of the ~, besides the obvious advantages of divisions of labor and the exchange of ideas, is also to create interdisciplinary networks.

Copyright **(copyright)** →Urheberrecht

***Copyshop* (copy center)** A commercial business in or near a university with various technology for reproducing documents (→Dokument). It is often used as a place for leaving lecture notes (→Skript) for students to copy.

Corrigenda (corrigenda) Lat. *corrigenda* = contents to be improved. Also: Errata. Information sheet with mistakes that were only discovered after printing a work but before it was delivered.

***Crashkurs* (crash course)** →Intensivkurs

CRUS (CRUS) Conférence des Recteurs des Universités Suisses, Conference of Rectors of the Swiss Universities.
www.crus.ch.

Cum laude (cum laude) Lat. *cum laude* = with distinction. Third level for scientific work, corresponding to an average grade (→Note 3). See also →summa cum laude and →magna cum laude. →rite →non rite.

cum tempore (literally: with time) Lat. *cum tempore* = with time. Indicates that an event starts 15 minutes after the time given (e.g. an event starting at "10 c.t." will start at 10:15). →akademisches Viertel

Curricularnormwert (total number of teaching hours required) The total number of teaching hours (→Deputatsstunden) required for the proper education of a student in a degree program.

Curriculum (curriculum) 1. Lat. *currere* = run. Organization and system of the learning process in terms of a certain study or education goal. 2. Lat. *curriculum* = course of events. The regulation of when the contents in a degree program (→Studium, →Studieninhalt) are taken. The true teaching of a subject at a university is in tension between the ~ and the freedom of research and teaching (→Forschung und Lehre), that is, the freedom of instructors to independently decide on the contents of what they teach.

Curriculum Vitae (curriculum vitae, résumé) Lat. *curriculum vitae* = résumé. Usually used in the context of applications. Representation of the most important stages of a career in the form of a list, possibly with brief descriptions.

CUS (CUS) Conférence universitaire suisse (SUK).
www.cus.ch.

Cusanuswerk (Cusanuswerk) Catholic organization located in Bonn with the purpose of supporting gifted students, named after the scholar Nikolaus von Cues, founded in 1956. Foreign students can only receive funding if they are EU citizens or if they are entitled to receive →BAföG under Sec. 8 (→Bildungsinländer).
www.cusanuswerk.de

D

Damenverbindung (sorority) →Studentenverbindung

Danksagung (acknowledgements) For longer scientific works, it is typical to thank people who helped. The ~ are normally placed in a prominent position, on a separate page at the beginning of the book, whereby everyone pays particular attention to the order of the people named, the number of the words used for the thanks, and the wording.

Datenmüll (data garbage) Also: Datenschrott (data trash). University jargon for the figures in scientific works that will probably not be noticed by readers and therefore only have a decorative purpose. Also refers to online data collections that are not from proven sources, not authored, and not able to be controlled, for example literature lists (→junk science).

Datenschutzbeauftragter (data protection officer) University employee responsible for compliance with the laws and ordinances on data protection and for giving advice on questions of data security based on the respective state data protection laws. These tasks include, among others: permissibility of data processing; processing of current personal data; objection rights of those affected; technical procedures for regular data transfer; organizational measures; maintenance issues; principles of system and process design; data protection audits; purpose-related saving, changes, and use of data; transfer of data within the public sector; transfer within the university; transfer of data to foreign, international, and other places; viewing of files, correction, deletion, and blocking; damages; reports of activities; data processing for scientific purposes; data processing for journalistic purposes; awards and honors; video surveillance and recording; data processing in service and employment relationships; personal data from former institutions.

Dean **(dean)** Also: →Dekan. At English-language universities, the dean is the head of a specific unit (department, college, etc.), or it is also used as a title at Anglistics institutes at German-language institutions.

Deckblatt (cover page) →Titelblatt

Definition (definition) A statement of the meaning of terms used. A ~ describes something completely and uniquely. That is why it is a key element of every scientific theory or hypothesis. The ~ shows the meaning in which terms are used. In particular, one can differentiate among the following types of ~: by type of word, functions, equivalencies, materials, categories, and doctrines or reference to authorities.

Dekan (dean) Lat. *decanus* = noncommissioned officer (cf. Ancient Greek: diakonos = servant). The original Latin term denotes only a military commander of ten men; later, it referred generally to a responsible person regardless of the number of people they commanded, e.g. in the church or diplomacy (→Doyen). Today, the title is usually used for the elected head of a faculty (→Fakultät), usually for 2 years, who represents the faculty externally and manages business matters. The ~ is represented by one or several vice-deans. The correct form of address for a ~ is →Spektabilität, or the Latin *Spectabilis* by his professorial colleagues.

Dekanat 1. (Dean's office) The office of the dean (→Dekan) including the employees and administrative tasks as the head of a faculty (→Fakultät). 2. **(faculty council)** In some *Länder*, the official term for the committee made up of a faculty's dean, vice-deans, and deans of study.

Deputat (teaching load) Lat. *deputatum* = assigned. Amount of teaching that must be done according to weekly contact hours per semester (→Semesterwochenstunden). The ~ of instructors can be reduced if they hold a university office so that they can focus more on administrative tasks.

Desiderat (desideratum) Lat. *desiderare* = to desire. Literature that is missing is called ~. This could be existing literature that has not yet been procured by a certain library, or it could be studies that are yet to be written. In the second meaning, ~ are also calls for future research.

Desideratliste (request list) Also: Desiderata. A list of books that the library management should order to expand the holdings. These lists are usually open and can be viewed and added to by all library users.

Desktop Publishing **(desktop publishing)** Modern connection between writing and formatting by an author on a computer. In earlier times, typewritten or handwritten manuscripts had to be typeset before printing. Digital manuscripts created by ~ are the norm today, which has significantly simplified and thus accelerated the production of books.

Deutscher Akademischer Austauschdienst (German Academic Exchange Service) The DAAD was founded in 1950 as a registered association (*eingetragener Verein, e.V.*). Initially it was founded in 1925, though, as a group of German universities with the goal of promoting international cooperation with scholarships (→Stipendien) or international projects. The core areas are: scholarships for foreign students at German universities; scholarships for German students at foreign universities; internationalization of the universities; promotion of the German language abroad; and educational cooperation with developing countries. The

projects are mainly financed with funding from the Federal Foreign Office and the Federal Ministry for Economic Cooperation and Development.
www.daad.de/en/

Deutsche Forschungsgemeinschaft (German Research Foundation) Also: DFG. The ~ develops and promotes research projects with financial support and coordination as well as network-building for all areas of science. The modern ~ was recreated in 1949 as a successor to the "Emergency Association of German Science," founded in 1920, with its headquarters in Bad Godesberg near Bonn.
www.dfg.de/en

Deutscher Hochschulverband (German Association of University Professors and Lecturers) Professional representation of German university instructors for university policies, legal positions, legal advice, financial support, further education, and promotion of young scientists.
www.hochschulverband.de

Deutsche Nationalbibliothek (German National Library) Central archive library and the national bibliographical center of Germany with the function of a national library. It has been responsible for collecting German and German-language literature, making it accessible, and bibliographically recording it since 1913. Since 1990 it has been joined together with the German Library in Leipzig as well as other institutions.
www.ddb.de

Deutsches Studentenwerk (German National Association for Student Affairs) Umbrella organization for the over 60 German student services organizations. It is located in Berlin and tasked with promoting the financial, social, health, and cultural state of students. According to its statutes, the ~ has three bodies: the general meeting, the executive board, and the secretariat for advising the educational policy actors at the federal and state level.
www.studentenwerke.de

DFG (DFG) Abbreviation for: German Research Foundation (→Deutsche Forschungsgemeinschaft)

*Dep*a*rtment* **(department)** One term for an academic unit (→Fakultät, →Lehrstuhl) at English-language universities and English-language institutes at German universities, for example at an Anglistics institute.

Dezernat (department) Unit of the central university administration, analogous to a ministry of a government. For example, Leipzig University has the following structure: Department 1: Budget and Finance; Department 2: Academic Administration; Department 3: Human Resources; Department 4: Planning and Technology; Department 5: Public Relations and Research Promotion; Rector's Office, Academic Continuing Education/Distance Learning, Office for Environmental

Protection and Occupational Safety, Internal Auditing, Legal Matters. (→Stabstelle)

Didaktik (didactics) Greek *didaskein* = teach. Professional preparation of scientific content so the listeners in a university course or school pupils can understand better and more easily. The subject ~ of particular disciplines (→Disziplin) is an element of the education program for teachers.

Dienstsiegel (seal) →Siegel

Dienstzimmer (office) The room at a university assigned to an instructor (→Dozent). Place where office hours (→Sprechstunden.) occur. In the ~ media (→Medien) from the library (→Bibliothek) on long-term loan can often be found.

dies academicus (dies academicus) Lat. *dies academicus* = academic day. Festive event at a university to honor members. Also other festivities in the context of special events, receptions, lectures, and concerts. Typically on ~ no regular courses take place. The institutions have the opportunity to present themselves and their employees to the university and external public.

Differenzierung (differentiation) Intellectual technique for distinguishing terms. The primary task of every scientist is to separate things that are different and then evaluate these differences.

Digest **(digest)** Overview of new publications, often in the form of a book or found online and structured according to topic to provide an easier overview of new publications in a subject. The pronunciation of the term can be German or English.

Diplom Greek *diploma* = folded, sealed.
1. **(Diplom)** Academic degree in natural science or technical subjects (→Abschluss), now phased out almost completely in favor of the Bachelor's/Master's system in the Bologna Process (→Bologna-Prozess). In the former GDR Diploms were also issued in contrast to academic traditions in the liberal arts, for example in German, for ideological reasons.
2. **(diploma)** Certificate to confirm academic or other achievements with a seal (→Siegel), description, and signature.

Diplomand (Diplom student) Student in the final phase of studying who is in the process of obtaining the Diplom degree (→Diplom), also a term for a staff member in a company during a Diplom semester.

Diplomarbeit (Diplom thesis) Scientific final thesis (→Abschlussarbeit) at the end of a Diplom degree program. The ~ can also be done at a company.

Diplomarbeitenbörse (Diplom thesis marketplace) A website based on a database with which you can view completed Diplom theses and possibly buy them, usually as digital publications.

Diplomgrad (Diplom degree) A degree in a specific subject area awarded after completion of a university examination, e.g. Diplom-Ingenieur (Diplom Engineer). This is different from the state examination. Universities, universities of applied sciences, art schools, and music schools, in some *Länder* also universities of cooperative education, may award a ~.

Diplomprüfung (Diplom examination) Final examination in Diplom degree programs to obtain the Diplom degree (→Diplomgrad), made up of a combination of the Diplom thesis, oral exams, and possibly written exams.

Diplomprüfungsordnung (Diplom examination regulations) Regulations with the provisions applying to Diplom examinations at a university such as deadlines or weighting of the coursework and examinations. There are no nationally valid ~, as each university or each faculty (→Fakultät) can – or must – pass its own ~. (→Prüfungsordnung)

Diplomsemester (Diplom semester) A university semester in which the student focuses primarily on completing the Diplom thesis.

Diploma-Supplement (diploma supplement) An explanation of a diploma certificate attached to the respective qualification in English and in the national language (German in Germany), required by the →Bologna Process. The ~ includes a description of the successfully completed degree program and may not contain value judgments, statements of equivalency with other qualifications, or suggestions on recognition.

Diplom-Vorprüfung (preliminary Diplom examination) An intermediate examination to complete the basic study period but not a separate, independent degree.

Direktstudium (on-campus program) In an ~, courses are offered directly at the university in contrast to a distance-learning program (→Fernstudium). Attendance is necessary. The ~ is the most common form of studying.

Disputation (viva voce, defense) Lat. *disputatio* = verbal argument. Also: Verteidigung. Oral examination in the context of a doctorate (→Promotion); a discussion of the contents and form of the dissertation (→Dissertation). This examination is usually public and can be attended by members of all the faculties (→Fakultät). The conditions of the ~ are determined by each university in the doctoral regulations (→Promotionsordnung).

Dissertant (doctoral candidate) →Doktorand

Dissertation (doctoral dissertation) Lat. *dissertare* = discuss. In slang, also: Doktorarbeit (doctoral thesis) or Diss. Independent scientific study of a relatively specific topic in the context of a doctorate (→Promotion) that is to provide new scientific findings. Depending on the subject, the effort, scope, and duration can vary greatly. After completion and publication of the work in the form of a book (traditional monograph dissertation) or several articles (cumulative dissertation, →Dissertation, kumulativ), the ~ must be defended in front of an examination committee. At the end of a successful examination, the candidate (→Kandidat) is awarded a doctorate.

Dissertation, approbierte (approved dissertation) Lat. *probare* = approve. Complete dissertation manuscript that has been recognized by the responsible advisor or corrector (→Korrektor) as being a sufficient basis for the defense (→Disputation).

Dissertation, kumulative (cumulative dissertation) Newer form of dissertation in Germany that is not written as a single monograph but as a series of articles on a related topic. Regulations differ among universities, but typical provisions include that the doctoral candidate (→Doktorand) must be the sole or primary author of a certain number of the publications or that a certain number must already be accepted for publication. When the ~ is finished, the candidate writes an introduction and conclusion discussing the results of the articles as they relate to one another and submits it for review by the advisor.

Dissertationsschrift (dissertation manuscript) The written form of the dissertation (→Dissertation) that follows the norms of the respective department or faculty and fulfills all scientific standards for publications (→Publikation). Usually, a ~ has between 200-300 pages, but this varies greatly among the different subjects (liberal arts ~ are usually the longest, medical ~ typically the shortest). The respective doctoral regulations of the university set down the number of copies to be submitted and the form of the publication: digitally, in the form of a book, or on another medium (→Medium).

Disziplin, wissenschaftliche (scientific discipline) →Fakultät

Disziplinarverfahren (disciplinary proceedings) Lat. *disciplina* = instruction, training. Administrative punishment of misconduct in the case of serious violations by university members such as embezzlement, negligence, evasion, accounting fraud at university clinics, or misappropriation. ~ are opened by the university management, usually in combination with a court case, and made public in a press conference. The goal of the proceedings is to clarify what happened and to suspend the accused from service if appropriate.

Dogma (dogma) Greek *dogma* = teaching. Binding doctrine; the term usually has a negative connotation. A ~ typically also denotes rules that are not to be questioned and is thus often a part of the self-understanding of religions or worldviews. The negative connotation of the term is modern.

Doktor (person with a doctorate) Lat. *Docere* = teach, instruct. A title and thus part of the form of address for a scientist with a doctorate. The correct form is: "promoviert werden" (to be granted a doctorate). At universities in the Middle Ages, the *doctores* already made up their own professional society apart from the students and the graduated scientists who did not yet have doctorates (→Fakultät; →Hochschulgeschichte). In German slang, "Doktor" is often used as the equivalent of "physician," which is not academically correct.

Doktortitel (doctorate title) Lat. *Docere* = teach, instruct. Academic title (→Titel) after completing the dissertation and passing the defense (→Disputation). One differentiates in particular among the following: Dr. des. (= *designiert*) is a candidate for the title; Dr. h.c. (= *Doktor honoris causa*) is a person with an honorary doctorate; Dr. habil. is a person with a doctorate and a habilitation (→Habilitation), e.g. Dr. phil. habil.; Dr. ing. = doctorate in engineering; Dr. jur. = doctor of law; Dr. med. = doctor of medicine; Dr. med. dent. = doctor of dentistry; Dr. paed. = doctor of pedagogy; Dr. phil. = doctor of liberal arts; Dr. rer. nat. = doctor of natural sciences; Dr. rer. pol. = doctor of economics and social sciences; Dr. rer. soc. = doctor of social sciences; Dr. sc. hum. = doctor of natural sciences in medicine; Dr. theol. = doctor of theology.

Doktortitel, historische Entstehung (historical development of doctorate title) At universities in the Middle Ages, the differentiation between professors and holders of doctorates was not as fully developed as it is today. Insignias of Middle Age doctors and professors were the hat, staff, ring, book, glove, and robe, and thus the traditional dress of doctors was similar to knightly clothing; acceptance into the *Collegium doctorum* was sometimes a very costly honor, but on the other hand it also meant acceptance into the nobility *de jure*, although it was likely an exception for them to be treated as equals to the born nobility. Formally, this equality could be seen with various privileges, for example waiving of customs taxes or being able to sit instead of stand in a court of law. In the course of the French Revolution, these privileges were stopped in Germany, as well. The doctor lost importance in comparison to the professor, which was younger in terms of university history. Today, a doctorate is typically a prerequisite for a professorship (→Juniorprofessor).

Doktorand (doctoral candidate) Doctoral student working on a dissertation (→Dissertation). After successfully completing the dissertation and finishing the examinations, the ~ is granted a doctorate in the discipline.

Doktorarbeit (doctoral thesis) →Dissertation

Doktorat (doctorate) Time in which a doctoral candidate (→Doktorand) completes a dissertation (→Dissertation). Usually, the ~ takes around three or four years with a great deal of variance from the relatively short doctorates in medical subjects to relatively long doctorates in the liberal arts.

Doktorgrad (doctoral degree) Term for the degree that a scientist with a doctorate has (→promovierter Wissenschaftler).

Doktorhut (mortarboard) A now very atypical, antiquated piece of clothing in Germany that expressed the social and legal status of a university's doctors in previous times. Today, the ~ is primarily awarded in the Anglo-Saxon countries together with the corresponding degree certificate in a ceremony (→Talarrecht).

Doktormutter ("doctor mother," advisor) Modern language for a female advisor (→Doktorvater)

Doktorprüfung →Promotion

Doktortitel (doctorate title) The title awarded after the successful conclusion of doctoral proceedings by the university to the doctoral candidate (→Doktorand). In Germany, the following titles are awarded:

Dr. agr. = Doctor agronomiae; Dr. e.h./E.H. = Doctor ehrenhalber; Dres.= Doctores (several titles outside of theology); Dr. habil. = Doctor habilitatus; Dr. h.c .= Doctor honoris causa; Dr.-Ing. = Doctor-Ingenieur; Dr. iur. = Doctor juris; Dr. iur can.= Doctor juris canonici (church law); Dr. iur. et rer. pol. = Doctor juris et rerum politicarum; Dr. iur. tripl. = Doctor juris triplicis (Roman, German, and canonical law); Dr. iur. utr.= Doctor juris utriusque (lay and church law); Dr. med.= Doctor medicinae; Dr. med. dent.= Doctor medicinae dentariae; Dr. med. vet.= Doctor medicinae veterinariae; Dr. mult. = Doctor multiplex; Dr. oec. Publ. = Doctor oeconomiae publicae; Dr. oec. troph.= Doctor oecotrophologiae; Dr. paed. = Doctor paedagogiae; Dr. phil. = Doctor philosophiae; Dr. phil. nat. = Doctor philosophiae (natural sciences in a philosophical faculty); Dr. rer. agr. = Doctor rerum agrarium; Dr. rer. comm. = Doctor rerum comercialium; Dr. rer. forest. = Doctor rerum forestalium; Dr. rer. hort. = Doctor rerum hortensiarium; Dr. rer. medic. = Doctor rerum medicinalium (University of Münster); Dr. rer. nat. = Doctor rerum naturalium; Dr. rer. oec. = Doctor rerum oeconomicarum; Dr. rer. pol. = Doctor rerum politicarum; Dr. rer. sec. = Doctor rerum securitatis; Dr. rer. silv. = Doctor rerum silvestrium; Dr. sc. = Doctor scientiae (GDR for Dr. habil.); Dr. sc. techn. = Doctor scientiarum technicarum; Dr. theol. = Doctor theologiae; Dr. troph. = Doctor trophologiae

Doktorvater ("doctor father," advisor) The professor or scientist with a →habilitation who supervises a dissertation. There are no standardized regulations or obligations for the extent of the supervision for a doctoral candidate. The differences in the quality of supervision can therefore be great, even within one department. The basis of the cooperation between a doctoral candidate and the ~ are regular discussions on the status of the dissertation (→Dissertation). At many universities, a doctoral agreement (→Promotionsvereinbarung) is now required between the candidate and supervisor that sets down the expectations of both parties and often requires written minutes of the meetings that must take place regularly (e.g. once a semester). In addition, the ~ is the most important partner in the defense (→Disputation).

Dokumentation (documentation) Lat. *documentum* = proof. A collection of sources on a set topic, usually in the context of research or project work.

Dokumentenlieferdienst (document delivery service) Commercial service provider who makes copies of journal articles, edited books, conference proceedings, etc., available via post or e-mail. The delivered documents are usually photocopies or scans. In Germany, SUBITO and GETINFO are the largest ~, but their services are not uncontroversial since the financial interests of publishing houses can be affected.
www.subito-doc.de
www.getinfo-doc.de

Domschule (cathedral school) Educational institution at diocesan towns in the Middle Ages from which the later universities and *Gymnasien* grew in terms of development history but not institutionally. In Germany, the Cologne ~ was famous, for example.

Don **(don)** Term at Anglo-Saxon universities for the head of a college (→*College*), a fellow (→*Fellow*), instructors in general (→Dozenten allgemein), or a tutor (→Tutor). (→*Superdon*)

Doppelstudium (double degree program) Working on two degree programs at once; at some universities the student must pay tuition for this.

Doyen **(doyen)** French *doyen* = dean (→Dekan). Term for the oldest or most senior representative of an expert group (→Nestor).

Doz<u>e</u>nt (instructor) →Hochschullehrer

DPO (DPO) Abbreviation for: Diplom examination regulations (→Diplomprüfungsordnung)

Drittmittel (external funding, third-party funding) Funds from third parties that are available to an institute or other institution in addition to the regular budget for the university. The procurement of ~ is a primary task of professors and institute directors. The amounts of ~ can vary greatly depending on the subject area: human medicine typically has the highest amounts, liberal arts the lowest (→Budget).

Drittmittelrelation (external funding ratio) Criterion for a university evaluation: What is measured is the total amount of external funds that a chair procures annually on average.

Druckfahne (proof) The print-out of a manuscript on large pieces of paper before cutting and binding into the final book form (→Desktop Publishing).

Druckkostenzuschuss (printing cost subsidy) Some publishing houses charge authors a portion of the publication costs in order to share the business risks of publication. This primarily affects young authors and particularly doctoral candidates, who are required to publish their dissertations and therefore have a weak negotiating position vis-à-vis the publishing houses. For this reason, the number of doctoral candidates who choose to publish electronically is greatly increasing.

DSH (DSH) Abbreviation for: Deutsche Sprachprüfung für den Hochschulzugang. Widely used test of German proficiency for foreign applicants for a university place. The examination is held at the individual universities and costs between 40-170 euros. Foreign students can obtain an exemption from the DSH for the following reasons: applicants who prove they have the necessary German proficiency, applicants who have the "Deutsche Sprachdiplom oder Kulturministerkonferenz" level 2, applicants who have successfully completed the Zentrale Oberstufenprüfung from a →Goethe Institute, applicants who have successfully completed the "Feststellungsprüfung" or "Abschlussprüfung" in a preparatory course (→Studienkolleg), or applicants who have completed part of their studies at a German university, e.g. as an exchange student. en.dsh-germany.com

DSW (DSW) Abbreviation for: German National Association of Student Affairs (→Deutsches Studentenwerk)

Du, studentisches (informal student form of address) Before 1968, the informal form of second person singular address "Du" was almost exclusively used within fraternities (→Studentenverbindung), but in the course of the student movement (→Studentenbewegung), it became a general custom at universities that now includes all students but not the instructors or non-scientific (e.g. administrative) staff.

Duales Studium (dual course of studies) Combination of studies and vocational training in which there are practical phases and study phases.

Durchfallen (fail, literally "fall through") University jargon for not passing an examination (→Prüfung). The term probably came originally from school slang.

Durchstarter **(overachiever)** University jargon for a student who completes their degree in much less time than the standard period of study (→Regelstudienzeit). The opposite of a long-term student (→Langzeitstudent).

E

e-Learning (e-learning) ~ denotes the use of modern technology (especially online, but also with other media) for purposes of teaching and learning. It can be used as a complement to traditional didactic methods, or a course can be given almost entirely using e-learning, for example in distance-learning programs (→Fernstudium). Commonly used e-learning tools at German universities for distance-learning or to complement traditional methods in a classroom include →ILIAS and →Moodle.

ECTS (ECTS) Abbreviation for: →*European Credit Transfer System*

Edu-Tainment (edutainment) popular science (→Populärwissenschaft)

Ehemalige (former student/staff member) →Alumni

Ehrenhalber (honorary) →honoris causa

Ehrendoktorat (honorary doctorate) Lat. *doctor* →*honoris causa* = honorary doctor. An honorary title given by a university based on achievements in or outside of the university.

Einführungsveranstaltung (introductory course) The first event in the semester for the newly enrolled students serves to orient the students at the university, institute, subject, or topic. In contrast to regular courses, the ~ is often a one-time event.

Einheit von Forschung und Lehre (unity of research and teaching) →Forschung und Lehre

Einleitung (introduction) Text on the first pages of a scientific work or the first page of a seminar paper that prepares readers for the contents. The purpose is to point out the focuses of the work and is therefore to be strictly separated from a foreword (→Vorwort) in terms of function.

Einschreibefrist (enrollment deadline, registration deadline) Last point in time at which an applicant can submit documents for a university place before the semester begins. If the student misses the deadline, then the right to a university place is lost.

Einschreibung (enrollment, registration) →Immatrikulation

Einwerbung (obtaining, procuring) external funding (→Drittmittel)

Elfenbeinturm (ivory tower) Metaphorical expression for an academia that is withdrawn from the world, hostile to the public, arrogant, and makes no effort to make its findings understandable to a general audience. This inaccessibility can be achieved with mathematical formulas or with terminology (→Terminologie) that is difficult to understand. The term is often used in discourses when new technologies are used, for example stem cell research or the use of nuclear energy. The physicist Robert Oppenheimer is often described as the archetype of a scientist (→Wissenschaftler) in an ~ in the literature due to his role in developing the atomic bomb, as the results of the research were more important to him than the possible dangers that could arise from non-scientists applying the knowledge (→Weltbild).

Elite-Hochschule (elite university) A much-discussed and cost-intensive type of German university according to the American model, the graduates of which are to be recruited as the next generation of managers in public service and the private sector. In contrast to regular universities, ~ make direct contact with the business world, offer better individual supervision and demand high tuition. Today there are no ~ in Germany in this sense, but there are universities with varying reputations, although the reputation usually varies among the disciplines.

Elite-Hochschule, amerikanische (American elite university) Usually private but state-supported universities in the United States, as they have existed for around 100 years. Characteristics are: high tuition fees, good student to teacher ratios, and excellent resources for teaching and learning, for example libraries that are open around the clock. There is no clear or legally binding definition of the term even in the USA. The average amount of tuition for private non-profit universities in the US was around $31,000 in 2014/15.

ELSA (ELSA) Abbreviation for: *European Law Students' Association*. Largest international association of law students, law interns, and career entrants in legal professions. www.elsa.org

Emeritierung (retirement to emeritus status) Retirement of a professor (→Emeritus).

Emeritus (emeritus) Lat. *emeritus* = retired, honorably discharged. A retired professor who continues to receive a full salary. The position of an ~ at a university is often described with the sentence: Relieved of obligations but not rights. That means that an emeritus professor may continue to be active at the university both in terms of courses and examinations as well as office hours (→Sprechstunden).

Empirie (empiricism) Greek *empereia* = experience. Data material obtained from observing nature and its analysis including conclusions about a general truth. ~ is a key method of all inductive sciences (→Wissenschaften), in particular of natural sciences. ~ is a contrasting method to hermeneutics (→Hermeneutik). (→Weltbild; →Wegestreit; →Logik)

Endnote 1. (final grade) The final evaluation in an examination process that can be made up of a (weighted) average from various grades such as the grades from oral examinations, coursework, and a final thesis.

2. **(endnote)** In contrast to footnotes (→Fußnoten), which are at the bottom of each page, ~ are collected at the end of a text and contain comments and/or citations with consecutive numbering.

Enzyklopädie (encyclopedia) Greek *kyklos* = cycle. Usually a multiple-volume set of books with the goal of describing the entirety of knowledge available in a particular academic or other subject: basic teachings of sciences and arts, online or in printed form. One of the most famous ~ is the Encyclopedia Britannica.
www.britannica.com

Erasmus/Erasmus+ (Erasmus/Erasmus+) Abbreviation for: European Action Scheme for the Mobility of University Students. EU initiative to promote international exchange and cooperation of universities in the EU. Students can travel as so-called "zero grant" students in which they enjoy the privileges and have the obligations of Erasmus+ students but receive no funding, or they can receive a grant to subsidize their stay abroad. In any case, students must apply to the Erasmus+ program through their home university and may also take advantage of language courses in the language of instruction for their upcoming program after acceptance. In 2008, Erasmus replaced the previous →Lifelong Learning Programme (LLP) and in 2014, Erasmus+ succeeded Erasmus. Each year, more than 250,000 students across Europe take part in the exchanges. The most popular destination countries are Spain, Germany, and France.

Erkenntnis (knowledge, insight, discovery) The goal of all research is a better understanding of how the world works. One speaks of the state of research (→Forschungsstand) in a discipline or topic if one wants to describe the sum of the published ~. The so-called cognitive sciences look into the psychological-medical functioning of human knowledge, epistemology investigates the philosophical aspects of the same question. Regardless of the discipline, obtaining ~ follows a certain path, such as: observation, memory, trial and error, comparison, and questioning (→Weltbild).

Errata (errata) →Corrigenda

Erstsemester (first-semester students) Term for newly enrolled students at a university. At universities in the United States, the corresponding term is "freshman" (→Freshman). In student slang, the slightly derogatory form is "Erstie."

Eselsbrücke (mnemonic aid, literally "donkey bridge") Help in memorizing numbers and facts with sayings, rhymes, or other ideas that have no relation to the actual topic (e.g. "I before E except after C..." as a spelling mnemonic or ROY G. BIV as an acronym mnemonic for the colors of the rainbow).

Ethik, wissenschaftliche (scientific ethics) Honor code that is unwritten or fixed in a university's mission statement (→Leitbild) for proper behavior within the sciences. For university operations, it is extremely important that it is adhered to. The following aspects make up the core of the rules of behavior:

The primary goal is striving for truth and knowledge, a lack of prejudice or overcoming prejudice and no superiority to any other groups, fair play, self-critical thinking, willingness to learn and develop further, willingness to engage in discussions, honesty and the recognition of others' work, not ignoring undesirable results, discipline, and hard work.

EU-Beschlüsse von Lissabon und Barcelona (EU decisions from Lisbon and Barcelona) In March 2000 and 2002, the EU member-state governments agreed on goals for economic and education policies toward more harmonization and quality assurance in European education according to standards that were yet to be set.

EURODOC (EURODOC) European association created in 2002 for doctoral candidates and young scientists. In 2015, it was made up of 32 national associations. According to the statutes, the objectives are: to represent doctoral candidates and junior researchers at the European level in matters of education, research, and professional development; to advance the quality of doctoral programs and the standards of research activity in Europe; to promote the circulation of information on issues regarding young researchers; organize events, take part in debates, and assist in the elaboration of policies about higher education and research in Europe; and to establish and promote cooperation between national associations representing doctoral candidates and junior researchers within Europe.
www.eurodoc.net

European Credit Transfer System **(European Credit Transfer System)** Also: ECTS. Point system to compare coursework completed within the EU in the framework of the Bologna Process (→Bologna-Prozess).

European Science Foundation **(European Science Foundation)** Foundation to promote scientific excellence in Europe, scientific exchange, and European projects.
www.esf.org

European University Institute **(European University Institute)** An institution founded by the member-states of the European Community in 1972 to promote doctoral candidates and dissertation projects, especially in the subjects history, law, economics, and political science.
www.iue.it

Evaluation (evaluation) Lat. *valere* = be worth.

1. The assessment of individual courses by the participants with a questionnaire that is more or less

standardized. The results of the ~ are usually not published and serve to give the instructors feedback to improve their teaching. Typical questions deal with: didactics, literature, understanding, speed of presentation, and possibilities for discussion.

2. In the framework of the debate on university reform (→Hochschulreform), a key term for the assessment of universities in general. The ~ has two particular focuses: quality assurance and accountability to performance transparency. Depending on the goal of the ~, the methods differ. On the one hand one can differentiate between quantitatively oriented ~ (e.g. number of students, external funding, number of intermediate examinations, dropout rates, number of graduates, semesters needed to complete a degree, doctorates, publications) and qualitatively focused procedures that are usually written by external reviewers as peer reviews (→*Peer Reviews*).

Evidenz (evidence) Lat. *evidentia* = proof. Sum of all empirical (→Empirie) proof and observations that provide the basis for scientific assessments. The philosopher Immanuel Kant called this basis discursive certainty (→Anschaulichkeit).

EX Abk. für: →Exkursion

Examen (examination) Lat. *examen* = examination. Academic final test (→Abschlussprüfung), in particular in the case of state examinations (→Staatsprüfung).

Exkursion (excursion, field trip, study trip) Lat. *excursus* = excursion. Academic educational trip to increase knowledge over a certain period of time with certain learning objectives for the participants, often held at the end of the semester.

Exlibris (exlibris, bookplate) Lat. *ex libris* = from the books, from the book collection. A label or stamp in a book to indicate its owner, often in the form of an artistic crest or detailed logo. The designs of the marks were often so demanding that they became their own art form, the so-called ex libris art. In contrast, the much simpler stamps from libraries are often found in several places in the book to prevent theft.

Exmatrikulation (de-registration, withdrawal) Opposite of enrollment (→Immatrikulation). Removal from a university's register of students (→Matrikel). The ~ can be done in various ways, either regularly after completing a degree program or forcibly, for example after missing the final deadline for re-registration (→Rückmeldung).

Expedition (expedition) Lat. *expeditio* = military campaign. Scientific research journey into an unknown area (→terra incognita), primarily for purposes of gaining knowledge, in contrast to an excursion (→Exkursion) for a course.

Experiment (experiment) →Versuch

Experte (expert) Lat. *experiri* = attempt, try. Person with experience and proven, especially practical, knowledge of a subject that goes beyond general knowledge. An academic education is not a requirement for being an ~ in an area.

Exposé (synopsis, summary) Lat. *expositum* = explanation. Draft of a scientific work, e.g. dissertation (→Doktorarbeit) to present to an editor, scholarship committee, or publishing house for evaluation in order to determine whether it is worth continuing the effort (→peer review) or, in the case of a scholarship, whether the student or doctoral candidate will be awarded a scholarship.

Externe Leistung (external achievement) Qualifications or degrees obtained or work, degree programs, internships, or other achievements completed outside of the university for which credit is given.

Extraordinarius (extraordinary professor) Professor without a separate chair (→Lehrstuhl) and with only few or no assistants.

Exzellenz der Hochschulen (university excellence) Collective term for the evaluation, improvement, and increase in performance for all universities in regards to the quality of activities in research and teaching, particularly in the context of the Bologna Process (→Bologna-Prozess). The discussion about the term and definition of "quality" or the indicators necessary to measure it is also linked to this. The ~ is also a term for the increasing competition among various universities.

Exzerpt (excerpt) Lat. *excerpere* = pluck. Extract from a work of research literature for the purpose of bundling the contents concisely depending on topic, for example when researching (→Recherche) an article (→Artikel) and leaving out information that is not relevant. ~ are the basis for evaluating the state of research.

Fachabitur (vocational university qualification) Originally: "Fachgebundene Hochschulreife" (subject-related university qualification), also used as a term for the qualification for entering universities of applied sciences. Secondary school degree that allows the person to study at a university of applied sciences. Without additional examinations, the ~ does not qualify the holder to study at a regular university.

Fachbereich (department) →Fakultät

Fächerkombination (subject combination) The permissible combination of two or three subjects for a degree program. In the case of Magister programs or education programs, these are usually one major and two minors or two majors. Not all subject combinations are possible. The degree program regulations (→Studienordnung) from the individual universities set down which combinations are allowed.

Fächerwahl, allgemeine (general selection of subjects) Must students at German universities choose subjects in legal, business, and social sciences. With around 822,000 students, this group of subjects makes up around 30% of the student body (2015). In recent years, this number has decreased by around 4%. The second most popular subject area is that of engineering with around 20% (→Nachwuchskrise).

Fachhochschule (university of applied sciences) Also: FH. Practice-oriented, professionally-focused university, usually with a strict →curriculum lasting around 8 semesters with less emphasis placed on research. Often in combination with high-level praxis semesters. Modern ~ increasingly have standards closer to that of regular universities.

Fachinformation (specialized information) Scientific or other information about a subject area that is made available by specialized providers: specialized libraries, newsletters, archives, specialized information centers, press agencies, associations, political parties, unions, or churches.

Fachmentor (Specialist mentor) →Mentor

Fachpublikum (specialist audience) The professional readers of scientific publications (→Publikation) or the entirety of scientists that follow the development of a subject with particular attention.

Fachreferent (subject specialist) Person responsible for an essential task such as semester planning in a faculty or institute. For example: internal communication, allocation of rooms and resources, or quality control.

Fachrichtung (subject area) Term for a degree program (→Studiengang) or the subject in general as a part of a faculty (→Fakultät).

Fachrichtungswechsel (change of subject) Changing the degree program or part of the degree program for various reasons (changing interests, suitability, strategy) with possible consequences for funding programs.

Fachschaft (student representatives for a department, student society) Originally a term for all students in a subject. However, it is now often used to denote a small group of students who volunteer to represent student interests within an institute or to advise individual students. There are often elections for the ~, and they usually have (a limited amount of) resources and their own rooms that can be used as common rooms.

Fachschaftsrat (student representative council) The permanent or ad hoc conference of members from the various departments' student representatives.

Fachschaftsvertreter (student representatives) The representatives for an institute's students vis-à-vis the institute management on a volunteer basis. The student representatives (→Fachschaft) are always organized as a grassroots democracy and are open for new members.

Fachschaftszeitung (student representative newspaper) Independent organ of the student representatives to announce certain activities, assess developments at the universities, and generally inform students. ~ are not a scientific medium.

Fachsemester (subject-related semester) Term for the number of semesters a certain subject has been studied. Leaves of absence count as university semesters (→Hochschul-semester) but not as ~, and the number of subject-related semesters can therefore be different from the number of university semesters. If a student changes degree programs (→Fachrichtungswechsel), this can also lead to a different number of university and subject-related semesters.

Fachsprache (technical language, jargon) Expressions within a subject area marked by word choice and type of argumentation that allow the specific problems of the discipline to be quickly communicated in a standard manner (→Terminologie).

Fachtagung (expert conference) →Kongress

Fahnenkorrektur (proof correction) One of the last stages in producing a book in which the typeset pages are once again checked for errors by the proofreader and author before going to print. Modern desktop publishing (→*Desktop Publishing*) transfers many of the tasks previously done by the typesetter to the author. Important tasks include: checking spelling and punctuation, formatting, position of graphics, and completeness. Content corrections and style improvements should be completed at an earlier point in the process. The special marks for ~ are set down in the DIN ISO 16511 and can be found in Duden or online.

Fahrender Schüler (traveling student) Antiquated term for a student traveling, usually during the time between two stays at universities. Also the name of a well-known student song from the 19th century (→Scholarenmigration).

Und die Straßen durchirr ich, die Plätze so schnell, ich klopfe von Hause zu Haus; bin ein fahrender Schüler, ein wüster Gesell, wer schützt mich vor Wetter und Graus?

Faksimile (facsimile) →Nachdruck

Fakultät (faculty, college, department, school) Lat. *facultas* = means, opportunity. Administrative unit for related subjects at a university. Not to be confused with a common use of the English "faculty" for the instructors at a university (→Lehrkörper). Universities in the Middle Ages only had four ~. Medicine, jurisprudence, philosophy, and theology. With the separation of natural sciences, more ~ were added. The ~ includes professors, mid-level instructors, students, administrative personnel, and technical staff members.

Fakultäten, Streit der (Conflict of the Faculties) An influential pamphlet published in 1798 by the philosopher Kant on the question of which of the classical university faculties (→Fakultäten) had the highest intellectual priority: philosophy, theology, medicine, or jurisprudence.

Fakultativ (elective) →Wahlfach

Fakultätsfarben (faculty colors) Individual faculties have been assigned colors since the Middle Ages and the rise of academic dress codes (→Kleiderordnung) so that the wearer of an academic robe or another piece of clothing could quickly be recognized as belonging to a certain faculty. These colors still exist in part today. In a chronicle for the University of Halle, in the year 1755 it was written that *the professors shall receive long robes according to the type worn at Oxford in England at the cost of the elector (Kurfürst), which they are to wear at all solemn occasions in the future. Theology had robes of fine black cloth trimmed with black velvet, and a four-cornered beret made of the same black velvet; jurisprudence scarlet; medicine flesh-colored; and philosophy violet.*

Fakultätsrat (faculty council) Organ of the faculty under the chairmanship of the dean (→Dekan) and participation of representatives from all faculty members to regulate all duties for which the faculty is responsible and not the chairs or the university.

Fakultätssiegel (faculty seal) Stamp or embossment to officially certify documents that were issued by the faculty in contrast to those of the

Falsifizierbarkeit (falsifiability) Lat. *falsum* = error. Scientific studies and theories must contain empirically verifiable conclusions. If this is not the case, then the theory is not falsifiable and thus not scientific. Important contributions on the topic of ~ were written by the philosopher Karl Popper. ~ differentiates true science from popular science (→Pseudowissenschaften) such as astrology or so-called paraphysics.

Famulatur (clinical traineeship, medical clerkship) Lat. *famulus* = servant. Internships for medical students in the clinical semesters lasting at least 3 months. The most famous representative in German literature is Wagner from Goethe's Faust.

Famulus (clinical trainee) →Famulatur

Faszikel (fascicles) Lat. *fasces* = bundle. Bundle of files, notebooks, or also an unbound partial volume of a work (→Werk), looseleaf collection.

Feedback (feedback) Reaction or critique of contents or form of courses, usually given to the lecturer in written or oral form by the student participants (→Evaluation) or in a standardized form. It can also be given within student study groups (→Lerngruppe).

Feldversuch (field trial) →Versuch

Fellow (fellow) Member of a college (→College) and thus, in English usage, a university employee with tasks in research and/or teaching (→Forschung und Lehre). The term is not used in a standardized manner, but ~ are normally at least graduates, usually scientists with doctorates (→promovierte Wissenschaftler) have a fixed-term contract. Permanent employees are more commonly called lecturers (→*Lecturer*).

Fernleihe (inter-library loan) Service offered by scientific libraries for a fee to procure books from the holdings of other libraries using the consortium system of library cooperation. In the catalog system of a library, titles can be included that are archived in other stacks (→Magazin), an external branch, or a connected library. In this case, the ~ is offered directly in the request form (→OPAC). (→Bibliotheksverbundsystem)

Fernstudium (distance-learning degree program, correspondence program) Studies done at home with books, lecture notes, and the internet. In some cases, the student must take examinations in person. (→Präsenzstudium)

Fernuniversität-Gesamthochschule (distance-learning university, open university) State university in Hagen offering only distance-learning programs leading to degrees such as Bachelor's and Master's as well as graduate studies. (→Mega University).

Festschrift (commemorative publication, *festchrift*) An edited book with essays published on a research focus for a special occasion in honor of a scientist, usually written and published by colleagues for a 65th birthday. ~ are often large volumes with two typical characteristics: the names of those offering congratulations are written on a *tabula gratulatoria*, although they do not necessary have to have written an essay for the publication, and: the foreword is often similar to a →laudatio. In the individual essays that follow, the accomplishments of the honored scientist are once again especially emphasized.

Flordame (no direct equivalent) Term from the language of fraternity students for a female visitor – possibly not a student – at a student event.

Fidibus (taper, punk, lighter) Old-fashioned term for a lighter in general or paper strips for lighting a flame in order to light a pipe. In the 17th century, smoking was prohibited for students at many universities (usually punishable by corporal punishment or a detention cell (→Karzer)). It wasn't until the revolution in 1848 in the course of the street battles that public smoking was generally tolerated by the authorities.

Fiebiger Plan (Fiebiger's Plan) An initiative named after the experimental physicist Prof. Nikolaus Fiebiger (University of Erlangen) to assist and promote young scientists at German universities.

Findbuch (inventory, index) Catalog of the archival units included in the holdings (→Bestand). The structure of the ~ shows the content organization of an archive (→Archiv).

Follow-up **Kontakte (follow-up contacts)** →Nachkontakte; →Alumni

Förderungshöchstdauer (maximum funding period) Time limit of a funding program such as (→Bafög) or a scholarship (→Stipendium) which can differ depending on the degree program, project, or other conditions.

Förderverein (booster club, organization of supporters) Group of friends, members, and former members of a university, usually in the form of a non-profit and recognized association (eingetragener Verein, e.V.) for the purpose of funding or otherwise supporting a university, e.g. with public relations work.

Format, DIN (DIN format) Formats established by the German institute for standardization of paper in 1922, approximately according to the length ratio of the so-called "Golden Ratio." The ~ has also become the standard in book formats for scientific publications.
www.din.de/en
DIN A0 = 841 x 1189 mm; DIN A1 = 594 x 841 mm; DIN A2 = 420 x 594 mm; DIN A3 = 297 x 420 mm; DIN A4 = 210 x 297 mm; DIN A5 = 148 x 210 mm; DIN A6 = 105 x 148 mm

Format, traditionelles (traditional format) The ratio between the width and length of a book or only the length. The traditional terms for the book formats have rarely been used since the introduction of the

DIN formats (→Format, DIN) and primarily serve to describe antique books, e.g. collections of rare books (→R̲a̲ra), incunabula (→Inkunabel), and manuscripts (→Handschrift).

Forschung (research) Science that is less focused on training new researchers than on obtaining new knowledge. German universities follow the principle of the unity of research and teaching that obligates all professors to fulfill both tasks. Pure research is thus primarily done at special institutions in the private sector, whereby research cannot be strictly separated from teaching here, either.

Forschung, Grenzen der (limits of research) Theoretically, every area could be the subject of academic research, but the possibilities for research can be restricted by technical and legal limits. In the first case, one speaks of parascience (→Parawissenschaften) if research is conducted despite technological inferiority. An example of the second case is embryo research, which reaches ethical and legal limits, e.g. if the basic rights of third parties are threatened. Here often no clear answer can be expected, or various solutions are offered depending on the legal system, the result of balancing interests, or the culture.

Forschung, interdisziplinäre (interdisciplinary research) Linking two different subjects to explain something is typical in both basic research (→Grundlagenforschung) as well as applied research (→Forschung). For example, sociologists, ethnologists, city planners, and epidemiologists could work together on projects to fight epidemics.

Forschung und Lehre (research and teaching) Principle of unity according to the ideal of the Humboldtian university reform (→Humboldtschen Universitätsreform) in the 19th century, whereby ~ are to make up a unified whole. According to Art. 5(2) of the Basic Law, art, science, research, and teaching are free. This is the foundation upon which the autonomy of content and administration at German universities is based. Universities are to be free from political, financial, and other dependencies or external interference to the greatest extent possible. That means: The universities govern themselves under the auspices of a ministry. In a decision by the Federal Constitutional Court, it was stated that "In favor of the freedom of science, the basic idea behind this right to freedom is to be taken into consideration: that science freed from the ideas of social utility and political relevance serves the state and society best in the end." (BVerfGE 47, 327 (370))

The freedom of ~ is not absolute, however. It is dependent on financing, teaching plans, framework laws, and parameters of the modern mass university.

Forschungsauftrag (research agreement) The goal formulated for a research plan by an educational institution or another authority to a scientist or institution. It is often linked to a waiver of teaching responsibilities.

Forschungsbericht (research report) With ~, scientists or scientific institutions inform their funders, contractors, the scientific community, or the general public about new knowledge and progress. The editorial context of a ~ can be a scientific journal or a separate publication series.

Forschungsdisziplin (research discipline) →Fachrichtung

Forschungsfreiheit (freedom of research) →Forschung und Lehre

Forschungsförderung (research funding) Funding of research by third parties, e.g. the state, quasi-state institutions, foundations, or other institutions connected to a specific project.

Forschungsfreisemester (sabbatical, literally: free semester for research) →Sabbatjahr

Forschungsgegenstand (object of research) The defined topic of scientific work or of an institution for which the focus is on obtaining new knowledge. The original challenge of scientific work is always finding the ~, describing it, and precisely delimiting it so that further systematic steps are possible.

Forschungslandkarten (research maps) Geographical list of research institutions according to their region with brief information. (→Wissenschaftsstandort)

www.forschungsportal.net

Forschungsliteratur (research literature) →Literatur

Forschungssemester (sabbatical, literally: research semester) →Sabbatjahr

Forschungsstand (state of research, state of the art) The status of knowledge at a particular point in time as can be found in expert literature (→Fachliteratur) including all consensuses and controversies (→Kontroversen). Recognizing and understanding the current state of research is the first goal in investigating a new object of research (→Forschungsgegenstand).

Forschungsvorhaben (research project) The concrete description of a scientific project with all of the sub-aspects (objectives, methods, data, research questions, state of research) is not only a precondition for proper scientific work but is also required for obtaining funding or other support by external parties (personnel, material, time).

Fortschritt, wissenschaftlicher (scientific progress) In a general sense, an improvement of the foundation for what is to follow. The intellectual-historical requirement for the term "progress" is a linear worldview (→Weltbild) instead of a circular one and thus the idea that the world changes or can be changed as has been prevalent in the European intellectual tradition especially since the French Revolution and the Enlightenment.

Frat (frat) →Fraternity

Fraternity **(fraternity)** A term for student societies (→Studentenverbindung) in connection with universities in the United States since the country's independence. The names are usually made up of three Greek letters, which is why the American fraternity and sorority system is also often called the →Greek System, and the students in the association can be referred to as Greeks. Student societies open only to women are called →sororities. The Greek letters usually stand as an acronym for the association's motto, which is often secret. In addition to assisting with social contacts, a key task of the ~ was to convey knowledge and skills to their members that were not elements of the traditional academic canon.

Frauenbeauftragter (women's representative, women's affairs officer) →Gleichstellungsbeauftragter

Frauenanteil (proportion of women) →Gleichstellung

Frauenstudium (women studying) This was known in antiquity and the Middle Ages but was very rare. It only became widespread after the end of the First World War – at the same time as women's suffrage in many countries. In Germany, the Kingdom of Wuerttemberg was the pioneer and introduced regulations in 1904 that not only allowed women to enroll at university but also supported them.

Fraunhofer Gesellschaft (Fraunhofer Gesellschaft) An initiative founded in 1949 by the state, companies, and universities in Germany and abroad oriented on practical research. It is named after the Munich physician Joseph von Fraunhofer (1787-1826).
www.fraunhofer.de/en

Freihandbereich (open stacks) →Lesesaal

Freie Rede (speaking freely) Speaking in front of an audience without or with only very few notes is one of the most important skills of a modern scientist and is expected as an element of a professional lecture.

Freischuss (free examination attempt, literally "free kick") →Freiversuch

Freitisch (free meals) Complete or partial discount of the cost of meals in the canteen for students in need.

Freiversuch (free attempt) Also: Freischuss. The possibility to take an examination without the results counting against the students who fail. Those who fail can re-take the examination without any penalty.

Freshman **(freshman)** Semi-official term at universities in the United States for a first-year student. Other terms are also given according to the year: Sophomore (2nd year), Junior (3rd year), and Senior (4th year).

Fulbright **Programm (Fulbright program)** Partnership program started in 1952 named after the US Senator J. William Fulbright and based in

Berlin with the aim of promoting bilateral contact on the basis of exchange programs between German and American students and researchers.

eca.state.gov/fulbright

Fußnote (footnote) Scientific method of referring to external texts, for example other publications, or to matters of marginal importance that would interrupt the flow of the main text. ~ are entered with running numbers at the bottom of a page below a line or the numbers can start anew on each page. (→Endnote).

G

GATE (GATE) Abbreviation for →*Guide to Academic Training and Education*

Gastdozent (visiting professor, guest professor) Member of a university who works for another university for a limited period of time in research or teaching, usually in the framework of an international exchange program. (→*Sabbatical*)

Gastdozentenhaus (housing for visiting professors) →Gästehaus

Gästehaus (guest house) Housing near campus for external guests staying for a short period of time, for visiting professors for a longer period of time (→*Sabbatical*), for university retirees, or for permanent residents.

Gasthörer (auditor, guest student) Someone attending a course who is not enrolled as a regular student. ~ cannot take any examinations, but they can obtain certificates of attendance for the courses.

Gastprofessor (visiting professor) →Gastdozent

Gastvortrag (guest lecture) In a general sense, a lecture by an external expert on a particular topic of a course or other event, e.g. in →Studium Generale is meant. "External" can mean: from outside of the university or only from outside of the course.

Gaudeamus Igitur (Gaudeamus Igatur) Lat. *gaudeamus igitur* = Let us rejoice! A student song from the 13th century known worldwide even at Asian and South American universities. The manuscript of the oldest German translation from the 18th century is in the West German library in Marburg. The Latin text of the first three verses is:

|: *Gaudeamus igitur, iuvenes dum sumus;:*| *post iucundam iuventutem* post molestam senectutem |: nos habit humus!:| Vita nostra brevis est, Brevi finietur, :| Venit mors velociter, *Rapit nos atrociter*, |: *Nemini parcetur.* :| *Ubi sunt, qui ante nos in mundo fuere? Vadite ad superos, transite ad inferos, hos si vis videre.*

Gaudeamus Igitur, English version In a popular translation by Mark Sugars from 1997:

1. While we're young, let us rejoice, Singing out in gleeful tones; After youth's delightful frolic, And old age (so melancholic!), Earth will cover our bones.

2. Where are those who trod this globe, In the years before us? They in hellish fire below, Or in Heaven's kindly glow, Swell th' eternal chorus.

3. Life is short and all too soon, We emit our final gasp; Death ere long is on our back; Terrible is his attack; None escapes his dread grasp.

Gedankenexperiment (thought experiment) Part of scientific methods (→Methode). With assumptions that contradict reality with one or more aspects, an attempt is made to find out what the essence of the correlation being investigated is. These investigations are based on counterfactual assumptions of the type: "What if..." One of the most ancient thought experiments comes from the Greek philosopher Xenophanes of Colophon. It is: *If god had not made yellow honey, people would think that figs were far sweeter.* (→Versuch).

Geistesblitze (flash of inspiration) Phenomenon that occurs when intensively studying an object in which an intellectual insight comes suddenly and can overcome an earlier block. The leap in understanding cannot be logically reconstructed (→Fortschritt). Characteristic for a ~ is the transfer of a principle between two essentially different areas: The construction of the steam machine by James Watt after observing a tea kettle or the calculation of the planets' orbits by Johannes Keppler after attempts to estimate the volume of wine casks are two examples of classic scientific ~.

Geisteswissenschaften (liberal arts, humanities) A term arising from a translation of the English term "moral science" for all academic subjects that deal with questions of the human condition, that is, the place of people in the world. The following subjects are included in the traditional canon: Greek-Roman antiquity, literary studies, philosophy, legal sciences, art history, religious studies, literary criticism, art criticism, history, archaeology, and political science.

Geländepraktikum (field course) Course in which independent work is done under supervision (→Praktikum).

Gelehrter (scholar) Essentially a non-academic term for a person whose profession consists of obtaining and passing on education in a general sense (universal scholar). This is not always linked to a position at a university. In today's usage, the term – which has become rare – usually refers to a scientist with academic degrees. The modern university, with the high degree of importance it places on specialization, no longer allows for the existence of more general scholars. As an ideal type of German ~, Gottfried Wilhelm Leibniz is often named.

Gen<u>ie</u> (genius) Lat. *genius* = protective spirit. A rare type of person who has talent in one or several subjects that is far above average.

Genieklausel (genius provision) Provision for exceedingly talented applicants for university places or applicants for an academic position that is intended to make acceptance easier (Sec. 44 German Higher Education Framework Act (*Hochschulrahmengesetz*), HRG).

German University Cairo **(German University in Cairo)** Joint project by the Universities of Stuttgart and Ulm in Cairo in the form of a private university financed by Egyptian investors. The degree programs offered there are: medical engineering, information technology, material sciences, management, pharmacy, and biotechnology.

Gesamthochschule (comprehensive university) Concept developed in the 1970s that is a combination of a regular university and a university of applied sciences.

Gesellschaften, wissenschaftliche (academic societies, scientific societies) Usually open associations structured as non-profit organizations whose goal is to increase the rate of dissemination and thus the acceptance of an academic discipline with lobbying. Well-known examples are the Royal Society, the *Académie Française*, or, the oldest, the *Accademia dei Lincei* in Rome.

Gesellschaftswissenschaften (social sciences) Application of scientific methods to social phenomena. In English they are sometimes referred to pejoratively as soft sciences. The ~ include sociology, political science, linguistics, communication science, business and economic science, and anthropology. It is difficult to clearly assign many subjects since there are overlaps (→Nexialistik) among the three basic types of sciences as well as individual forms, special statuses, and many points of contact, so that the traditional separation into natural sciences, humanities, and social sciences has become questionable.

GEW (GEW) → Gewerkschaft Erziehung und Wissenschaft

Gewerkschaft Erziehung und Wissenschaft (German Union for Education and Science) Also: GEW. Trade union for the interest representation of all persons employed in the area of education from preschool to university.
www.gew.de

Gleichstellung (gender equality, equal opportunity) The attempt to equalize the numerical imbalance between men and women in the higher career stages at universities. While the number of women enrolled at universities has developed very positively, women are still greatly underrepresented in higher positions. The proportion of first-year students who were women was 49.8% in 2014/2015 in Germany. The proportion of female graduates was even higher with 50.6%. The proportion (→Frauenanteil) decreases to only 45.5% for doctorates and 27.8% for habilitations (→Habilitation). These numbers are very high in comparison to the past, but they are far from equal (→*affirmative action*; →Chancengleichheit).

Gleichstellungsbeauftragter (gender equality officer, equal opportunity officer) Special function at a university or in a faculty to equalize the representation of men and women, which is still very different, or to object to disadvantages and discrimination, and to increase the number of female students e.g. in technical subjects. The key areas of focus are: applications, "gender-specific" continuing education offers, mentoring for women (→Mentoring), assisting in finding daycare spots, documentation, work in various committees and working groups, and support for women and gender studies.

Globalhaushalt (globalized budget) The lump sum provided to a university from the *Land* that the university can allocate for the most part independently and autonomously. These funds are only rarely sufficient, however, and the universities must therefore request funding from others, so-called external funding (→Drittmittel).

Glossar (glossary) Collection of explanations of difficult terms or specialized terminology (→Terminologie). Usually found in the form of a list, especially at the end of a specialist publication.

Glosse (gloss) Greek *glossa* = tongue, langauge. Comment (→Anmerkung) on an academic subject with a definition, position, or more detailed description, for example in the context of a publication.

Go-in **("go-in")** The ~ was developed as a method of political protest in the time of the student movement (→Studentenbewegung). An event was attended in order to force a discussion by means of a provocative demeanor or systematic disruptions. The ~ was used in particular in the 1960s at universities in the United States and is successfully used in protest actions (→Protestaktionen) and strikes up to the present. Occupations and protest marches in general have a very long tradition, and there is evidence that they took place at schools in antiquity.

Goethe-Institut (Goethe Institute) Institution founded in 1952 with its headquarters in Munich to spread and maintain the German language and cultural communication between the Federal Republic of Germany and foreign countries as well as to provide education for foreign teachers of German.
www.goethe.de/en

Göttinger Sieben (Göttingen Seven) Group of professors in Göttingen who protested against the abolition of the constitution of the Kingdom of Hanover in 1837 and were therefore fired and some even sent into exile. They included: Wilhelm Eduard Albrecht, constitutional law expert; Friedrich Christoph Dahlmann, historian; Heinrich Ewald, Middle East specialist; Jacob Grimm, German specialist; Wilhelm Grimm, German specialist; Georg Gottfried Gervinus, literary historian; Wilhelm Eduard Weber, physicist.

Göttinger Achtzehn (Göttingen Eighteen) Group of atomic physicists who spoke out against the planned arming of the *Bundeswehr* with atomic weapons in 1957. They included: Fritz Bopp, Max Born, Rudolf Fleischmann, Walther Gerlach, Otto Hahn, Otto Haxel, Werner Heisenberg, Hans Kopfermann, Max von Laue, Heinz Maier-Leibnitz, Josef Mattauch, Friedrich-Adolf Paneth, Wolfgang Paul, Wolfgang Riezler, Fritz Strassmann,

Wilhelm Walcher, Carl Friedrich von Weizsäcker, and Karl Wirtz.

Göttliches Prinzip (divine principle) The relationship between religion and science has always been problematic, whereby the mutual influences have displayed nearly every practical and imaginable facet between irreconcilability and mutual inspiration depending on the age from antiquity until the present. Links between the triumph of the sciences in Europe and the Judeo-Christian tradition of a legally oriented monotheism have often been discussed (→Weltbild; →Lebenswissenschaften).

Graduieren (to graduate) Lat. *gradi* = to step. Complete an academic degree (→Abschluss) and obtain a title (→Titel).

Graduiertenförderung (graduate assistance, graduate funding) Support for graduated students for further academic development after their →Master's degree, for example to work on a doctorate (→Promotion). (→Stipendium)

Graduiertenkolleg (research training group) Academic continuing education measure for students who have completed a degree, for example doctoral candidates who would like to prepare themselves to continue their studies and thus an academic career. ~ are usually supported by third parties, e.g. the German Research Foundation (→DFG) and make it possible to work on specific, time-consuming or resource-consuming, and intensive research that cannot be done by individual researchers.

Graduierter (graduate) An academic (→Akademiker) who recently completed university successfully and has not yet entered a career.

Gräkum (examination on Ancient Greek, Graecum) Proof of good knowledge of the Ancient Greek language. Together with the examinations on Latin (→Latinum) and Hebrew (→Hebraikum), it is part of the classical language education.

***Grandes Ecoles* (Grand ecoles)** French *grandes écoles* = grand schools. Group of the most important French universities, comparable to the →Ivy League in the United States. The education is of various lengths up to three years depending on the institution. Although there is no authoritative list of ~, examples are the Ecole Normale Supérieure (ENS), the Ecole Nationale d'Administration (ENA), and the Ecole Polytechnique in Paris. For historical reasons, the German university system (→Hochschullandschaft) has no corresponding term for the group of the most important universities. That is why the discussion about elite universities (→Elitehochschulen) in the Federal Republic has a different significance than in France or the United States.

Gravitas (gravitas, dignity, seriousness) Lat. = weight, heaviness. Demeanor of professors that emphasizes the importance of the contents being discussed or the person himself. ~ includes gestures, facial expressions, and the tone of the lecture or the actual or supposed dignity in the general demeanor as it is expected from a professor but not from students. The typical habitus of professors has always been a welcome opportunity for mockery.

Greek System **(Greek system)** Most student societies (→Studentenverbindung) at universities in the United States (→fraternities and →sororities) use two or three Greek letters as an abbreviation for the full, secret name, but the letters are usually written in the Latin alphabet, (e.g. alpha kappa tau). Members of these societies, also called *student corporations* or *academic corporations*, are thus sometimes collectively called the ~. Most of the societies have certain rituals that arose in connection to the Masonic traditions and identifying signs.

Gremium (body, committee) Lat. *gremium* = lap, bosom. Body or organ of a university. Important ~ include: the senate (→Senat), rector's office (→Rektorat) or executive committee (→Präsidium), other committees, and the constituted student body (→verfasste Studentenschaft). Due to the differing charters (→Grundordnung) of German universities, there is no standard terminology as relates to the ~.

Großmuttertest (grandmother test) Joking term for the prudent requirement for academic texts that they be written in a language that is understandable to the general public. A text that cannot be understood by an outsider (personified by the grandmother) has failed the ~ and should be rewritten. The basic idea is that the scientific character (→Wissenschaftlichkeit) arises from the methods (→Methode) and not primarily from the use of technical jargon.

Grundlagenforschung (basic research, fundamental research, frontier research) The scientific handling of basic questions of a subject, the compilation, verification, and discussion of principles of a science, particularly in the natural sciences, that is often uncertain in the applicability of the findings. It is therefore different from applied science, which is always conducted on behalf of a precise question.

Grundmittel (basic funds) Funds from institutions that support the university are the primary source of funding. In 2011, the total was around 21.9 billion euros. The ~ are complemented by so-called external funding (→Drittmittel). In 2011, for example, the average amount of external funding for each professor at every kind of university in Germany (with the exception of the administrative universities) was 160,800 euros. However, there is a great deal of variation depending on the subject area (→Grundmittel).

Grundordnung (charter, basic order) The university constitution. One can differentiate between the more modern executive committee constitution (→Präsidialverfassung) and the traditional rector constitution (→Rektoratsverfassung). These university statutes are usually limited by the provisions of the *Land*'s higher education act, and that is in turn shaped by the German Higher Education Framework Act (→Hochschulrahmengesetz). According to this, the universities have a great deal of autonomy but are not completely sovereign (→Forschung und Lehre).

Grundordnungsversammlung (charter meeting) When a university is founded, the ~ is a committee that meets to consult on the charter (→Grundordnung). The result of the meeting is a kind of constitution according to the stipulations of the *Land*'s higher education act. The ~ decides whether there will be an executive committee or rector constitution, about the size and make-up of the individual bodies, the division of the faculties, and the terms of office.

Grundstudium (basic study period) The first semesters of studies before the intermediate examination (→Zwischenprüfung) in contrast to the advanced study period (→Hauptstudium). The ~ serves primarily to learn the basic techniques of academic work and terminology (→Terminologie). The focus is thus less on contents or current research and more on the canon of a subject, the way the library functions, the citation methods, organization of sources and materials, etc. Depending on the subject, the ~ can be highly structured. With the introduction of the Bachelor's/Master's system (→Bologna-Prozess), the term ~ is not used as frequently, as the division between the ~ and the advanced study period with the intermediate examination no longer exists.

Gründungsmythos (founding myth) Legends exist about the founding date and circumstances of many universities; for example Oxford University claims to have been founded by survivors of the Trojan War, in particular by the hero Aeneas and thus a son of the goddess Venus and an ancestor of Julius Caesar. The University of Paris, somewhat more humbly, names Charlemagne as its founding father.

GS (GS) Abbreviation for: →Grundstudium

GUC (GUC) Abbreviation for: →*German University Cairo*

***Guide to Academic Training and Education* (Guide to Academic Training and Education)** With the initiative of the →DAAD and the German Rectors' Conference (→HRK), a consortium of German universities founded with the goal of advertising Germany as a place to study and to inform about possibilities for study and research in Germany. The university consortium is supported by the German federal government as part of a comprehensive marketing strategy.

Gutachten 1. (expert review, report) Term from the applied sciences (→angewandten Wissenschaften).

Evaluation of a practical research project by an expert (→Experte), for example by a structural engineer if construction is planned. ~ are usually an important source of income or a part-time job (→Nebentätigkeit) for researchers whose field is open for practical application.

2. (review, evaluation) Assessment report of an academic work by a corrector (→Korrektor) or reviewer, usually in the context of a Master's thesis (→Master-Arbeit) or dissertation (→Dissertation).

Gymnasium (secondary school) Greek *gymnos* = naked. Secondary school that goes until the twelfth or thirteenth grade and ends with a certificate that qualifies the graduate to attend university (→Abitur or Matura). The ~ can have different concentrations, for example languages, natural sciences, technical areas, and music. At English-language universities, and increasingly in Germany, as well, the term "gym" still denotes the hall in which sports are played, as the term was originally used.

Habilitand (habilitation candidate) Typically a researcher with a doctorate who is working on a habilitation (→Habilitation).

Habilitation (post-doctoral lecturing qualification, habilitation) Lat. *habilitare* = enable. Highest academic degree (→Grad) awarded on the basis of an extensive scientific work or collection of publications (cumulative habilitation), an academic discussion (not an examination in the traditional sense), and a lecture. At the end of a successful ~, the habilitation candidate obtains a lecturing qualification (→*venia legendi*).
The provisions for the ~, which are set down in the habilitation regulations (→Habilitationsordnungen) of the individual universities can differ. However, the degree obtained is Dr. habil (but not: →Professor).

Habiltitationsordnung (habilitation regulations) The provisions valid at a university on habilitations. Important aspects relate to the habilitation committee, acceptance as a habilitation candidate, the review and acceptance of the postdoctoral thesis, the trial lecture and colloquium, the expansion of the teaching qualification, and provisions about the regulations taking effect.

Habilitationsrecht (right to award habilitations) The right of a university to award the lecturing qualification (→*venia legendi*).

Habilitationsschrift (postdoctoral thesis, habilitation treatise) A written work of research often made up of several volumes, usually longer than an average →dissertation, the most advanced type of final thesis and a condition for the lecturing qualification (→*venia legendi*).

Habilitationszahlen (habilitation statistics) Overview of the number of habilitations awarded according to *Bundesland*. In 2014, there were a total of 1,627 in Germany. According to *Bundesländer*: Baden-Wuerttemberg: 266; Bavaria: 311; Berlin: 110; Brandenburg: 22, Bremen: 6; Hamburg: 72; Hesse: 133; Mecklenburg-Western Pomerania: 35; Lower Saxony: 112; North Rhine-Westphalia: 264; Rhineland-Palatinate: 45; Saarland: 24; Saxony: 92; Saxony-Anhalt: 43; Schleswig-Holstein: 35; Thuringia: 57

Hambacher Fest (Hambach Festival) Mass political event at Hambach Castle near Neustadt a.d. Haardt, where around 30,000 participants including many students and professors stood up for democratic reforms, freedom, civil rights, and a modern constitution in 1832.

Handschriftenlesesaal (manuscript reading room) Special room in a library for viewing expensive and rare, handwritten manuscripts, some of which are on parchment or papy-

rus, whereby the actual originals are only rarely given out. Instead, reprints or digital versions are preferred. One of the most expensive manuscripts in the German-speaking countries is the so-called *Codex Manesse*, the Heidelberg manuscript of songs (*Liederhandschrift*) from the 14th century that can be viewed in its entirety online in digital form:
http://digi.ub.uni-heidelberg.de/cpg 848

Härtefall (hardship case) A regulation for exceptions or relief that can be applied under particular conditions to repeat failed examinations, for example after illness, blows of fate, or accidents. The requirement is an approved hardship case request. There are also usually provisions or even quotas for ~ when applying for admission to degree programs.

Handapparat (seminar binder) →Seminarapparat

Handbuch (handbook) Term for a comprehensive reference work with important basic information on a subject or topic. In libraries they can usually be found in the open stacks and as part of the non-lending collection.

Handout (handout) Concisely formulated informational sheet designed to accompany and complement a presentation. It is handed out at the beginning of a presentation or lecture. A ~ usually includes the title of the course including all information on the lecturer, the presenter, the date, and the topic of the presentation. In addition to information on key literature, information is included that is meant to make it easier to understand the presentation but does not repeat it. It is important that the description of the main points is understandable. The ~ and the presentation complement each other. Clarity and conciseness are key for a ~.

Handout, Bewertung (evaluation of a handout) The following criteria are often used to assess the quality of a handout. This is relevant for grading. The paper and format: DIN A4, white, printed, few bolded words/sections, with page numbers, font Times or Arial 12 point, clearly designed with good graphics; top section: course, instructor, semester, faculty, university, date, name, subject combination of presenter, title of presentation; middle section: outline of presentation, key theses on the topic, key names, dates, graphs, tables, important citations or illustrations, not a repetition of the presentation but complementary, not too full of information; bottom section: important literature, photo credits, page numbers (e.g. 1 of 2), footnotes or endnotes only when necessary.

Hauptstudium (advanced study period) Term for the period of studies after the basic study period and before the degree. In the advanced study period, more in-depth knowledge of academic working methods are required (→Grundstudium).

Hauptseminar (advanced seminar) Term for seminars in the advanced study period with stricter formal requirements and advanced contents than in the introductory seminars (→Proseminar) in the basic study period (→Grundstudium). The credits earned for ~ make up the basis for registering for the final degree examination (→Abschlussprüfung). After the introduction of the Bachelor's/Master's system (→Bologna-Prozess), the term ~ is rarely used, as the more advanced seminars are now part of the Master's programs.

Hausarbeit (seminar paper, essay) Paper to be written by students according to precise formal requirements including an academic research question without independent research between 10 and 25 pages depending on the course. A ~ includes the following parts: →title page, table of contents, introduction, structured main section, conclusion, annexes, and literature (→Literaturangaben).

Hausarbeitenbörse (seminar paper exchange) Database-supported website on which completed seminar papers (→Hausarbeit) can be published and downloaded. ~ serve for informing other students about methods but can also be abused as a source for plagiarism (→Plagiat).

Hebraikum (examination for Hebrew) Proof of good knowledge of Hebrew. Together with the examinations for Latin (→Latinum) and Ancient Greek (→Gräkum), it is part of the classical language education.

Herausgeber (editor) The person responsible for a publication (→Publikation) in contrast to an author; often in connection with anthologies or journals, whereby an editor can also be an author. Editorship and authorship must be strictly separated in the literature references (→Literaturangaben).

Herbarium (herbarium) Lat. *herbarium* = herb garden. Collection of dried plants for the purposes of teaching and research.

Hermann von Helmholtz Gemeinschaft Deutscher Forschungszentren (Hermann von Helmholtz Association of German Research Centres) Association of 15 research centers between universities and industry with technical equipment and in international cooperation. www.helmholtz.de/en

Hermeneutik (hermeneutics) Greek *hermeneutike* = translate, interpret. The term can be traced back to the Greek god Hermes, who had the task of passing on messages from the father of the gods, Zeus, in an encrypted form to people, which is why ~ is the art of deciphering. The philosophers Schleiermacher and Gadamer described ~ in general as the art of understanding. In contrast to empirics (→Empirie), ~ is used in particular in relation to art, literature, and music as well as in theology when interpreting Biblical passages.

Hierarchie (hierarchy) Greek *hierarchia* = rule of a high priest. Term for the structure of organizations according to the rank of the authorities or offices from top to bottom. The hierarchical structure of many institutes and departments is described as an obstacle to innovation by critics; in Germany and Austria, discussions on this also touch on the status of civil servants (→Beamtenstatus) and the habilitation (→Habilitation).

Hilfskraft (student assistant) Usually a student employee in a department (→Lehrstuhl), responsible for preparing and following-up on courses (→Lehrveranstaltung), organizing appointments, making copies, preparing seminar binders (→Seminarapparat), and assisting the professors for low wages. The origin of the abbreviation "Hiwi" is controversial. It is possible that it is derived from the term "Hilfswilliger" (voluntary helper) from the Second World War in the occupied areas, including the meaning of "collaborator."

Hippokratischer Eid (Hippocratic Oath) Traditional oath now usually only taken note of for the sake of completeness. It is a self-obligation of physicians written by the Greek physician Hippocrates. The full oath in a translation by James Copland in 1825 is:

I swear by Apollo the physician, and Aesculapius the surgeon, likewise Hygeia and Panacea, and call all the gods and goddesses to witness, that I will observe and keep this underwritten oath, to the utmost of my power and judgment.

I will reverence my master who taught me the art. Equally with my parents, will I allow him things necessary for his support, and will consider his sons as brothers. I will teach them my art without reward or agreement; and I will impart all my acquirement, instructions, and whatever I know, to my master's children, as to my own; and likewise to all my pupils, who shall bind and tie themselves by a professional oath, but to none else. With regard to healing the sick, I will devise and order for them the best diet, according to my judgment and means; and I will take care that they suffer no hurt or damage.

Nor shall any man's entreaty prevail upon me to administer poison to anyone; neither will I counsel any man to do so. Moreover, I will give no sort of medicine to any pregnant woman, with a view to destroy the child. Further, I will comport myself and use my knowledge in a godly manner. I will not cut for the stone, but will commit that affair entirely to the surgeons.

Whatsoever house I may enter, my visit shall be for the convenience and advantage of the patient; and I will willingly refrain from doing any injury or wrong from falsehood, and (in an especial manner) from acts of an amorous nature, whatever may be the rank of those who it may be my duty to cure, whether mistress or servant, bond or free. Whatever, in the course of my practice, I may see or hear (even when not invited), whatever I may happen to obtain knowledge of, if it be not proper to repeat it, I will keep sacred and secret within my own breast. If I faithfully observe this oath, may I thrive and prosper in my fortune and profession, and live in the estimation of posterity; or on breach thereof, may the reverse be my fate!

HIS (HIS) Abbreviation for: →Hochschul-Informationssystem

HISinOne (HISinOne) Web-based management system for universities for the entire student process as well as all other university management tasks. Many German universities began to introduce the new system between 2013 and 2015, although in most cases it is a process that takes several years.

Hiwi (student assistant) Abbreviation for: →Hilfskraft, studentische

hochgestellte Ziffer (superscript number) In bibliographical references, the number of the edition is usually placed as a superscript Arabic numeral directly after the title in order to specify the edition, as the page numbers of the individual editions can differ due to the revisions. Alternatively, the edition can be given in parentheses after the title.

Hochschule (higher education institution) Summarizing term for various types of universities (→Hochschularten) that are set up according to the principle of research and teaching (→Forschung und Lehre) and give a scientific education as regulated by the German Higher Education Framework Act (→Hochschulrahmengesetz) or the state higher education acts. A ~ has the following basic structure:

A rector's office or executive committee, a chancellor and central administration, a senate, faculties, institutes, departments, chairs, computing center, advising offices, office of international affairs, and libraries.

Hochschul-Informationssystem (university information system) Service company founded in 1969 for universities and state university planning. It provides software solutions for universities to increase effectiveness and manage university administration, the use of university institutions, duration of studies, drop-outs, changes in degree programs, and career chances.
www.his.de

Hochschulabsolvent (university graduate) →Absolvent

Hochschularten (types of universities) In Germany, one differentiates among universities (→Universität), technical universities (Technische Universität), equivalent universities (gleichgestellte Hochschule), universities of applied sciences (→Fachhochschule), comprehensive universities (→Gesamthochschule), and pedagogical universities (→Pädagogische Hochschule). There are also less common types of universities such as music academies, mountain academies, and church universities. Universities can also be separated according to the supporting institutions: public or private, whereby the Bundeswehr

Universities in Hamburg and Munich have a special status.

Hochschulautonomie (autonomy of universities) Legally guaranteed independence of the universities and their charters (→Grundordnung), or the regulated right of the universities to freedom in research (→Forschung und Lehre).

Hochschulbetrieb (university operations) Term for the entirety of all ongoing activities done at a university – both scientific and non-scientific and thus the object of campus novels (→Campusromane).

Hochschulevaluation (university evaluation) Assessment of universities in order to create a ranking list (→Ranking). Key criteria are: student to instructor ratio (→Betreuungsrelation); external funding quota (→Drittmittelquote); doctoral candidate quota (→Promotionsquote); duration of studies (→Studiendauer); citation index (→Zitations-index); and patent index (→Patentindex).

Hochschulfeiertag (university holiday) →*dies academicus*

Hochschulfreiheitsgesetz (HFG) (Freedom of Institutes of Higher Education Act) Regulates the new structure of universities in North Rhine-Westphalia as of 1 January 2007. There are four basic areas: independence of higher education institutions as public law entities, that is, independence from the state; new structure of university management as an expression of the new autonomy. The university council is thereby comprised primarily of non-university members. The goal of the law was to dismantle bureaucracy and achieve more flexibility. North Rhine-Westphalia was the first *Bundesland* to enact such a law.

Hochschulgottesdienst (university church service) Often an ecumenical but it can also be a confessional church service for student groups, faculties, or the entire university, usually under the direction of an ordained member of the clergy, who can also be a university professor (→Hochschulkapelle).

Hochschulgruppe (student group) Group of students who are voluntary members and who come together for common political, religious, or cultural purposes or on the basis of other values and interests. In contrast to the student societies (→Studentenverbindungen), however, the group is not organized around one living area. (→Lerngruppe)

Hochschulkapelle (university chapel) Usually an ecumenical institution for university church services or prayer services. One of the most famous ~ is the King's College Chapel in Cambridge.

Hochschullandschaft (university system) Entirety of the various types of universities in a *Land* or region. The term is often used in the reform debates to describe the quality of the universities in Germany. In contrast to the Anglo-Saxon ~, in Germany it is relatively homogeneous.

In the winter semester 2014/2015, there were a total of 427 universities in Germany including 129 scientific universities (regular universities, pedagogical universities, and theological universities) and 298 universities of applied science or administrative universities.

Hochschullehrer (professor) →Dozent

Hochschulort (university location) In contrast to a university city (→Universitätsstadt), this term refers to the location of the university within a city, not to the city itself.

Hochschulpädagogik (university pedagogy) Academic subject dealing with teaching at universities and thus both the object of research and the method of teaching. In Germany, up to the present there is no obligatory education in ~ for university instructors (→Dozent). This becomes noticeable in international university rankings. In these, German universities do not have top positions. This serious disadvantage is often discussed by critics of the German university system.

Hochschulrahmengesetz (German Higher Education Framework Act) Federal act that sets down provisions for the specific higher education acts at the level of the *Länder*. The content includes in particular: Sec. 3 Equality of Women and Men; Sec. 4 Freedom of Art and Science, Research, Teaching, and Studies; Sec. 5 State Funding; Sec. 6 Evaluation of Research, Teaching, Promotion of Young Scientists, and Gender Equality; Sec. 7 Objectives of Studies; Sec. 8 Academic Reform; Sec. 9 Coordination of the Order of Studies and Examinations; Sec. 10 Degree Programs; Sec. 11 Standard Period of Study Until First Degree Qualifying for a Profession; Sec. 12 Postgraduate Degree Programs; Sec. 13 Distance-Learning Programs, Multimedia; Sec. 14 Student Advising; Sec. 15 Examinations and Credit Point System; Sec. 16 Examination Regulations; Sec. 17 Early Completion of the Examination; Sec. 18 University Degrees; Sec. 19 Bachelor's and Master's Degree Programs; Sec. 20 Studying at Foreign Universities; Sec. 22 Tasks and Coordination of Research; Sec. 24 Publication of Research Findings; Sec. 25 Research with External Funding; Sec. 26 Development Projects; Sec. 27 General Prerequisites; Sec. 29 Standards of Education Capacities; Sec. 30 Setting Admission Numbers; Sec. 31 Central Allocation of University Places; Sec. 32 General Admission Procedure; Sec. 33 Special Admission Procedure; Sec. 34 Prohibition of Discrimination; Sec. 35 Admission is Not Dependent on Nationality; Sec. 36 Membership; Sec. 37 General Principles of Participation; Sec. 41 Student Body; Sec. 42 Scientific and Artistic Personnel Primarily Employed by the University; Sec. 43 Professional Duties of Professors; Sec. 44 Preconditions for Hiring Professors; Sec. 45 Appointing Professors; Sec.

46 Status of Professors; Sec. 47 Academic and Artistic Assistants; Sec. 48 Status of Academic and Artistic Assistants; Sec. 48a Senior Assistants and Senior Engineers; Sec. 48b Status of Senior Assistants and Senior Engineers; Sec. 48c University Instructors; Sec. 48d Status of University Instructors; Sec. 49 Application of the Regulations of the Civil Service Framework Act; Sec. 50 Special Service Regulations; Sec. 52 Additional Jobs for Professors; Sec. 53 Research and Artistic Associates; Sec. 54 Personnel with Medical Duties; Sec. 55 Adjunct Professors; Sec. 56 Instructors for Special Tasks; Sec. 57a Fixed-Term Limits of Employment Agreements; Sec. 57b Material Reason for the Fixed Term; Sec. 57c Duration of Employment Agreement; Sec. 57d Termination when External Funding Stops; Sec. 57e Private Service Agreement; Sec. 57f First-Time Use; 58 Legal Form and Self-Administrative Right; Sec. 59 Supervision; Sec. 70 Recognition of Institutions; Sec. 71 Equivalency of Degrees from the Notary Schools; Sec. 72 Adjustment Periods; Sec. 73 Deviating Provisions; Sec. 76 Protection of Vested Rights in Retirement of Civil Servants; Sec. 76a Transitional Provisions for University Assistants; Sec. 77-80 (Changes in Legal Provisions); Sec. 81 Agreements with the Churches; Sec. 83 (Entry into Force)

Hochschulranking (university ranking) →Ranking

Hochschulrat (university council) Advisory body (→Gremium) or controlling body vis-à-vis the rector's office. The ~ is made up of university members and/or non-members (private sector representatives), although there can be significant differences among the universities.

Hochschulreform (university reform) Attempt undertaken by the state or a university to adapt a university's administrative structures to new realities. Key aspects of a ~ usually deal with questions of admission, evaluation of research and teaching, funding, tuition fees, status of lecturers, participation rules, and general modernization and technical equipment for new forms of teaching. Important topics in the German debate include: the introduction of staged degrees according to the international model (BA, MA); reform of salary laws for civil servants; introduction of junior professorships (→Juniorprofessuren); unemployment of academics (→Akademikerarbeitslosigkeit) and vocational education; tuition fees (→Studiengebühren); university ranking; strengthening the universities with financial autonomy; and attractiveness of the university abroad.

Hochschulrektorenkonferenz (HRK) (German Rectors' Conference) Voluntary association of state and state-recognized universities in Germany, currently with 268 members, whose students make up around 97% of all students in Ger-

many. The ~ is the voice of the universities in politics. Its tasks include: information about the universities; formulating their interests; PR work; consulting for politics, business, and the public; quality assurance at the universities; international contacts; archiving and documentation.
www.hrk.de

Hochschulsammlung (university collection) Exhibition of historical insignia (→Insignien) from a university, e.g. book of statutes (→Statutenbuch), rector's chest, university sceptor, robes (→Talare), mortarboards, chronicles, registration books (→Matrikelbücher), and other historical, often very valuable objects from the history of a university.

Hochschulschrift (university publications) Book publications, usually in the form of a series of monographs (→Monographien) from an academic publishing house on related topics, subjects, or the programmatic focus of the publishing house, whereby the individual contributions can be independent of one another and could come from different authors.

Hochschulsemester (university semester) Total number of →semesters that a student has been enrolled at a university, including semesters spent in degree programs that a student dropped out of and semesters in which the student took a leave of absence. It must be differentiated from the number of subject-related semesters (→Fachsemester), which is calculated differently.

Hochschulstatistik (university statistics) Entirety of all figures that describe the existence and work of universities on a statistical basis. The most important ~ are documented at:
www.bildungsserver.de and www.destatis.de

Hochschulsystem, amerikanisches (American university system) Entirety of the universities in the USA, usually especially the →Ivy League. In general usage, the term primarily refers to the in part very high tuition fees required from enrolled students and to the better student to instructor ratio as compared to the German system. This is possible in the ~ due to the division of labor between professors and lecturers (→Lecturers). The quality of the universities is very heterogeneous compared to the German system. The ~ is built on colleges. One differentiates especially between two-year colleges, four-year colleges, and research universities with different possibilities for degrees from an Associate's degree to a doctorate (→Promotion).

Hochschulsystem, britisches (British university system) Great Britain's university structure differs greatly from the system in continental Europe. The universities in the ~ are some of the oldest in Europe, including Oxford, founded in the 13th century, Cambridge, founded in

1284, the University of St. Andrews, founded in 1411, Glasgow, 1451, and Aberdeen, 1494. The reputation of the two British *ancient universities* corresponds to the →Grandes Ecoles or the →Ivy League and are often referred to as *Oxbridge*. Other than these, no other universities were founded in England until the 19th century. Characteristic for these universities is the college system (→College-System): university members are first and foremost members of a college and only secondarily of the university. With the exception of Edinburgh, the Scottish universities were founded by churches, and colleges therefore do not play a key role.

Hochschulsystem, deutsches (German university system) An educational system on the basis of various types of universities, with the principle of the unity of research and teaching (→Forschung und Lehre), in which students usually do not have to pay tuition fees (→Studiengebühren) other than a small semester contribution (→Semesterbeitrag), which is low in international comparison. Many find the current structure of research, teaching, and administration to be over-regulated. Characteristic for the ~ are also: the system of ordinaries, the absence of college structures and elite universities, and a large number of participants in courses.

Hochschulverfassung (university charter) →Grundordnung

Hochschulversion (university version, academic version) Some computer program manufacturers offer cheaper versions of their products for purposes of research and teaching. These programs often contain small changes. The condition for purchasing a ~ is proof that one is a student or employed by the university.

Hochschulwechsel (change of university) A change of university is usually done after the basic study period (→Grundstudium) by deregistering from the old university and enrolling (→Immatrikulation) at the new one. The new Bachelor's/Master's system introduced by the Bologna Process (→Bologna-Prozess) is intended to make this process easier, as students can conclude their Bachelor's degree at one university and apply for a Master's degree at a different university without going through the administrative processes of getting recognition for credits already earned.

Hochschulzeitung (university newspaper) Regular publication (→Publikation) from a university with the press department (→Pressestelle) as the editors for the purpose of public relations. ~ are official publications by the university in contrast to newspapers from the student departmental representatives (→Fachschaftszeitungen) or student newspapers (→Studentenzeitungen).

Hochschulzugangsberechtigung (university entrance qualification)

Degree or qualification that allows a person to enroll at a university (→Abitur). If the ~ was obtained abroad, then it will need to be submitted for evaluation and recognition as described in the admission procedures.

Honorarprofessor (honorary professor) Term for an academic honor that can be awarded to independent university lecturers who have earned their qualification or to other adjunct instructors from the private sector or otherwise. The position as a ~ is usually lost when the person obtains a regular university position.

honoris causa (honoris causa) Also: Dr. h.c. Lat. *honoris causa* = for an honorary purpose. A title awarded by a university to well-known people from politics, business, culture, and society regardless of their academic education, whether they have written a →dissertation, had a defense, or completed other qualifications (→Doktor).

Honors **(honors)** Term for the grade given at English-language universities for outstanding academic work.

Honors Program **(honors program)** Possibility for particularly gifted or high-achieving students to take part in special offers based on above-average work in early semesters (→Honors).

Hörer (listener) Participant in a course, usually referring to lectures. Here one differentiates primarily between regular listeners and auditors. (→Hospitieren; →Seniorstudent; →Studium Generale).

Hörsaal (lecture hall) Usually a room built in tiers for a large audience in which lectures can be held. In contrast to seminar rooms (→Seminarräumen), ~ often have technical equipment permanently installed (Video, microphone, projector, large blackboard/whiteboard, etc.). Ideally, they also have good acoustics.

Hospitant (guest student) Lat. *hospitare* = to be a guest. Term for an auditor (→Gaststudent) who attends a course out of interest but not to obtain credits (→Leistungsnachweis), whereby a university student can be a guest student (→hospitieren) in other faculties.

Hospitieren (to be a guest student, sit in on someone's lecture) Lat. *hospes* = guest. Attending a course that is not part of the student's regular schedule (→Stundenplan), especially due to interest in the instructor's didactic skills or to get a personal impression of the listeners, topic (→Thema), room, or the instructor's rhetorical abilities (→Evaluation).

HRG Abbreviation for: →Hochschulrahmengesetz

HRK Abbreviation for: →Hochschulrektorenkonferenz

HS Abbreviation in the course catalog (→Vorlesungsverzeichnis) for: advanced seminar (→Hauptseminar) or advanced study period (→Hauptstudium). If it is listed as the location, then it is the abbreviation for lecture hall (→Hörsaal).

Humboldtsche Reformen (Humboldtian reforms) Named after Wilhelm von Humboldt (1767-1835), important reformer in the early 19th century of Prussian educational policy and in particular of the Berlin university later named after him according to the principle of the unity of research and teaching (→Forschung und Lehre) – the so-called Humboldtian Principle – based on the philosophies of Immanuel Kant, Johann Gottlob Fichte, and Friedrich Daniel Schleiermacher. (→Ordinarienverfassung)

Hypoth<u>e</u>se (hypothesis) Greek *hypothesis* = basis, supposition. Important tool for research to formulate preliminary assumptions that can be modified, confirmed, or falsified by the studies, argumentation, experiments, tests, and research. ~ can come at the beginning or the end of a section in a research paper. With experiments, ~ can be verified.

Idiotikon (dialect dictionary, regiolect dictionary, specialized dictionary) Greek *idios* = uniquely one's own, peculiar to an individual. Collection of special linguistic or dialect expressions that either make up a specialized language or are the object of specialized language (→Glossar).

Ikone (icon) Greek *eikon* = picture, representation. Renowned researcher with "cult status," referring to the use of the term for pictures of saints in the Orthodox Church. Often the individual style or presence of the person is better known than their actual scientific theses and achievements. Many ~ come from more abstract areas of subjects such as physics, medicine, and psychology. Examples are Sigmund Freud, Albert Einstein, or Stephen Hawking (→Wissenschaftler, der verrückte), who understood how to awaken broad public interest in their basic theoretical insights.

ILIAS (ILIAS) Abbreviation for: Integriertes Lern-, Informations- und Arbeitskooperations-System. An open source, online e-learning (→E-Learning) tool used by many German universities. The extent to which the system is used varies greatly, but instructors can use it to provide access to required reading for courses, to open up forums for student discussion, to provide a folder for students to upload handouts or assignments, to conduct surveys (including evaluations), and even to carry out examinations.

Illumination (illumination) Artistic decoration of a book for aesthetic purposes, usually in the context of old and rare books as well as a factor in determining the value of antique volumes (→Illustration).

Illustration (illustration) Lat. *illustris* = bright, shining. Graphics and pictures in a text for didactic purposes. The sources of ~ in an academic paper are cited just as quotes are.

Illustrationsverzeichnis (list of illustrations) →Bildnachweis

Immatrikulation (enrollment, registration) The process of registering an admitted applicant for a place in a degree program (→Matrikel). Without enrolling, a student is not officially a university member and cannot take advantage of any benefits (e.g. semester ticket for public transportation, student ID).

Immatrikulationsamt (admissions office, enrollment office, registration office) →Immatrikulationsbüro

Immatrikulationsbescheinigung (certificate of enrollment) Proof of successful enrollment at a university, usually in the form of a DIN A4 piece of paper with several sections. Some sections are for specific purposes (e.g. →BaföG, semester ticket for public transportation). (→Leporello)

Immatrikulationsbüro (admissions office, enrollment office, registration office) Administrative office at a university to organize and document all records for enrolled students and thus the contact point for students for all questions dealing with applying to the university, re-registration, and de-registration.

Immatrikulationsfeier (matriculation ceremony, enrollment ceremony) Depending on the tradition of the individual university, it is a more or less formal ceremony to greet the newly enrolled and successfully re-registered students for the coming semester. The other members of the university also participate (→Aula).

Immaturenprüfung (alternative university entrance examination) Actual name: Prüfung für Studieninteressenten ohne →Hochschulzugangsberechtigung (examination for prospective students without a university entrance qualification). If the prospective students pass, they can obtain the right to enter a university to study a particular subject.

Impact-Factor **(impact factor)** Controversial measurement tool to evaluate the influence of a publication on the scientific community's dialogue by measuring the number of other publications that have cited the publication being evaluated.

Impressum (legal notice, imprint, disclaimer) The typical and legally required list of authors, creators, responsible editors, publisher's location, and other information on the company such as tax number, managing director in print media and websites (→Titelei).

Inauguration (inauguration) Lat. *inauguratio* = initiation. Term for the assumption of office or official introduction, e.g. of a university rector (→Rektor) in office.

Index 1. (annex) →Anhang

2. Lat. *index librorum prohibitorum* (list of prohibited books) = A list first published in 1559 of books forbidden by the Holy See for believers. Many scientific as well as literary works were included. As of 1950 it included: Honoré de Balzac, René Descartes, Denis Diderot, Alexandre Dumas (father and son), Heinrich Heine, Immanuel Kant, Maurice Maeterlinck, Voltaire. In 1966, the Vatican stated that while the list still held moral authority, there were no longer any penalties for reading the books on it.

Induktion (induction) Lat. *inducere* = induce, introduce. Academic's tool in which a conclusion is generalized from an individual case. ~ is therefore characteristic for the empirical sciences that reach general statements based on experiments (→Versuch) and observations. The more systematic and controlled such an experiment is set up, the more significant the inductive conclusion can be (→Deduktion).

Infotag (informational day) Open door day at a university during which the individual departments (→Fachbereich) and libraries (→Bibliothek) present themselves to the public, sometimes with spectacular programs depending on space and capabilities. The ~ primarily serves for marketing and public relations purposes (→Pressestelle).

Infotainment (infotainment) →Populärwissenschaft

Inhaltsverzeichnis (table of contents) Section at the beginning of a scientific work in which the order, position, and length of individual chapters are shown in a list. Usually in decimal classification. In addition to the literature information, the quality of the ~ is one of the most important criteria for instructors when evaluating a seminar paper (→*style sheet*).

Inhaltsverzeichnis, abstraktes (abstract table of contents) Standardized guidelines for orientation when structuring scientific texts that can be filled with the respective questions and topics of the work.

Cover page;
Table of contents
1. Introduction; 1.1 Research question: Objective of the work; 1.2 Methods and definitions of terms in the work; 1.3 State of research and sources; 1.4 History and genesis of the term being investigated; 2. First main point; 2.1 General description and particularities; 2.2 Main point in relation to external parameters; 2.3 Main point in relation to internal parameters; 2.4 Summary; 3. Second main point; 3.1 General description and particularities; 3.2 Main point in relation to external parameters; 3.3 Main point in relation to internal parameters; 3.4 Summary; 3.5 Conclusion and outlook for the entire work;

Annexes: 4. Timeline; 5. List of abbreviations; 6. Tables; 7. Index (index of people, locations, and objects); 8. Information on sources and literature; 9. Other proof

Inkunabel (incunabelum) Lat. *incunabula* = swaddling clothes, cradle. Work from the early period of printing up to 1500 CE. Can only be viewed in special reading rooms and often very expensive or even unique. The ~ in the German-speaking world are cataloged and archived in the Bavarian State Library. Around 30% of the specimens preserved worldwide are kept there.

Insignien (insignia) Lat. *insignia* = mark, badge. Symbolic sign of a person or entity's office, usually with certain props or clothing such as a mortarboard (→Doktorhut), robe (→Talar), rector's scepter (→Rektorstab), registry book (→Matrikelbuch), or book of statutes (→Statutenbuch) (→Universitätsgeschichte). At early universities, these were important symbols of the legal independence of the students and instructors but also other members (→Pedell).

Inskription (inscription) Lat. *scribo* = write. Term for enrollment (→Immatrikulation) at Austrian universities.

Institut (institute, department) Lat. *institutum* = establishment, custom. Term for an organizational unit at a university that can include several chairs (→Lehrstuhl) but is below the level of the faculty (→Fakultät, →Seminar).

Insufficienter (unsatisfactory) Lat. *insufficienter* = insufficient. The worst grade (→Note): failed, if a deadline is missed or total failure. The Latin form of grades is becoming less common.

Intellektueller (intellectual) In general usage, a person whose career and authority is based in education (→Bildung) and who participates in public life based on this authority. The ~ include primarily authors, journalists, publicists, and academics (→Akademiker). The term can also take on negative connotations in certain cases (in the sense of impractical, →Elfenbeinturm).

Intensivkurs (intensive course) Also: *Crashkurs*. Course in which the contents are condensed to the necessary minimum and conveyed in a relatively short period of time. ~ are often offered in the semester breaks (→Semesterferien) for language courses (→Sprachkurse).

Interdisziplinarität (interdisciplinarity) Academic cooperation beyond the boundaries of a single subject (→Fach) to overcome the often strictly observed boundaries of the faculties (→Fakultäten, →Nexialistik).

***International Academy of Science* (International Academy of Science)** International and interdisciplinary academy founded in 1980 across the boundaries of the East-West conflict. The IAS has around 1500 members from over 100 countries, including many Nobel Prize winners. Members include: Linus Pauling, Karl Popper, Hans Jonas, Andrej Sacharow, and Konrad Lorenz.
http://www.ias-icsd.org

Intitulationseid (oath of intitulation) At universities in the Middle Ages and Early Modern age, the ~ had to be said to the constitution and to maintain absolute loyalty to the university and its rector. The ~ was to be said before the largest number of witnesses possible by everyone who entered the university, whether as a student or instructor. It included the promise to study diligently, refrain from breaking the law, obey authorities and supervisors, and recognize the legal sovereignty of the rector.

ISBN (ISBN) Abbreviation for: International Standard Book Number. Each title has its own ~ with 10 or 13 numbers (13 if it was assigned after 1 January 2007). In academic bibliographical references (→Literaturangaben), the ISBN is usually not given (→*style sheet*).

ISSN (ISSN) Abbreviation for: International Standard Serial Number. Analog to the ISBN, the ~ is a system for numbering journals and periodicals. It is made up of 8 numbers without a country or publisher code. In academic literature references (→Literaturangaben), the ISSN is usually not given (→*style sheet*).

Iteration (iteration) Lat. *iteratio* = repetition. The repeated, refining approach to a research question at a higher level after the first round is completed and preliminary results have already been found. Iterative work is one of the foundational scientific techniques in all disciplines (→Disziplin).

***Ivy League* (Ivy League)** Term for a group of universities (→Hochschule) in the United States with demanding admission requirements and high tuition fees (→Studiengebühren). The ~ includes: Brown University, Columbia University, Cornell University, Dartmouth →College, Harvard University, University of Pennsylvania, Princeton University, and Yale University.

J

Journal (journal) French *journal* = journal, diary. Term for a regularly published academic magazine (→Zeitschrift). The pronunciation is traditionally French, whereby the modern variation, English, is becoming ever more common. The English-speaking world also differentiates between *science magazines* as publications of popular science and *scientific journals* as publications for an academic expert audience (→Fachpublikum).

Junior (junior) →Freshman

Juniorprofessor (junior professor, assistant professor) In Germany, this is a newly created and not uncontroversial position for academics with a doctorate in order to more quickly be able to work independently. The goal is to make an academic career more attractive for young scientists.

Junk-science **(junk science)** Contemptuous term for results of a scientific review that are in the interest of the (often non-academic) contractor, for example the automobile or alcohol and tobacco industry, that are against good scientific practice, e.g. because the researcher is worried about funding, follow-up projects, or bad press. ~ is the opposite of sound science. The term ~ is sometimes used by contractors of reviews in regards to unwanted scientific studies or findings in order to be able to avoid undesirable consequences.

Kalter Blick (dispassionate analysis) Scientists' intellectual ideal of approaching and studying a topic neutrally and without any bias, that is, not burdened by any feelings, whereby the findings cannot be clear from the beginning of the study. The ~ is muddied by many factors in everyday life, for example by time pressure, pressure to succeed, budget restrictions, hopes for the content, impatience, controversies with colleagues, pressure to publish, vanity, or as a consequence of previous falsifications. (→Weltbild)

Kandidat (candidate) Lat. *candidatus* = dressed in white. In ancient Rome, the applicants for public offices appeared in a white toga. From this tradition, the term was transferred to applicants in general, especially those for academic honors who had to take an examination (→Prüfung). The ~ in an academic subject is a student who will soon take the final exam (→Examen) and has already completed the other requirements for the degree.

Kanzler (chancellor, administrative director) Lat. *cancelli* = lattice, gate. Head of the university administration, in particular responsible for the budget (→Budget), the non-scientific personnel, and other administrative and legal tasks.

Karlsbader Beschlüsse (Carlsbad Decrees) Regulations passed in 1819 to monitor the universities (→Hochschule) and student body in order to prevent attempts at democratic reform. As a result of the ~, numerous publications (→Publikation) were prohibited, professors were fired, and students were expelled from the universities (→Göttinger Sieben).

Karteileiche (inactive member, member who only exists on paper) Term for the name of a person on a list of members or similar list who is no longer an active member.

Kartenteil (map sheet) Part of the annex (→Anhang) in which geographical, political, or other maps and images are shown.

Kartenverzeichnis (list of maps) List ordered alphabetically or otherwise in the annex (→Anhang) to give references for all maps or similar images in a scientific work.

Karzer (detention cell) Lat. *carcer* = prison. University prison for students (→Student) who were guilty of misconduct such as: smoking in public, disturbing the peace, skinny-dipping, or physical attacks on instructors (→Dozent). The ~ was the clearest expression of the internal university jurisdiction. The walls of the ~ were traditionally written and drawn on with rust and candle wax, usually in the style of a guest book. The ~ in Heidelberg is one of the best known—it was built in 1387 and is currently used as a museum.

Kasino (canteen) Italian casino = small house, but also: "pigsty" or brothel. At the university of the →Bundeswehr, the term for the canteen (→Mensa).

Katalog (catalog) Greek *katalogos* = register, list. A list of the books that are actually or supposedly present in a library (→Bibliothek). ~ can be ordered according to various criteria, e.g. alphabetically according to the authors' names, titles, or according to keywords in the topic. When looking for current titles, online catalogs (→OPAC) are the first place to look in order to check the holdings (→Bestand). Sometimes, though, not all titles in the library are also listed in the digital catalog. Most libraries have several catalogs (→Magazin).

Katheder (lectern, teacher's desk) Greek *cathedra* = seat. Typical term for a chair (→Lehrstuhl) starting in the 16th century but very rare today. An explanation given *ex cathedra* is thus a doctrine stated at a university or in the church by virtue of office (→Dogma).

Kausalität (causality) Lat. *causa* = cause. The connection between the cause and effect is called ~, and in many disciplines (→Disziplin) it makes up the basic questions of the time, order, occurrence, and free will, especially in physics, computer science, philosophy, and law. Important theoreticians of ~ were Democritus, David Hume, Arthur Schopenhauer, Albert Einstein ("God does not play dice!"), and Alan Turing.

Kinder-Uni (children's university) An offer usually provided by a university in the summer months of the semester holidays (→Semesterferien) for children and youth. The university teaches them about working methods and the university's offers in the context of an open door day, usually with courses especially designed for children. First developed by the University of Tübingen, later adopted by many other universities.

Kirchliche Abschlussprüfung (final church examination) Final examination in the basic study program for Catholic or Protestant theology as a condition for beginning service in the church or as a priest. Members of the examination committee include representatives of both the university and the respective church.

Klassifikation (classification) Structure of the holdings in a collection, an archive (→Archiv), or a library according to topics designed to make research (→Recherche) easier. The ~ of an archive is a fundamental decision when setting up collections and archives and can only be changed with a great deal of effort.

Klausur Lat. *clausura* = lock, enclosure.
1. (written exam) Written examination (→Prüfung) at a university under the supervision of the examiner (→Prüfer) or an invigilator within a

set time limit. The result of the ~ is part of the final grade, similar to tests at school.

2. (retreat, conclave) Term for meetings, conferences, evaluations, or study periods that are not open to the public.

Kleiderordnung (dress code) Rules for what could or could not be worn at universities in the Middle Ages and Early Modern age. If students violated the rules, both they and the tailors could be fined; the fines were to be paid to the rector. In the 16th century, large, slitted hats were forbidden as well as Turkish trousers. Instead, according to a ~ of the University of Erfurt from 1562, what was desired was:

That the doctors and licentiates (...) wear long clothing so that the skirts are a hand's width below the knee (...) and no velvet or silk skirts and no velvet, beret, or train. The students of all faculties should not wear torn or short clothing, instead their clothing should be honest and of an honorable length because it is a great show of carelessness and abuse when the youth go out in public in short clothing where honest and virtuous women and virgins can see them (→Talarrecht).

Today, questions of ~ are primarily relevant within university hospitals and labs and deal with occupational safety and hygiene regulations.

KMK Abbreviation for: →Kultusministerkonferenz

Kodex, wissenschaftlicher (scientific code) →Leitbild, →Weltbild

Kölner Runde (Cologne Group) Network of student initiatives dealing with economics since 1991. www.koelner-runde.de

Kolleg (college, lecture) Originally a term for a lecture at universities in the Middle Ages in which first a classic literary work was read aloud and then interpreted. Also called "Lesung" ("reading") from Latin *lectio*. Today in Germany, it is usually a term for a non-university course, for example a "Tele-Kolleg," while the *lectio* turned into "lecture" at Anglo-Saxon universities. The German ~ is comparable to evening secondary school, but the participants cannot have jobs. (→Burse, →Studienkolleg)

Kollege (colleague) Lat. *collega* = associate, fellow. Traditional way of addressing or term for instructors (→Dozent) amongst each other according to the model of the Roman magistrates.

Kolloquium (colloquium) Lat. *colloquium* = to talk together. Event for instructors (→Dozent) and advanced students on various projects of the participants, who present their work. The ~ is also a special form of oral examination (Prüfung) for the post-doctoral lecturing qualification (→Habilitation). (→Oberseminar)

Kommilitone (fellow student) Lat. *commilitium* = fellowship in time of war. Student term for students in the same or different semesters and in the same or a different subject, or for the instructors to their students. The term for fellow combatants is derived from the solidary organizational form of early universities (→Burse), but it might also be related to the frequent conflict situations between the university and the sovereigns.

Kommers (commercium) Term from the language of fraternity students (→Verbindungsstudent). Festive variation of a gathering with strict ceremony, festive speeches, and representatives of other corporations (→Korporation), also: term for any type of loud event.

Kompendium (compendium) Lat. *compendere* = weigh, balance together. Traditional term for a concise but also a tried and true textbook (→Lehrbuch).

Kompilation (compilation) In a general sense, a collection of sources, data, citations, texts, illustrations, e.g. in the form of a file or a collection of papers, in order to make the introduction to the topic easier. In particular: Part of the seminar binder (→Seminarapparat).

Konferenz (conference) Lat. *conferentia* = meeting. Scheduled meeting or gathering with a set agenda dealing with subject-related or administrative questions, sometimes on a regular rotation in university operations (→Gremium).

Kongress (congress) Lat. *congredi* = meet. Expert conference on a certain scientific topic (→Thema) with a set program for discussion among experts with an open or closed audience.

Konsistorium (university council) Lat. *consistorium* = place of assembly. The ~ is usually made up of members of the rector's office (→Rektorat) or executive committee (→Präsidium) and other university members. The task of this body (→Gremium) is determining the university constitution, electing the management, and reviewing the annual report. There are large differences among the individual universities in regard to the competencies and name of the ~.

Konsultation (consultation) Lat. *consulere* = consult. Discussion between two or more instructors at a university in order to decide on a grade or evaluate an examination (→Prüfungsleistung), or a term for a general academic evaluation.

Kontroverse (controversy) Lat. *controversia* = turning against, debate. Academic debate between two or more researchers on an unresolved question that can be carried out with publications (→Publikation) and discussion contributions that respond to one another or appearances at expert conferences. A famous ~ in Germany was the socalled "Historikerstreit" (historian's quarrel) in 1986 and 1987, during the course of which a fundamental debate on the historical evaluation of National-Socialism and in particular the Holocaust was conducted by many parties.

Konvent (faculty council) →Fakultätsrat

Konzertexamen (concert examination) Degree at music universities for post-graduates who already have an artistic →Diplom.

Konzertreife (concert level, concert performance) Final examination of the post-graduate degree program of ~ or soloist level for graduates (→Absolvent) of the basic level degree programs at music universities if the performance in the final examination was particularly outstanding.

Konzil (council) Lat. *concilium* = association, gathering. The names for the individual decision-making bodies (→Gremien) at German universities is not standardized. One term can therefore refer to different bodies at different universities. At many universities, however, the ~ is responsible for passing decisions on the charter (→Grundordnung) and changes to it.

Korporation (association) Lat. *corporatio* = corporation. Collective term since the start of the 20th century for student societies (→Studentenverbindungen).

Korrektor (proofreader) Term for a reader who checks a manuscript for errors but does not necessarily prepare a publication like an editor (→Lektor). Checking for errors (→Korrekturlesen) is an essential step in producing every kind of text and should be repeated several times.

Korrekturlesen (proofread) Essential step before every publication in which the text is repeatedly checked for mistakes or inaccuracies. Important types of errors are: spelling errors, errors in reasoning, unintended humor, redundancies, stylistic blunders, formatting mistakes, and errors in phrasing. Ideally, the ~ is done by a publisher's editor, but for seminar papers or other texts that are not published, the work must be done by a fellow student since an author cannot neutrally check his own work.

Krambambuli (Krambambuli) A very sweet, spiced liquor made in Danzig, known since 1598 and a favored drink of students until World War I. The ~ became known to the broader German public with a short story of the same name by the poet Marie von Ebner-Eschenbach.

Krankenversicherung (health insurance) ~ is a requirement for enrolling (→Immatrikulation) at a university. It is usually offered to students with cheaper premiums. Foreign students can either provide proof that their ~ in their home country will cover any medical expenses they incur in Germany, or they can purchase German ~. Often exchange organizations will offer ~ to students in their programs

Kultusministerium (Ministry of Education and the Arts) Highest authority in the *Länder* for issues related to education, science (→Wissenschaft), and culture, especially for schools, universities, and adult education as well as general art and cultural conservation. Most *Länder*

have both a ~ and a separate ministry for science and research.

Kultusministerkonferenz (Standing Conference of the Ministers of Education) Full name: Ständige Konferenz der Kultusminister der Länder in der Bundesrepublik Deutschland. Before the Basic Law was passed, this coordinating and voluntary association of the ministers of education was formed in 1948 to deal with questions related to culture and education with nation-wide relevance. The organs of the ~ are the plenary, the executive committee, and the rector. The plenary meets at the ministerial level three to four times per year. www.kmk.org

Kunsthochschule (art college, university of the arts) Type of university for degree programs related to fine, creative, and visual arts as well as the corresponding sciences. Admission requirements include a university entrance qualification and proof of artistic talent, whereby the second criterion is more important than the first. In some *Länder*, studies at a ~ can be started without a university entrance qualification.

Kuratorium (board of trustees) Lat. *cura* = concern. Term for a supervisory committee (→Gremium) at a university, for example the supervision of the university's art collection. The tasks of different boards of trustees at different types of universities vary.

Kurie (Curia) Lat. *curia* = senate, meeting house. Term not used in a standardized way to denote or divide the members of a university in professional groups, e.g. students, instructors, and professors.

Kurs (course) Lat. *cursus* = course, direction. Series of events. Usually in connection with practical contents (dance course, language course) or other classes in contrast to a more theoretically oriented seminar (→Seminar).

Kürzel (abbreviation) →Abkürzungen

Kustodie (curatorship) Lat. *custos* = guard, warden. The supervision of the museum, collection (→Sammlung), or archive of a university. In addition to art treasures, it also often includes documentation, copies, or originals of old articles of daily use from the university's history.

KVV Abbreviation for: →kommentiertes Vorlesungsverzeichnis

LA Abbreviation for: →Lehramt

Lab (lab) →Labor

Labor/Laboratorium (laboratory) Lat. *labor* = labor, exertion. Place of work for practical experiments (→Versuche) often with extensive technical equipment for processing, simulating, and measuring. Essential and expensive element of many research institutions. Also: term for an institute as a whole.

Laborpraktikum (lab course, practical) Course with supervised independent work (→Praktikum).

Landeshochschulgesetz (state higher education act) →Hochschulrahmengesetz

Langzeitstudent (long-term student) Not a term with a standard definition. Typically students who have studied for at least four semesters more than the general standard period of study are called ~. According to this definition, around 10% of the students enrolled at German universities are ~.

Langzeitstudium (long-term studies) Exceeding the standard period of studies by one or more semesters. This term, which is difficult to define precisely, is also a form of failure (→Studienversagen).

Lapidarium (lapidarium) Lat. *lapis* = stone. Collection of carved stones or sculptures, for example pillars, monuments, or boundary stones, usually from the Greco-Roman times for purposes of teaching or exhibition, also often in the form of copies or plaster casts of delicate originals.

Latein (Latin) International language of science from antiquity until the 18th century. With the emancipation of the natural sciences, lessons taught in the national languages became more common. In Germany, this was first done in 1687 temporarily in Leipzig, then later in Halle with the Enlightenment philosopher Christian Thomasius. Starting in 1848, ~ was mostly replaced by German as the language of instruction. The Latin examination (→Latinum) remains a requirement for many subjects today, however, for example for theology or most historical sciences.

Lateinische Ausdrücke (Latin expressions) Latin expressions or terms commonly used in scientific texts that have the purpose of implying typical thoughts in a shortened form. Common ~ include:

a fortiori = from yet a stronger reason; *a posteriori* = in retrospect, known from experience; *a priori* = known before the event; *ab hinc* = from here on; *ab initio* = from the beginning; *ad hoc* = to this, improvised; *ad hominem* = personal, emotional attack; *ad infinitum* = going on forever; *ad interim* = in the meantime; *animal rationale* = man as a rational being; *animal sociale* =

man as a social being; *conditio humana* = human condition; *contradictio in adiecto* = contradiction between two parts of an argument; *coram publico* = in front of the public eye; *cum grano salis* = (take something) with a grain of salt; *de jure* = by right, according to the law; *de minimis* = concerning minimal things; *ex ante* = before the event (based on forecasts); *ex cathedra* = with the full authority of office (with the right to teach); *ex negativo* = (to define something) from the opposite; *ex nihilo* = out of nothing; *ex nunc* = from now on; *ex officio* = by virtue of one's office, authority; *ex post facto* = with retrospective action or force; *ex tempore* = extemporaneous, impromptu; *ex termini* = by force of the term, according to the definition; *ex tunc* = from the outset; *expressis verbis* = explicitly; *ibidem* = in the same place; *id est (i.e.)* = that is; *in loco* = in the place; *in memoriam* = in memory of; *in vitro* = in a laboratory; *in vivo* = within a living being, under real life conditions; *ipso facto* = by that very fact or act; *locus classicus* = classical source, source typically quoted for something; *magnum opus* = a great work; *modus operandi* = method or procedure; *mutatis mutandis* = the necessary changes having been made; *nota bene* = note well!; *opera posthuma* = posthumous works; *opere citato* = in the work cited; *pari passu* = ranking equally; *pars pro toto* = a part taken for the whole; *passim* = here and there; *per annum* = per year; *per caput* = per capita; *per se* = in and of itself; *prima facie* = at first sight; *reductio ad absurdum* = reduction to absurdity; *sensu stricto* = in a narrow or strict sense; *sic!* = intentionally so written (used when an error is contained in a citation); *sine anno* = without year; *spiritus rector* = ruling or guiding spirit; *status quo ante* = the way things were before; *status quo* = the existing state of affairs; *terra firma* = firm ground; *terra incognita* = unfamiliar territory; *ultima ratio* = the final argument, last resort; *vice versa* = conversely

Latinum (Latin examination) Proof of solid knowledge of Latin. Together with the examinations in Hebrew (→Hebraikum) and Greek (→Gräkum), a part of the classical humanist language education.

Laudatio (laudation, encomium) Lat. *laus* = praise. Speech of praise for a scientist, often in combination with other honors such as an award ceremony or when retiring (→Emeritierung) or having a birthday. (→dies academicus)

Laufbahn (career path) →akademische Karriere

Lebenslauf (résumé) →*curriculum vitae*

Lebenswissenschaften (life sciences) Collective term for all research activities dealing with human life, from medicine to biology, from philosophy to theology with the overarching task of working on a comprehensive meaning of human existence in various areas of science. The questions of ~, for example, are related to genetic research, brain research, discussions on assisted suicide, and consciousness research.

Lecture (lecture) A speech on a specific and more or less set topic. Especially in the context of universities in Britain and the United States, a course in which the instructor gives a speech for the sessions (→Vorlesung) instead of basing the course on discussions with the students (→Seminar), and in Germany increasingly used as a fashionable word. Popular scientific and non-academic speeches can also be called ~.

Lecturer (lecturer) Term for an employee or instructor at an English-language university with a doctorate that does not have a professorship but has researching and teaching tasks. One differentiates in particular among lecturers, senior lecturers, and readers. At some universities in the United States, ~ have the primary task of supervising first-semester students and are thus freed from research tasks.

Legion, akademische (Academic Legion) An armed student association founded in 1848 in Vienna. The objectives of this political organization were: freedom, democracy, a constitution, and reform. The ~ played an active role in the revolutionary fighting in 1848 (→Karlsbader Beschlüsse; →Göttinger Sieben; →Hambacher Fest).

Lehramt (teaching profession, teaching post) Goal of students in degree programs for education – typically a civil servant (→Beamte) position at schools. At universities, this is in contrast to students who are in programs for degrees such as Bachelor's or Master's.

Lehrangebot (range of courses) The entirety of all courses (→Veranstaltung) for students at a university as listed in the course catalog (→Vorlesungsverzeichnis).

Lehrbeauftragter (adjunct professor, contracted lecturer) An instructor (Dozent) at a university who is hired for a semester or other limited period of time. The ~ usually has a doctorate but no habilitation with a weak status and low pay (→Assistent), usually external experts, for example judges in legal subjects.

Lehrbetrieb (teaching operations) The entirety of all activities related to teaching at a university (→Hochschulbetrieb).

Lehrbuch (textbook) Comprehensive, introductory description of a subject or topic that was written for teaching purposes, not research purposes. Colloquially, usually with the status of a classic. Formal distinctive characteristic: textbooks often do not list the literature used in an annex but directly after the respective chapter (→Monographie).

Lehrbuchsammlung (textbook collection) Area of a library in which the books often used for courses are available. These books can usually not be borrowed but only viewed in the reading room (→Präsenzbibliothek).

Lehre (teaching) →Forschung und Lehre

Lehreinheit (taught unit) Also: Unterrichtseinheit. A thematically and didactically separate sub-area within a course, comparable to a chapter in a book.

Lehrkörper (faculty, instructors) Entirety of all university members dealing with teaching. The term is used primarily at schools, however, and less frequently at universities, where they are often referred to as →Dozenten (→Kollegium).

Lehrkraft für besondere Aufgaben (instructor for special tasks) Instructor who is usually not a regular part of a department (→Lehrstuhl) and who takes on many teaching tasks. They are usually given fixed-term contracts.

Lehrstuhl (chair, department) Planned position for a professor (→Professor) or several professors for life including their staff. A ~ can include many staff members and could have the following structure: One or two professors heading the ~, then an academic director who could also be a professor with a post-doctoral lecturing qualification, then four senior research associates who could also be scientists with post-doctoral lecturing qualifications or research associates who are working on their doctorates, then the adjunct professors and honorary professors, student assistants, and tutors assisted by a secretary's office.

Lehrstuhlinhaber (professor with chair, head of department) Term for the head of a department (→Lehrstuhl). →Ordinarius.

Lehrstuhlstiftung (chair endowment) Establishment of a chair by the university, faculty, or a third party. The so-called "Lukasische Lehrstuhl," for example, was endowed by the British MP Henry Lucas in 1663 in Cambridge. The financial basis of this endowment is an estate. Famous professors who held the chair include Isaac Newton in 1669 and Stephen Hawking since 1979.

Lehrveranstaltung (course) →Veranstaltung

Lehrveranstaltung, fakultative (optional course) Courses (→Veranstaltung) the students are not required to attend and whose contents are not necessarily included in a general examination (→Prüfung). →Studium Generale

Lehrveranstaltung, obligatorische (required course) Lat. *obligare* = obligate. Course (→Veranstaltung) that is required to complete a degree.

Lehrverpflichtung (teaching responsibility) Depending on the position and commitments in other offices, the ~ is time an instructor must spend on teaching expressed in weekly hours per semester (→Semesterwochenstunden, →Deputat).

Leibniz-Preis (Leibniz Prize) Germany's most highly endowed award from the DFG with the goal of improving the working conditions of outstanding scientists, expanding their research possibilities, relieving them of their administrative work, and making it easier to employ particularly well-qualified young scientists.

Leistungsnachweis (certificate of achievement, credit certificate) Document of the grade and participation in a course (→Lehrveranstaltung) on the basis of work completed (→Referat, →Hausarbeit, →Protokoll, →Rezension, →Übung, →Seminar, →Praktikum) that is necessary to register for an examination. In university jargon, it is also often called a "Schein." Depending on the university and degree program, students may be required to collect the ~ to be admitted to the final examination for the degree.

Leitbild (mission statement) Catalog of the ethical values of a university as documented in the charter. Typical values in a ~ are: combining humanity and science, readiness for innovation and reform, social responsibility, consciousness of tradition, unity of research and teaching (→Forschung und Lehre), conveying knowledge, building personalities, motivation, joy in development and responsibility, preservation of academic traditions, promotion of young scientists, self-responsibility, equal opportunity, autonomy of the university, participation, internationality, being open to the global community.

Lektionsbogen (instructor's information sheet) A document completed by instructors. It includes: personal data, subject, and courses from the last four or five semesters. The comparison and coordination of ~ makes it easier to coordinate course offers.

Lektor 1. (editor) Term for a staff member in a publishing house who evaluates the quality of submitted manuscripts (→Manuskript) and optimizes it together with the author (→Autor)

2. (lecturer) Translation of the term for an instructor (→Dozent) at Anglo-Saxon universities who is primarily tasked with teaching. →Lecturer

3. (language instructor) Term for a native-language instructor, for example at the →DAAD.

Lektorat (editorial office) Lat. *legere* = read. Department at an academic publishing house to review and evaluate submitted manuscripts (→Manuskript) in order to ensure the quality of the publisher's program and to coach authors.

Lektüre (reading) Primary task of a scientist (→Wissenschaftler) according to units of time. Reading one's own or others' texts as well as the broader sense of considering what has been read without necessarily correcting (→Korrekturleistung) the texts. With the large amount of scientific texts (→Wissensexplosion), selective reading becomes necessary, which restricts concentration to certain parts of a scientific text that are directly relevant for one's own topic while leaving out all other parts. To aid in ~, excerpts (→Exzerpt) are prepared.

Lemma 1. (lemma) The content expressed in the title of a literary work (→Werk).

2. (headword) The keyword (→Stichwort) of a lexicon entry or the basic form of a word as listed in a dictionary (e.g. nominative singular for nouns, the infinitive for modern verbs, or the first person singular for verbs of ancient languages).

3. (lemma) Subsidiary part of a mathematical proof.

Lemmastrecke (character string) Section from an alphabetically sorted list, for example a volume of an encyclopedia with many volumes or another reference work, in the form of the starting letters (e.g. "Bo-Mer").

Leporello (accordion format, sheet with certificates of enrollment) Originally the term for a form folded in an accordion format. Today the term for a printed version of the certificates of enrollment (→Immatrikulation) at a university. A ~ is sent to each student via post and includes a student ID (→Studentenausweis), certificates of enrollment (→Immatrikulationsbescheinigung), deposit slip for semester fees (→Semestergebühr), re-registration confirmation (→Rückmeldeerklärung), and a page for the course record book (→Studienbuch). The name can be traced back to the character of the same name in Mozart's opera *Don Giovanni*, whose task was to record the morally questionable adventures of the title character in a small but continually growing book.

Lerngruppe (study group) A self-organized group of students on a voluntary basis. A ~ serves to prepare for an examination or deepen understanding of course material throughout the entire semester. Work in a ~ helps the participants to make up for the weaknesses of the individual members and achieve better results in oral presentations (→Referat) or written exams (→Klausur) by exchanging ideas and studying together.

Leserpsychologie (reader psychology) Aid for optimizing your own reading performance, in particular: concentration, textual comprehension, comparison, and evaluation. Successful reading is also dependent on the abilities of skimming, generalizing, reconstructing, and memorizing.

Lesesaal (reading room) Large area of a library (→Bibliothek), often close to the open stacks or reference section (→Präsenzbereich). ~ are sometimes divided into notebook areas and areas in which electronic devices are not permitted.

Literatur (literature) Lat. *littera* = letter. Term for the entirety of scientific texts that are available on a particular topic or in general. Knowledge of the ~ is thus an essential requirement for scientific work, and the discussion of the ~ is one of the primary tasks. One differentiates first between primary literature (→Primärliteratur), that is, sources, on the one hand and secondary literature (→Sekundärliteratur) or research literature on the other. Both are divided into sub-categories depending on the literary genre, and these categories can vary according to the subject. To collect and categorize the ~, bibliographic references (→bibliographische Angaben) are used.

Literaturangaben (literature references, bibliographical references) List or reference to titles of texts that were used to complete a scientific work. The evaluation of a scientific text is based to a significant extent on the evaluation of the literature used. All sources used to write a scientific work must be listed in the ~. The typical structure of the ~ includes the name of the author(s), the title of the publication, the location of publication, and the year (→Bibliographie), although this information can vary depending on the type of source and discipline.

Literaturliste (reading list) List of relevant book titles that is passed out at the beginning of a semester and serves to orient the students in a course. The quality of a ~ is a key aspect in the evaluation or grading. With the term ~, a list of literature that must be read can be meant, for example in the context of a seminar (→Seminar).

Literaturverzeichnis (bibliography) →Literaturangaben.

Lizenziat (licentiate) Also: Lizentiat. Academic degree (→Abschluss) in Switzerland for theology or the liberal arts.

LLM (LLM) Abbreviation for *Legum Magister*. Multiple post-graduate specialization for lawyers (simple: LM) in relation to certain legal areas, but not a protected title and not a qualification that allows for admission. The requirement for acquiring a ~ is a regular legal degree, for example a *Juris Doctor* (USA) or an LB (*Bachelor of Laws* in Great Britain).

Logik (logic) Logic as a science of valid conclusions investigates connections between individual statements and creates relationships between them in order to determine whether a statement is true or false. In the context of a ~ course as offered by philosophical or mathematical institutes, the terms of ~ can be learned. One differentiates between two key types of ~: deductive and inductive. Logic as a scientific discipline (→Disziplin) rests on the systematic work of the Greek philosopher Aristotle, to whom the term syllogism can be traced. Important logicians were also Leibniz, Russels, Gödel, and Wittgenstein.

Logik, deduktive (deductive logic) The teaching of valid reasoning in the form of the following statement from the antiquity: *If all men are mortal and if Socrates was a man, then Socrates was also mortal.* ~ is thus the process of forming conclusions about something specific from something general and is used primarily in the mathematical disciplines or where empirics (→Empirie) plays only a small or no role. Pure ~ is thus important for mathematics and some areas of philosophy but is rarely used in subjects such as political science or theology and is in essence entirely unimportant in subjects such as art history or literary science.

Logik, induktive (inductive logic) In contrast to deduction, it is the not universally valid technique of drawing conclusions about the general from the specific, for example in the following sentence: *I only see white sheep here and therefore conclude that (almost) all sheep here are white*. The conclusion must include restrictions in order to be valid. ~ is a key tool in all empirical subjects and represents the majority of natural science argumentations and descriptions.

Loseblattausgabe (looseleaf edition) Form of publication in contrast to bound books. ~ are often published in the form of notebooks, individual sheets, or binders so that regularly published expansions can be included without problems. ~ are often sold as subscriptions and periodically delivered by the publisher.

Losverfahren (lottery procedure) Selection procedure under neutral supervision if there are more applicants than university places and other selection criteria such as examinations (→Prüfung), etc., can no longer be used or are not prudent.

M

M.A. (Magister, Master) Abbreviation for: Magister Artium (→Magister) or Master of Arts (→Master)

Magazin (closed stacks) Area of a library (→Bibliothek) that is usually not immediately accessible for visitors. Location for storing books and other media (→Medien) such as microfilms (→Microfilm), digital data carriers, etc., that are not kept in the reading room (→Lesesaal) or open stacks. Depending on the size of the library, ~ can contain several million volumes (→Bände). That is why modern logistics plants like in the industrial sector are necessary in most libraries. Additional key aspects of the structure of closed stacks include the efficient use of the room, temperature, humidity, speed of access, structure systematics, protection against dust and fire, and the ability to expand the holdings.

Magister Artium (Magister Artium) Lat. *magister artium* = Master of Arts. →Magister. Abbreviation: M.A.

Magister (Magister) Lat. *magister* = tutor, teacher, expert. Also: M.A. Academic degree (→Grad) or title (→Titel) at universities, usually liberal arts (→Geisteswissenschaften) after around 10-12 semesters and corresponds to a →Diplom but usually includes two majors or one major and two minors. The title is usually not used in Germany, that is, not placed on business cards or letterheads, in contrast to Austria, where the title is relatively common. The degree is being phased out in favor of the Bachelor's/Master's system. As the standard period of study was often approximately 5 years, it is in some respects considered equivalent to a Master's degree.

Magisterprüfungsordnung (Magister examination regulations) Provisions that regulate the procedure for obtaining a Magister degree. The focus is on regulations for the examination procedure (→Prüfung), the evaluation, and the timeline. A university's ~ are approved by the *Land*'s ministry of science. →Prüfungsordnung

magna cum laude (magna cum laude) Lat. *magna cum laude* = with great distinction. Second-best evaluation of academic work, corresponds to the grade 2 (→Note 2).

magna cum tempore (15 minute delay) →akademisches Viertel

Magnifizenz (His/Her Magnificence) Lat. *magnificentia* = nobleness, greatness. Official, antiquated form of address for the rector (→Rektor) of a university, but not necessarily for the head of a university's executive committee (→Präsident).

Mahngebühr (overdue fee) Usually a small fee that can be assessed for library media not brought back on time.

Major **(major)** Term for "→Hauptfach" at universities in the United States.

Manuskript (manuscript) Lat. *manus* = hand.

1. Term for a text not yet ready for print or another text with a draft character as well as a term for written notes, e.g. notes from a lecture or a prepared outline of a draft.

2. Term for valuable individual pieces in the sense of 1. but from famous writers or works, for example handwritten ~ of Middle Age poetry. (→Handschriftenlesesaal)

Marie-Curie-Programm (Marie Skłodowska-Curie actions) Collective term for several EU initatives to support European research with a budget of 6.16 billion euros between 2014 and 2020 for research training and mobility programs for young scientists (→Nachwuchswissenschaftler).

Massenfach (subjects attended in large numbers) In contrast to the rare subjects (→Orchideenfach), the ~ are subjects taken by a large number of applicants, for example business and economic sciences.

Massenuniversität (mass university) The phenomenon that more applicants and enrolled students (want to) study at a university than there are places (→Studienplätze). The resulting overfull courses means that the quality of teaching greatly suffers. In connection with the ~, tuition fees are often discussed (→Mega-Uni; →Evaluation). In Germany, around one-third of each secondary school class studies at university, but the universities are not organizationally set up for this. The introduction of the Bachelor's programs (→Bachelor) are supposed to combat this, as they allow students to leave university earlier but with a degree as long as they do not want to pursue an academic career.

Master (Master's degree) Academic degree that can be obtained as a further degree after 1-2 years at a regular university or university of applied sciences. Together with the Bachelor's degree (→Bachelorabschluss), the ~ is part of the newly introduced system of successive degrees that in part still exists parallel to the traditional degrees (Diplom, Magister, Staatsprüfung). These traditional degrees are being largely phased out, however. After a successfully completed Bachelor's degree (→Bachelorstudiengang), a more in-depth academic education can be pursued. However, it is usually necessary to apply to a Master's program. After completing the ~, the graduate once again has the choice of entering into a career or continuing academic education with a doctorate (→Promotion).

Master-Arbeit (Master's thesis) Written work representing independent research usually done at the end of a Master's program. The ~ is typically longer than a Bachelor's thesis, and students can receive anywhere between 3-6 months to complete it, depending on the program.

Matrikel (register) Lat. *matricula* = public register. Catalog-like list of all students at a university (→Immatrikulation) according to year. These lists are important sources (→Quelle) for research on universities.

Matrikelbuch (registration book) At old universities, the ~ was usually a highly decorated, large book of the enrolled students, but these have long since been replaced by IT databases. The ~ is one of the insignia of a classical university and serves as a source for university historians. In libraries, historical ~ can be viewed and serve to document the respective university's history (→Alumni; →Ahnengalerie).

Matrikelnummer (student number, matriculation number, registration number) A unique, unchangeable identification number given to a student that is noted in the university's register (→Matrikel) and the certificate of enrollment (→Immatrikulationsbescheinigung, →Leporello).

Matura (secondary school leaving certificate) Lat. *maturitas* = ripeness. Term for the qualification to enter university (→Abitur) in Austria, Liechtenstein, and Switzerland, whereby in Switzerland it is called "Maturität."

Master of Business Administration (Master of Business Administration) A degree primarily known as an MBA becoming ever more common in Germany as a secondary degree (→Zweitstudium) on the topic of management. Often in connection with high tuition fees (→Studiengebühren), especially at private universities.

MC-Test (multiple-choice test) Abbreviation for: →Multiple-Choice-Test

MD **(MD)** Abbreviation for Medical Doctor (→PhD)

Medium (medium) Lat. *medius* = mediator. The physical carrier of contents or information in libraries (→Bibliothek): Books (→Buch) as print media, CDs or USB sticks as electronic media, microfilm, video, and audio recording are the most common forms.

Medizinertest (test for prospective medical students) A test for applicants to medical degree programs that was discontinued in 1996. The ~ was a combination of an intelligence and concentration test that was done at upper-level secondary schools.

Mega-Uni (mega online university9 Term for a distance-learning university (→Fernuniversität) whose capacity for university places (→Studienplätze) is unlimited, at least in theory. Examples include the Fernuniversität Hagen, Open University in Great Britain, or the University of Maryland, USA.

Meisterklassenexamen (master class examination) Conclusion of a postgraduate master class at music universities after a basic level degree program (→Studiengang) and a successful admission examination.

Meisterschüler (master student) A title given by art universities to particularly talented students after they have presented their artistic abilities to a jury. In slang, it is also a term for an excellent student in any subject.

M̱ensa (canteen, refractory, student dining hall) Lat. *mensa* = meal, table. A university canteen with relatively low prices and varying quality – anything from prize-winning private companies to lackluster efforts are possible. Usually it is supported by the local Student Services organization (→Studentenwerk). The online ~ menu is usually one of the most frequently visited pages on the university website.

Menschenbild, akademisches (academic conception of humankind) Both the methods and objectives of universities (→Hochschule) are based on the conviction that it is possible for people to obtain new knowledge and develop intellectually, and that these abilities will in the end benefit the general public. The ~ is based on the ideals of: intellectual upbringing to independence; maturity and awareness; intellectual courage; an investigative spirit; goodwill and the readiness to critique other academics; joy in discovery; readiness to debate; and openness to new ideas. Another key element is the conviction that it is worth looking for new explanations for both new and familiar facts and measuring these against the opinions of others (→Weltbild). The ~ is thus equally characterized by the ideas of communication and competition.

Mensu̱r (duel) Lat. *mensura* = measure. Term from the language of fraternity students. Carrying out a fencing duel with sharpened weapons and precisely defined rules. The wounds are cared for by a so-called "Paukarzt." If there is a scar from a ~, this is called a "Schmiss." Only a small number of fraternities (→Verbindung) still have ~.

Mentor (mentor) Professor or other university member who advises students. Named after the Greek hero ~, in whose form the goddess Athena (→Athene) advised her protégé Telemach.

Mentoring (mentoring) The systematic support and expert instruction of a student by a professor or other successful graduate of the university. The mentor (→Mentor) doesn't necessarily need to have an academic background but could also be in a management position at a company, for example.

Methode, wissenschaftliche (scientific method) Systematic procedure to investigate a posed question. The respective ~ of a study is directly relevant to its success, as it can determine even before starting whether there is a possibility of gaining knowledge. Research methods themselves are the object of the theory of science (→Wissenschaftstheorie). Science as an iterative process (→Iteration) covers the following stages: Finding questions, observing phenomenon including documentation (→Dokumentation), collecting and structuring material, creating preliminary hypotheses (→Hypothese), systematically repeating trials or thought experiments (→Gedankenexperiment), proving or falsifying your own or others' hypotheses, publishing the results of the project, and reporting, discussing, or teaching about the results.

Microfiche (microfiche) Medium that is cheap to produce and saves minimized texts the size of postcards for documents, magazines, or final papers. To enlarge them, special reading devices (usually not digital) with large screens are necessary. The reading head of the devices is moved over the cards and the enlarged picture is shown on the screen.

Microfilm (microfilm) Analog storage medium for pictures and text material in the form of a black 35 mm-wide role with a lifespan of around 500 years under good climatic conditions. To enlarge them, special reading devices with screens are necessary. In contrast to microfiche (→Microfiche), which is made up of a single card, ~ are suitable for saving newspaper contents since they are rolled onto spindles and can therefore also handle larger formats. Most daily newspapers, for example, are saved on this medium as are maps and sheet music.

Microthek (microform collection, microform area) Greek *mikros* = small and Greek *theke* = board. Area of a library (→Bibliothek): Collection point for microfilm (→Mikrofilme) and microfiche (→Microfiche) as well as other media based on optically minimized contents. There are also corresponding catalogs, reading devices, and special copiers.

Miszellen (miscellaneous) Lat. *miscellanea* = mixed dish. Section in scientific journals with brief notifications about various current research projects (→Forschungsvorhaben), or the term can refer to these contributions themselves.

Mitarbeiter, wissenschaftlicher (research associate, academic assistant) →Lehrstuhl

Mitarbeiterinformation (staff information) Internal communication path, for example with a mailing list (e-mail or post). Important topics include: job postings, purchases, people who are leaving, HR policies, and general news.

Mitbestimmungsrecht (participation right) The guarantee of participation in the respective charter for all curiae (→Kurien) in important internal processes, votes, and elections (→Wahlen), on questions of the budget and appointments in the context of the regular work of university committees (→Hochschulgremien). Students often believe their ~ is insufficient.

Mitschrift (notes) The written information from an oral speech such as a lecture (→Vortrag) or presentation (→Referat) that can vary greatly depending on the previous knowledge, interest, or education of the listener. ~ are therefore often compared when preparing for exams and are often the only documentation of historical lectures, for example Georg Wilhelm Friedrich Hegel's lectures on the philosophy of law, which were able to be reconstructed in this way. (→Exzerpt)

Mitverfasser (co-author) Second, secondary author of a work (→Werk), whereby the name of the ~ must also appear on the publication (→Autor).

Mittelbau (mid-level faculty, non-professorial teaching staff) Term for the group of academic personnel (→Personal) at a university that does not include the professors (→Professorenschaft) or the non-academic personnel. It typically refers to research staff and civil servants (→Beamte). These staff members usually have doctorates and in some cases also have post-doctoral lecturing qualifications (→Habilitation).

Modell, wissenschaftliches (scientific model) Term from scientific theory to denote a theoretical construct that can be used to better explain, study, and predict complex relationships. Constants and variables are necessary as is a certain degree of abstraction, idealization, and simplification, for example in the case of Bohr's model of the atom. The globe is also a ~ (→Weltbild).

Modul (module) Term for an element of a degree program in the context of the Bologna Declaration. Modules are defined as "self-contained, formally structured learning experience" that can be made up of several courses (e.g. lecture and exercise course). In terms of time, modules usually do not stretch over more than two semesters. A ~ includes up to a maximum of 20 ECTS points. One also differentiates between compulsory and semi-elective modules.

Monographie (monograph) Greek *monos* = single; *graphein* = write. A work by an author or group of authors of varying length that deals with a single topic in detail and comprehensively. Together with articles (→Aufsatz), ~ are the most important source of information for students.

Moodle (Moodle) ~ is an acronym for "modular object-oriented dynamic learning environment." It is an open source e-learning software program for distance-learning courses or e-learning aspects of regular courses.

Motto (motto) Ital. *motto* = word. →Wahlspruch

Mütze (cap) Head covering with a brim. Part of the traditional and previously mandatory dress code for students, today still typical for some student societies (→Studentenverbindungen). First attested in Jena in 1808 (→Pedell; →Burse).

***Multiple Choice Test* (multiple-choice test)** Type of written examination in which answers are marked without the possibility to state an independent position or evaluation, used in particular in subjects that are highly structured (→verschult) in order to be able to manage the high number of participants in examinations. The disadvantages of ~ become apparent in cases of questions that are not stated clearly or if existing, correct answer possibilities are not included by the creator of the test. Innovative or creative solutions are also not possible.

multi-tasking **(multi-tasking)** Simultaneously taking care of several tasks without decreasing the quality of any.

Musen, die (muses) In Greek mythology, the most important gods of the sciences and arts together with Athena (→Athene) and Apollo (→Apollon). The ~ were daughters of Zeus and the goddess of memory, Mnemosyne. There is disagreement about the number of ~, but usually three or nine (= three times three) are named. In the second case, the names are: Calliope (epic poetry), Clio (history), Erato (lyric poetry), Euterpe (music), Melpomene (tragedy), Polyhymnia (hymns), Terpsichore (dance), Thalia (comedy), and Urania (astronomy).

Musikhochschule (music academy, college of music) Type of university for degree programs in musical subjects as well as the corresponding sciences (→Wissenschaft). Admission requirements are a university entrance qualification (→Hochschulreife) and proof of artistic talent, whereby the second criterion is more important than the first.

N

Nachdruck (reprint) Also: Faksimile-Ausgabe. Unrevised printing of an older version for the aesthetic value so that a physically new book is similar to an old volume (→Band) without its disadvantages, e.g. brittleness, mold, or other defects. ~ are primarily relevant for researching the history of a subject, whereby critical editions are always to be preferred.

Nachkontakte (alumni networking) Also: *Follow-up*-Kontakte. The personal relationships that result from studies, including those that are independent of the subject or class (→Alumni).

Nachlass (estate) After the death of a writer, for example, material that is to be archived because it is unstructured. The professional management of the documents is usually very time-intensive and makes up its own research project (→kritische Ausgabe; →Archiv).

Nachrückverfahren (succession procedure, move-up procedure) When allocating university places, students who receive a place but do not or cannot accept thus give other students who did not receive a university place in the primary admission procedure a chance to move up. The systematic and comprehensively conducted ~ are intended to shorten waiting times.

Nachwuchskrise (young talent crisis) The long-existing problem at German and Austrian universities of getting talented young scientists to stay in the long-term. Attempts to counteract this include providing attractive career prospects or equivalent working conditions as in the university system in the United States. The introduction of junior professorships (→Juniorprofessur) is one measure intended to alleviate the problem.

Nachwuchswissenschaftler (young scientists, up-and-coming scientists) Term for academics with a doctorate who are preparing for a →habilitation or another academic career (→Karriere), for example at a private research institute. In the Federal Republic, working conditions for ~ are considered comparatively difficult. Reasons for this include: strong competition from universities in the United States, strict hierarchies at German universities, high costs, and poor career opportunities.

Namensregister (name index) Part of the annex (→Anhang) in which all names of people mentioned in a work, not including the names of authors in the footnotes and endnotes, are given in alphabetical order with the corresponding page numbers in the work.

Nationes (nations) Lat. *natio* = birth. Term from early universities to denote the student body, which was always organized according to nationality. The so-called *"universitas magistrorum et scholarium,"* the entirety of instructors and students, became the core of today's university (→Universität). At the University of Paris, for example, the following *nationes* were differentiated: the Gauls, Normans, Picards, and English. Students and instructors belonged to these main groups. The German students, for example, belonged to the group "English"; the *nationes* of the University of Prague were called: Bohemian, Bavarian, Saxon, and Polish (→Burse; →Hochschulgeschichte).

Naturgesetz (natural law) Observable regularity that can be replicated by experiments and exists in animate and inanimate nature. Whether ~ are descriptions of e.g. physical processes or whether their functioning itself belongs to nature is controversial. The term "law" is thus not unproblematic. An example for a ~ is the inability to genetically pass on acquired characteristics. The physicist Werner Heisenberg was one scientist who was occupied with the question of ~. Here the determination that natural laws can also be falsified is important or, more precisely, the hypothesis that a particular correlation could be a ~.

Naturwissenschaften (natural sciences) Study of phenomenon in the external world, that is, animate and inanimate nature, with scientific methods primarily on the basis of observations and experiments, whereby the term "nature" is to be understood in contrast to the cultural world made by humans and includes: biology, chemistry, mineralogy, geosciences, physics, etc. Traditionally, mathematics has been considered part of the ~, but this has been increasingly questioned in recent decades. The study of ~ is often more cost-intensive than subjects in the liberal arts due to laboratory classes (→Praktika) and excursions (→Exkursion), and the external funding procured is also higher on average.

Naturwissenschaftler (natural scientist) Researcher who investigates objects of animate or inanimate nature in contrast to scholars of the humanities (→Geisteswissenschaftler). People may be the object of study, but as part of nature and not as the object of cultural values or ideas or in regards to their position in the world. For ~, empirical approaches to scientific questions are of primary relevance, that is, observations and conclusions drawn from them. That is why elaborate devices are often necessary for research (→Labor).

N.C. Abbreviation for: →Numerus Clausus

Nebentätigkeit (side job, part-time job) Use of professional abilities for a third party or freelance work outside of the university, for example as a reviewer (→Gutachtertätigkeit) and thus an important additional source of income for many academics.

Nestor (doyen) Term for a scientist who significantly influenced her discipline for many years (→Ikone). The name is from Homer's Iliad in which Nestor, the old king of Pylos, gave advice considered particularly wise.

Networking **(networking)** The social and professional contacts made during studies that can prove to be very valuable later when looking for a job (→Alumni).

Neuerscheinung (new release) Publications new on the market are often reviewed for an expert audience (→Fachpublikum) in scientific journals close to the publication date (→peer review).

Nexialistik (nexialism) Term for interdisciplinary thinking by scientists and the inclusion of ancillary sciences. For example in the numerous points of contact between biology and medicine. The structure of sciences according to faculties is questioned by ~ but not due to the administrative organization of the degree programs.

Nichtwissenschaftliches Personal (non-academic personnel, non-scientific personnel) Collective term for all employees at a university who only indirectly have contact with research, if at all, but are necessary for the functioning of the university: secretaries, librarians, lab assistants, drivers, facility managers, graphic artists, technicians, and programmers.

N.N. Abbreviation for: →Nomen Nominandum

Nobelpreis (Nobel Prize) The most famous prize worldwide. It was endowed by the Swedish industrialist (dynamite products) Alfred Nobel in 1901. It is awarded each year to important scientists in the areas of physics, chemistry, physiology and medicine, literature, and peace. Since 1969, it has also been awarded for economics.
www.nobelpreis.org

Nobelpreisträger, deutsche: Chemie (German Nobel Prize winners in chemistry) Hermann Emil Fischer 1902, Adolf von Baeyer 1905, Eduard Buchner 1907, Wilhelm Ostwald 1909, Otto Wallach 1910, Richard Martin Willstätter 1915, Fritz Haber 1918, Walther Hermann Nernst 1920, Richard Adolf Zsigmondy 1925, Heinrich Otto Wieland 1927, Adolf Otto Reinhold Windaus 1928, Hans Fischer 1930, Friedrich Bergius 1931, Carl Bosch 1931, Richard Kuhn 1938, Adolf F. J. Butenandt 1939, Otto Hahn 1939, Otto P. H. Diels 1950, Kurt Alder 1950, Hermann Staudinger 1953, Karl Ziegler 1963, Manfred Eigen 1967, Ernst Otto Fischer 1973, Georg Wittig 1979, Johann Deisenhofer 1988, Robert Huber 1988, Hartmut Michel 1988

Nobelpreisträger, deutsche: Medizin oder Physiologie (German Nobel Prize winners for medicine or physiology) Emil von Behring 1901, Robert Koch 1905, Paul Ehrlich 1908, Albrecht Kossel 1910, Otto F. Meyerhof 1922, Otto H. Warburg 1931, Hans Spemann 1935, Gerhard Domagk 1939, Feodor Lynen 1964,

Karl von Frisch 1973, Georges J. F. Köhler 1984, Erwin Neher 1991, Christiane Nüsslein-Volhard 1995, Günter Blobel 1999

Nobelpreisträger, deutsche: Physik (German Nobel Prize winners for physics) Wilhelm Conrad Röntgen 1901, Philipp Lenard 1905, Ferdinand Braun 1909, Wilhelm Wien 1911, Max von Laue 1914, Max Planck 1918, Johannes Stark 1919, Albert Einstein 1921, James Franck 1925, Gustav Hertz 1925, Werner Heisenberg 1932, Walther Bothe 1954, Max Born 1954, Rudolf Mössbauer 1961, J. Hans D. Jensen 1963, Klaus von Klitzing 1985, Gerd Binnig 1986, Ernst Ruska 1986, Johannes Georg Bednorz 1987, Wolfgang Paul 1989, Herbert Kroemer 2000, Wolfgang Ketterle 2001

Nomen nominandum (yet to be named) Lat. *nomen nominandum* = a name yet to be named. Also abbreviated: N.N. in course catalogs (→Vorlesungsverzeichnis) if the instructor had not yet been set by the editorial deadline. Not to be confused with the abbreviation "n.n." in footnotes (→Fußnoten), where it comes from the Latin *nomen nescio* = I do not know the name.

Nominalstil (style using many nouns) In scientific and official German texts, this is the typical style with a high number of sometimes long noun constructions, noun-verb phrases, prepositions, and genitives with relatively few verbs and a comparatively high number of passive sentences. Most entries in a lexicon are written in this style. The ~ is in contrast to the style of spoken language (Verbalstil).

Non rite (unsatisfactory) Lat. *non rite* = insufficient. Grade for a dissertation (→Dissertation). Corresponds to the grade 5 (→*insufficienter*).

Normseite (standard page) Measurement unit for text with 30 lines per page and 60 characters per line: totaling 1800 characters per page. (→Format DIN)

Nostrifizierung (nostrification) Lat. *nostrificare* = make ours. Term for recognizing degrees from foreign universities. At Austrian universities, also for recognizing credits obtained from foreign universities.

Noten (grades, marks) Lat. *nota* = mark, sign. Scale for evaluating student work. Three main systems are used: single-digit numbers (Central Europe), letters (Anglo-Saxon areas), and percentages (Italy, Ireland, and many African countries). The ~ in Germany and Austria go from 1 (best grade) to 6 (worst grade) or 1 (best grade) to 5 (worst grade).

Noten, deutsche (German grades) The German grading system has six different grades.
1 = very good = summa cum laude; 2 = good = magna cum laude; 3 = satisfactory = cum laude; 4 = sufficient = rite; 5 = poor/insufficient = non rite; 6 = unsatisfactory = also: non rite

Noten, Bedeutung der (meaning of grades) The following evaluations of work are usually used as a basis for grades:
Very good (sehr gut) = excellent, brilliant presentation, above-average fulfillment of all evaluation criteria, linguistically outstanding and independent. Problems are minor, corrector's expectations were far exceeded; good (gut) = evaluation criteria were fulfilled, the work held a certain appeal, there are problems but they are not major, the corrector's expectations were not disappointed; satisfactory = all important requirements were fulfilled, the work is "proper" but a certain something is missing, there are clear problems that should have been corrected, the corrector's expectations were mostly fulfilled; sufficient = the work is "not bad" and is sufficient for credit, it is clear that the author made an effort, the corrector did not enjoy reading the work, problems are very clear; fail (poor or unsatisfactory) = the work does not even fulfill the minimum requirements, the corrector was frustrated when reading the work.

Notenabzug (grade deduction) The following errors usually lead to a lower grade: failing to address the issue, literature used is old or unsuitable, research question is missing or unclear, work only states known truths, imprecise citing, lack of necessary academic distance from topic, insufficient linguistic skill in the case of native speakers.

Notizen (notes) Written documentation of thoughts and tips on paper or a digital medium (→Medium) without necessarily any structure for the purpose of later evaluation in a systematic work. ~ can be taken during an oral lecture (→Mitschrift), important points found in written sources, or they can be a collection of one's own thoughts.

Numerus clausus (numerus clausus, degree program with restricted admissions) Lat. *numerus clausus* = closed number. Limit on the number of students (→Studentenzahl) in a particular degree program and semester. Also: NC. The criterion for admission is usually the Abitur (→Abitur) grade, and "NC" is therefore often used to mean "minimum grade required for admission." Applicants with a grade lower than the NC can have waiting semesters counted and circumvent the NC regulation. There are federal and state-wide admission restrictions (→Zulassungsbeschränkung).
www.hochschulstart.de

O

Oberseminar (advanced seminar) Course for advanced students or doctoral candidates in which the individuals' research projects are presented and discussed under the supervision of the doctoral advisor or one of the advisor's assistants.

Objektivität (objectivity) Lat. *obicere* = object, oppose. A term already used in the Middle Ages to describe that which is not influenced by subjects, for example people. ~ is therefore used for the neutral and unbiased attitude of an observer vis-à-vis the object of study in contrast to subjectivity and is one of the key conditions for evaluating a statements' scientific character (→Wissenschaftlichkeit). Pure ~ can rarely or never be achieved, however, as the sociologist Max Weber or the physicists Werner Heisenberg and Erwin Schrödinger believed to have proved. The observer, no matter how unbiased he might be, always affects what he is observing (→Wissenschaftlichkeit; →Weltbild).

Obligatorisch (obligatory, compulsory) →Pflichtfach

Observatorium (observatory) Lat. *observare* = observe. Place with optical or electronic equipment for observing space. Traditionally on a hill and removed from densely populated areas (light pollution) and mounted on a moving base. Example: The *Royal Greenwich Observatory* in London became the reference point for the Zero Meridian for the international coordinate system in 1884. That is why world time, *Greenwich Mean Time*, is oriented on this ~.

Ockhams Rasiermesser (Ockham's razor) Named after the Middle Age scholar Wilhelm von Ockham, but essentially an ancient Greek maxim for scientific economy: If there are several equal theories, the simplest and shortest is to be preferred. The principle of ~ is also applied when shortening fractions.

Ombudsmann (ombudsman) Swedish *Ombudsman* = advocate. Representative of student interests to the university management especially in cases of suggestions for improvement or complaints and objections. The ~ is usually a professor and is elected by the university senate. His tasks include passing on critique from students in an anonymized form. Ombudsmen can also be appointed to handle cases of suspected violations of scientific integrity among professors or other academic personnel.

Ombudsmann der DFG (DFG ombudsman) An advisor available to all scientists directly and independently from participation in the German Research Foundation (DFG) for advice and support on questions of good scientific practice or improbity. The ~ has the function of an advisor and mediator, in particular when advising persons who have brought scientific misconduct to the attention of investigation committees and experience sanctions from other institutions for this reason.

OPAC (OPAC) Abbreviation for: *Online Public Access Catalogue*. Internet-based library catalog (→Katalog) with differentiated search possibilities, e.g. according to author, title, year of publication, keywords, and other parameters. When researching (→Recherche) a new topic, it is often the first place to go in order to get an overview of existing literature.

Orchideenfach (rare subject) A subject rarely taken with a special status in a faculty and a very low number of enrolled students, e.g. Celtic Studies. If universities are forced to save money, the ~ are often particularly affected.

Orientierungstutorium (orientation course, orientation tutorial) Course for first-semester students held by older students to give information about basic methods of working at a university, for example looking for literature, how the library works, and scientific working methods. At some universities, courses such as these are also offered by the university institutions.

Orientierungswoche (orientation week) Introductory events stretching over several days for first-semester students in which older students or university employees introduce degree programs or university institutions to the newly enrolled students.

Ordinarienverfassung (professorial structure) The structure of a university based on chairs/departments as the smallest organizational unit; these are combined into seminars or institutes, and these are then combined into faculties. The beginnings of this system can be seen in the university statutes of the 16th century when the separation of departments in the faculty of arts (→Artistenfakultäten) into their own faculties started and thus also the concentration on a relatively small subject area. The responsibility of professors in the Middle Ages for several subjects was ended with the ~.

Ordinarius (full professor) Lat. *ordo* = row, order, series. Term for a regular professor, the holder of a chair in contrast to an adjunct professor or an honorary professor. The term is thus related to university administration and not an academic degree.

Ortsregister (index of places) Section of an annex (→Anhang) in which all places named in a work are listed alphabetically with the corresponding page numbers in the work.

OS Abbreviation for: →Oberseminar

Österreichischer Austauschdienst (Austrian Exchange Service) Initiative started in 1961 to support academic cooperation (→DAAD). www.oead.ac.at

***Oxbridge* (Oxbridge)** Term for all institutions, members, and alumni (→Alumni) of the two oldest British universities Cambridge and Oxford, which served as role models for the entire Anglo-Saxon world (→Hochschulsystem, britisches). In essence, these universities are consortia of free and autonomous colleges (→College) with their own budgets. That is why it is possible for a college to have more funding than the university of which it is a part. Both the university and the colleges hire personnel (→Fellow; →Don).

P

Pädagogische Hochschule (pedagogical university, university of education) Special form of university to prepare teachers, usually with programs lasting 6 semesters.

Paginierung (pagination) Organization of page numbers within a text or book. Citing (→Zitieren) works can be problematic if different editions of a text have different ~ (kritische →Ausgabe).

The following structure is typical, for example: even page numbers on the right, odd page numbers on the left, new chapters start on the right-hand page.

Number	Contents	Page Start
1-4	Title no page number	left
5	Dedication no page number	right
6	empty no page number	left
7	Motto no page number	right
8	empty no page number	left
9	Foreword pages given	right
10	2nd Foreword pages given	left
11	Table of Contents pages given	right
12	More Contents pages given	left
13	End pages given	right
14	empty no page number	left
15	Introduction pages given	right
16	End of Introduction pages given	left
17	1st chapter pages given	right
87	End of chapter pages given	right
88	empty no page number	left
89	2nd chapter pages given	right

Paper **(paper)** Term for a short essay, seminar assignment, or information about a research project before its publication (→Publikation) in a scientific journal.

Paradigma (paradigm) Greek *paradigma* = pattern. Term influenced strongly by Thomas S. Kuhn for what is scientifically observed and checked and what is asked in relation to a topic; it also includes the way in which questions are asked and the general direction and interpretation that should be taken or made. The term is therefore often used as a synonym for "perspective." The ~ is a key term when describing a scientific view of the world.

Paradoxie (paradox) Also: Paradoxon. Greek *para* = counter, *doxa* = view. Contradiction in logical connections, often through a reference back to something already mentioned, e.g. in the antique example: "The Cretan Epimendies said that all Cretans are liars." In academic texts, ~ are not popular as a stylistic device, as they themselves are often the object of academic research. That is why the (attempted) resolution of a logical contradiction, for example in mathematics, is always connected to a certain amount of progress (→Fortschritt) as in the case of Russell's paradox when considering the set of all sets that are not members of themselves.

Parawissenschaften (parasciences) Greek *para* = beside. Branch of science that focuses on studying unproven phenomena. In contrast to pseudosciences (→Pseudowissenschaften), which are not true sciences, here the doubts are not about the methods but about the sense and claims of the research, for example when studying supposed phenomena of parapsychology.

Parität (parity) Lat. *pars* = part. Filling a committee (→Gremium) with a set number of representatives from the various groups in order to ensure balance, or to ensure majorities (→Kurie).

Parkstudium ("parking spot" studies) Also: Verlegenheitsstudium. Enrollment (→Immatrikulation) at a university in a degree program to bridge the waiting time for the degree program the student actually wants to study. However, this time is not typically counted as waiting semesters (→Wartesemester).

Partnerhochschule (partner university) Usually international partnerships between two universities for the purpose of more intensive exchanges of instructors and students as well as other cooperation projects. Since each university can have many ~, a global network results through the respective partnerships that often develops analogous to the city's partnerships.

Partneruniversität (partner university) →Partnerhochschule

Party (party) Important and ubiquitous part of studies in the form of first more organized and then ever less organized social gatherings.

Patentindex (patent index) Criterion of university evaluation (→Hochschulevaluation). The attribution of patent registrations to universities is not unproblematic. In subjects with a strong link to practical applications, ~ is considered a measurement for the quality of research and flows directly into the ranking (→Ranking). In other subjects, it is usually only given for informational purposes. In Germany, the Fraunhofer Institute (→Fraunhofer Institut) carries out studies on this.

Pauken 1. (cram) Student slang for rote memorization, not necessarily comprehension of the material.

2. (duel training) Term from the language of fraternity students (→Verbindungsstudent). Practicing

fencing duels or preparation for a duel (→Mensur).

PC-*Pool* (computer pool) A computer center for students under the supervision of the computing center (→Rechenzentrum) with access to research tools, the internet, intranet, printers, terminals, scanners, and other computer-based tools and applications.

Pedell (caretaker) Late Latin *pedellus* = servant. Traditional term not commonly used today for a facility manager at a school or university. In earlier times an important official in the function of a factotum. The ~ was considered to be so important that at universities in the Middle Ages it was prohibited under threat of punishment for them to leave the university city for more than one day without the permission of the rector. Important tasks included: carrying the scepter for ceremonial processions, administration and maintenance, internal information service, supervision of instructors and reporting to the president about their conduct, and additional ceremonial functions as well as supervision of the detention cell (→Karzer, →Burse).

Peer Review **(peer review)** Method for checking manuscripts (→Manuskript) submitted to academic publishers. The review (so-called "screening") is primarily to check whether the texts fulfill the standards of the respective discipline (→Disziplin). At the end of the process, a recommendation to the editor (→Herausgeber) is made: accept, reject, or revise and resubmit (→Sokal Affäre).

Periodika (periodicals) Regularly published expert journals (→Journal) to provide information on new developments on a more or less narrowly defined topic.

Person*a*l (personnel, human resources) The entirety of all people employed at a university (→Hochschule), whether full-time or part-time. One can differentiate between academic or artistic and non-academic personnel (→nichtwissenschaftliches Personal). The academic personnel primarily employed by the university are determined by the Higher Education Framework Act (→HRG) for all of Germany and includes four groups: professors (→Professor), instructors (→Dozent) and assistants (→Assistent), research associates (→wissenschaftliche Mitarbeiter), and instructors for special tasks (→Lehrkräfte für besondere Aufgaben). At the end of 2014, 675,146 people were employed by German universities, 56% of which were academic personnel.

Personalrat (staff council) Labor law representation of the three *professional* groups (→Angestellte, →Arbeiter, and →Beamte) who work at a university. The tasks of a university ~ correspond to those of a works council in the private sector, that is, the representation of employee interests especially on questions of occupational safety and layoffs.

Pertinenzprinzip (principle of pertinence) Lat. *pertinere* = concern, extend. Principle of organization of a collection or an archive according to subjects regardless of how the archive material or collection items developed (→ Provenienzprinzip).

Pflichtexemplar (obligatory copy for submission) Term for a copy of a newly released title (→Titel) that must be submitted to a state library, committee, or the university examination office (→Prüfungsamt) for purposes of documentation (→Dokumentation) and evaluation.

Pflichtfach (compulsory course) Course required by a curriculum (→*Curriculum*). The course must be successfully completed in order to register for the final examination (→Abschlussprüfung). (→Wahlfach)

Pflichtmodul (compulsory module) →Pflichtfach

***PhD* (PhD)** This Anglo-American term is confusing because it does not only refer to the subject of philosophy, even though PhD is short for Doctor of Philosophy. Instead, it describes the type of degree, that is, a research project lasting around 4 years analogous to the German dissertation (→Dissertation, →Promotion). The use of the title is also not standardized in the Anglo-American countries. In Oxford, for example, the corresponding title is *DPhil*. In contrast to the German doctorate title, the ~ is placed after the name. The ~ serves to differentiate from the so-called professional degrees such as the medical doctor, MD. In Germany, ~ programs have started to be introduced, for example at the University of Osnabrück.

Phantomstudent (phantom student) →Pseudostudent

Philister (Philistines) Lat. *philistini* = Name of a people in the Bible. The term for non-students, people who are hostile to culture and the arts, or "old men" from a fraternity (→Studentenverbindung) now in the professional world is derived from the role of the Philistines in the Bible, who appear as the heathen opponents to God's chosen people the Israelites. With the use of the term, students are compared to a chosen people, although this is done somewhat ironically.

Philosophicum (philosophy examination) Traditional term for the conclusion of the first three of a total of seven liberal arts (→*artes liberales*), which was the requirement for continuing studies. The so-called trivium subjects were also taught outside of universities, and academics thus considered them "trivial." At the university, the ~ served to refresh knowledge from school or make up the knowledge in case the subject matter had not been handled at school. The ~ has hardly been used in Germany since the 1970s (→Fakultät).

Physikum (preliminary medical examination) Traditional term for the intermediate examination (→Zwischenprüfung) in medical professions as required by the license regulations (→Approbationsordnung).

Piltdown-Affäre (Piltdown Affair) Case of scientific fraud (→Betrugsfall) in 1908, when a human skull with the lower jaw similar to an ape was "found." The Piltdown Man was considered the missing link in mankind's evolution. But when the bones were re-examined in 1953 after the development of the radiocarbon method, it was determined that both the jaw and the skull were only a few years old and had also been manipulated. The jaw belonged to an orangutan and the skull to a human. The list of suspects was long at first and even included the author Sir Arthur Conan Doyle until finally the curator of the British Museum of Natural History was discovered to be the perpetrator. He likely wanted to harm his supervisor's reputation with this fake find.

PISA-Studie (PISA study) International comparison of performance in the area of education that led to the so-called "PISA Shock" in Germany due to the unexpectedly poor results. The ~ was carried out by the Organization for Economic Cooperation and Development (OECD). (→Hochschulreform)

Plagiat (plagiarism) Lat. *plagium* = kidnapping. Disregard for the intellectual property of third parties by purposely neglecting to cite sources (→Quellenangaben) or by unauthorized copying. The content of the work copied is irrelevant: Whether a seminar paper (→Hausarbeit) or a habilitation thesis (→Habilitationsschrift), when ~ is discovered it can have serious consequences including the revocation of academic degrees (→Grad) or the loss of the right to examinations (→Prüfungsanspruch). The guidelines on scientific integrity from the →DFG in 1998 formulated an honor code for scientists in order to ensure standardized good scientific practice; →VroniPlag.
www.dfg.de/antragstellung

PO Abbreviation for: →Prüfungsordnung

Polemik (polemic) Greek *polemos* = war. A confrontation or contribution to a debate usually done emotionally with harsh methods, whereby attacks on the content and the person can be mixed (→Kontroverse). Often caricatures are used that are designed to make certain perspectives look ridiculous. In contrast to satire, polemics usually have a serious concern and are not primarily for entertainment purposes.

***Political Correctness* (political correctness)** Also: PC. Linguistic rules to avoid discriminating word choices originally coming from US universities and now very controversial (→*affirmative action*).

Polytechnikum (polytechnic) Technically-oriented educational institution without the atmosphere of a university. The term has been in use since the mid-19th century. Usually an institute to educate engineers and officers.

Populärwissenschaft (popular science) Specific form of publishing scientific content for a non-scientific audience in contrast to pseudoscience (→Pseudowissenschaft), the contents of which are not scientific (→wissenschaftlich). Modern media uses ~ for providing entertaining information for interested laypeople (Also: Infotainment or Edutainment), whereby techniques from the media industry are linked to techniques of academic teaching (→Lehre). From the perspective of "pure" or true academic science, this type of presentation is usually lacking in terms of the necessary detail and restrictions. The choice of topic is predestined for the more dramatic areas of the sciences, for example: history: war; medicine: diet; biology: epidemics; physics: black holes (→Wissenschaftlichkeit; →Parawissenschaften; →Protowissenschaften).

Postdoc **(postdoc)** Young scientist after a completed doctorate (→Promotion) who continues to be active at a university and is pursuing a →habilitation, for example.

Postdoc-**Programm (postdoc program)** Program to support young scientists (→Nachwuchs) starting from the time they successfully complete their doctorate (→Promotion). Often with the goal of supporting the completion of a →habilitation.

Postgradualer Studiengang (postgraduate program) Term for an additional or consecutive degree program (→Studiengänge) that concludes with a certificate or another university degree but not with a doctorate (→Promotion).

Postgraduierter (postgraduate) →Nachwuchswissenschaftler

Praktikant (intern) Holder of an internship position (→Praktikum)

Praktikum Greek *praktike* = Knowledge of practical action. 1. (internship, work placement) Experience in the practice with no or only very low pay, often in a business or another non-academic organization. Important and desirable addition to an applicant's résumé (→Lebenslauf). Under some conditions, interns in Germany are now subject to minimum wage and thus paid better than in the past. 2. (lab hours, practical) A term for lab hours as part of a natural science course (→Labor) where the students conduct practical experiments themselves under supervision.

Prädikatsexamen (examination with honors) Degree (→Abschluss) with honors or particular distinction. (→summa cum laude)

Präsident (president, chairperson of executive committee) Chairperson of a university (→Hochschule) that is organized according to an executive committee model (→Präsidialverfassung). In contrast to a rector (→Rektoratsverfassung), the ~ is freed from teaching obligations. In addition, the ~ of a university is also the chairperson of the senate (→Senat). Some confusion can come to the term in English, as "Rektor" is sometimes also translated with "President."

Präsidialverfassung (executive committee constitution) While most universities used to have so-called rector constitutions (→Rektoratsverfassung), the ~ has become ever more common. The advantage of a ~ is that a president can completely focus on her administrative duties; this is in contrast to the rector, who must also fulfill teaching obligations in addition to administrative tasks. The Universities of Freiburg, Heidelberg, and Hohenheim, for example, have rector constitutions while Mainz, the HU Berlin, and Mannheim have a ~.

Präsidium (executive committee) The leading body (→Gremium) of a university organized according to an executive committee constitution (→Präsidialverfassung) to represent the university externally. The ~ has a relationship of checks and balances with the senate (→Senat), whereby the principle of the separation of powers only exists to a small degree.

Präsenzbestand (non-lending collection) Part of a library's holdings that cannot be borrowed. For various reasons (cost, archival reasons, fragility, security, irretrievability), they must remain in the library. The ~ often includes: handbooks (→Handbücher), atlases (→Atlanten), newspapers and magazines (→Zeitschriften), incunable (→Inkunablen), rare books (→Rara), and handwritten manuscripts (→Handschriften).

Präsenzbibliothek (reference libary) Traditional form of library (→Bibliothek) from the antiquity to Early Modern times when the idea of lending was unknown or undesired due to the cost of books. Most libraries (→Bibliothek) today combine the principle of ~ with lending by declaring some areas to be reading rooms where the holdings may not be borrowed.

Pressestelle (press office) Department for public relations work at a university. It usually also operates the university website and university newspaper (→Hochschulzeitung).

Primärliteratur (primary literature) The original sources for a topic are called ~, as they always have a higher priority in comparison to secondary literature (→Sekundärliteratur). A rule of thumb is: ~ does not age while secondary literature does. ~ includes all publications of original texts, data collections, lab findings, excavated artifacts, letters, diary entries, or field books on sediments or fossils (→Quellen).

Privatdozent (private lecturer, adjunct professor) Academic with a lecturing qualification who does not have a regular professorship and is thus not a full professor (→Ordinarius) but may be applying for professorships.

Privatgelehrter (private scholar) Not precisely defined, somewhat antiquated term for a scientist (→Wissenschaftler) or researcher who does not have a permanent position at a research institution or university or only has a part-time job there and concentrates on his private studies.

Privatuniversität (private university) Non-state educational institution financed by tuition fees (→Studiengebühren), donors, and in some cases with state support; usually in connection with business (→Wirtschaftswissenschaften) subjects. In Germany in 2005, fewer than 2% of students were enrolled at a German ~.

Prodekan (vice-dean) Assistant to the dean (→Dekan) elected by the faculty council (→Fakultätsrat) from among the professors (→Professorenschaft).

Professor (professor) Lat. *profiteri* = declare, profess.

1. University instructor with a postdoctoral lecturing qualification (→Habilitation) and a permanent position who has the right to teach at a university, conducts research and teaching (→Forschung und Lehre), and has the right to examine (→Juniorprofessur).

2. In countries such as Italy and France, it can also be a term and form of address for teachers with an academic education at state or private schools.

Professor, außerplanmäßiger (extraordinary professor) An honor conveyed by a university to a scientist with a →habilitation for special achievements in research and teaching. At art and music academies, a corresponding position can also be given to applicants without an academic background. This is an important difference to a full professor (→Ordinarius). The title is usually awarded 6 years after the habilitation.

Professur (professorship) Generally used as a synonym for chair/department (→Lehrstuhl), whereby one must differentiate among the various salary grades and functions of the officials (→Professor; →Honorarprofessor).

Projektarbeit (project work) Course (→Lehrveranstaltung) during the advanced study period (→Hauptstudium) that is focused on the practice, especially in natural science and technical subjects and can be designed to assist in practically implementing research results together with a company in the context of a general contract.

Proklamation (proclamation) Lat. *clamare* = call out. An announcement, for example of a new appointment for an academic position or a doctorate. It is traditionally a task of the dean (→Dekan) or vice-dean of a faculty (→Fakultät). Today they are usually made in written form.

Proletariat, akademisches (academic proletariat) Joking but negative term from the Anglo-Saxon countries for academically trained people who cannot achieve academic positions due to their social background and instead are active in professions or jobs for which an academic education is not necessary. The term can also be heard in connection with the introduction of the Bachelor's degree (→Bachelor) at German universities for the Bachelor's program graduates.

Promotion (doctorate) Lat. *promovere* = move forward. Obtaining a doctorate degree (→Doktorgrad) after another advanced degree such as a Master's (→Master) by completing a dissertation (→Dissertation) and an oral examination (→Disputation) according to a university's doctoral degree regulations (→Promotionsordnung). It is often falsely used as a synonym for dissertation (→Dissertation), which only means the extensive academic work.

Promotion, grundständige (fast-track doctorate) Procedure to award a doctorate degree (→Doktorgrad) without a previous degree such as a Master's or comparable degree on a direct path.

Promotionsordnung (doctoral degree regulations) University-specific regulations on the doctorate (→Promotion). There are no national standards for the requirements. The most important contents are:
The right to award doctorates, admission requirements, admission to the doctorate, dissertation, initiating the doctoral proceedings, doctoral committee, review of the dissertation, acceptance of the dissertation, dissertations that are not accepted, oral examination, evaluation of the oral examination, defense, evaluation of the defense, setting the overall grade for the doctorate, publication of the dissertation, awarding the doctoral degree, right to complaints and objections, doctoral file, honorary doctorate, revocation of the doctorate, final provisions.

Promotionquote (doctorate quota) Criterion for university evaluations (→Hochschulevaluation). What is measured is the number of successful doctorates per professor each year. An exception are the business and economic sciences, as the Federal Statistical Office states that these cannot be clearly assigned to certain personnel.

Promotionsvereinbarung (doctoral agreement) Measure being introduced at many universities to ensure better supervision of dissertations. The doctoral candidate and advisor agree on the project, timeline, how often they will meet (usually a minimum of once per semester), and often on milestones to be met before the next meeting. The agreement is updated after each meeting if there are changes.

Propädeutikum (preparatory course) Greek *propaidaia* = preparatory lesson. Introductory course in the basic study period (→Grundstudium) (or at an earlier point in time, thus also called: Vorsemester (presemester)) in which the basic parameters of a subject or a topic are presented. In contrast to a tutorial (→Tutorium) or an introductory seminar (→Proseminar), the ~ is usually not relevant for final examinations.

Prorektor (vice-rector, prorector, vice-president) A deputy of the rector (→Rektor) elected from among the professors (→Professorenschaft). Responsible for particular tasks in research and teaching (→Forschung und Lehre) or the university structures.

Proseminar (introductory seminar) Course for students in the basic study period in which the key working methods of the subject are presented. For older types of degrees (→Diplom, →Magister), proof of attendance of various ~ is required to complete the intermediate examination (→Zwischenprüfung).

Protestaktionen, studentische (student protest actions) Due to the relatively weak political position of the students at a university (→Hochschule) in certain situations, the ~ are a necessary defensive measure vis-à-vis the university management (→Hochschulleitung). The organizational form of ~ is usually grassroots and ad hoc, for example in the case of a threatened closure of small subjects, increase of tuition fees, or extremely overfull courses. Typical forms of ~ are: strikes, trespassing, insults, occupation of administrative rooms, posters, demonstrations, appearances in costume, and media contact. Atypical but documented cases are: hunger strikes, symbolic burning, coercion, unlawful detention, and violence against people or property, for example the murder of the poet August von Kotzebue by the student Karl Ludwig Sand in 1819.

Protokoll (minutes) Greek *protokollon* = first sheet glued onto a manuscript. Term for the documentation of an event according to what happened (Verlaufsprotokoll) or the results of the discussions (Ergebnisprotokoll) according to set guidelines. ~ are often required to obtain credit for a course.

Protowissenschaft (protoscience) Description for new research areas that have not yet become commonly accepted or have been replaced by true sciences throughout history, for example alchemy was replaced by chemistry. Philosophy can be considered a ~ in a similar sense, as modern disciplines such as mathematics, physics, and literary science developed from it. If scientific expectations of a ~ are not fulfilled, the ~ may be moved to the realm of pseudoscience (→Pseudowissenschaft).

Provenienzprinzip (provenance principle) Structuring principle for a collection or archive according to the criteria of the origin and creator. The ~ is therefore an alternative to the principle of pertinence (→Pertinenzprinzip).

Prüfer (examiner) Term for an instructor (→Dozent) in his function of holding an examination (→Prüfung). Together with an observer (→Beisitzer), the ~ holds a discussion with the candidate (→Kandidat) to evaluate the candidate's knowledge of a previously set topic. One typically differentiates between strong and weak ~, whereby the first play a dominant role in examination discussions and talk a lot themselves, while the latter give the candidate more time to talk.

Prüfung (examination) Method to evaluate student performance, usually at the end of the semester in the lecture-free period (→vorlesungsfreie Zeit) by one or more examiners (→Prüfer), whereby the individual ~ have precise regulations, the so-called examination regulations (→Prüfungsordnung) that can vary depending on the degree program and faculty (→Fakultät).

One differentiates among the following types of ~: written examinations (→Klausur), oral examinations (→mündliche Prüfung), and practical examinations, for example in handling technical equipment.

Prüfung zum Nachweis deutscher Sprachkenntnisse (examination to prove German proficiency) Language examination for foreigners applying for a university place, usually held in a language center or at the university. Generally accepted tests include the →DSH or the Zentrale Oberstufenprüfung (→Goethe Institut).

Prüfungsanspruch (right to take an examination) The right of every regularly enrolled student to be examined in the courses taken according to the respective examination regulations (→Prüfungsordnung); under certain conditions it can be lost, for example if cheating (→Betrugs- und Täuschungsfällen) or plagiarism (→Plagiat) is discovered, if a student fails the examination the maximum number of times allowed, or if a student misses an examination without an excuse.

Prüfungsamt (examinations office) Administrative unit at a university (→Hochschule) to manage examination registration, examination grades, and student problems dealing with examinations.

Prüfungsangst (test anxiety) Term for a special kind of fear related to examinations, a feeling of uncertainty combined with typical stress symptoms such as blanking out, losing your voice, excessive anxiety, or other blocks. At most universities, psychological counselling services offer courses to help students deal with ~.

Prüfungskommission (examination committee) Depending on the type of examination, a group of varying size made up of instructors participating in the examination. It is made up of a chair, additional members (professors and instructors), and observers (→Beisitzer) who have at least the same qualification as the candidate being examined.

Prüfungsleistung (work counted towards final grade, examination, graded coursework) A ~ is any work done that counts toward the final grade. Because the term "Prüfung" is often used to describe a written examination, ~ is often mistakenly understood as a written exam. While a written exam may be a ~, oral examinations, presentations, lab reports, or other work may also be counted towards the final grade and are therefore also considered ~.

Prüfungsordnung (examination regulations) Set of rules for carrying out examinations including deadlines, requirements, credit for courses, and combination of subjects depending on the degree. The ~ determine the legal framework for a final examination, are legally binding, and their interpretation and compliance with them can be brought before an administrative court. In addition, the rights and obligations of the participants are set down. The contents include provisions on:
Study objectives, structure of studies, name of the academic degree to be awarded, requirements for admission to the examination, standard period of study, recognition of coursework and examinations, examination procedure, examination dates and registration deadlines, regulations if examinations are missed, withdrawal, cheating, evaluation of examination results, grading, forms of examination, and possibilities for repeating the examination.

Prüfungsreferat (examination unit) A term used at Austrian universities for the examinations office (→Prüfungsamt).

PS (PS) Abbreviation for: →Proseminar

Pseudonym (pseudonym, pen name) Greek *pseudein* = to deceive. Alias of an author that is different from the actual name either to hide the true identity, which can be necessary for political reasons, or to create a second identity in another framework, for example for test purposes for possible reactions from an audience. In academic publishing, it is highly unusual to use a ~.

Pseudostudent (fake student) Student enrolled for purposes of insurance or discounts that can come from having a student status but who does not attend courses or complete examinations or has no intention of obtaining a degree.

Pseudowissenschaft (pseudoscience) Teaching or subject area that does not fulfill the most basic requirements of scientific methods (→Wissenschaftlichkeit) but is usually vehemently defended by its proponents. ~ are usually in ecological explanatory niches of sciences where serious research is not or hardly active or does not appear to be worth the effort: supposed earth rays or water veins, divining, astrology, creationism, reincarnation, or palm-reading, for example, and these are often linked to a quasi-religious background. In contrast, what is interesting is the in part common origin of ~ and serious sciences in antiquity when there was no difference made between astronomy and astrology or alchemy and chemistry. That is why pseudo-scientific approaches often contain information about the history of how knowledge is gained in general. What is very problematic and in part even criminal is the oft-found claim of ~ to the exclusive truth (→Weltbild).

Psychologische Beratung (psychological counselling) Initiative at universities by the central student counselling services (→Studienberatung) to offer assistance in the case of family, psychological, and general problems of students. One key task of ~ is also to help in crises, for text anxiety (→Prüfungsangst), and writing blocks (→Schreibhemmung) as well as general counselling for life planning.

Publikation (publication) Work that is published in the context of new academic knowledge or proclamations (→Proklamation). The number of publications is often a key part of an academic's reputation.

Publikationszwang (requirement to publish) University doctoral regulations (→Promotionsordnung) require that the →dissertation is published after the candidate has completed the defense. This can be done in the form of a book, in various publications of articles in journals in the case of a cumulative dissertation (→Dissertation, kumulative), or in digital form.

***Publish or Perish* (publish or perish)** Key phrase and critical description of the requirement in modern academic operations to continually publish new articles or books in order to be perceived as a serious academic (→*impact factor*) or to receive research funding or other recognition.

Q

Qualifikation (qualification) General term for the required knowledge within a subject that does not necessarily have to be academic in character. In a more narrow sense, ~ also refers to the degrees and examinations completed in relation to a later task.

Quästur (bursar's office) At Austrian universities, term for the academic financial administration and its oversight according to the model of the office of the same name in ancient Rome.

Quellen (sources) Primary literature (→Primärliteratur). Term for all material that serves as a basis for academic research that is not in a commented or interpreted form. Sources could be, for example: official documents, data, photographs, diary entries, coins, etc. The interpretation of the sources in writing is called secondary literature (→Sekundärliteratur).

Quellenbeleg (citation) Footnote (→Fußnote), →endnote, or parenthetical reference. Term for a reference to a source in the primary literature (→Primärliteratur). These kinds of references serve as a mark of the academic nature of a text.

Quellenedition (source edition) Collection of sources on a topic that can be published as a critical edition (→kritische Ausgabe) or an uncritical edition. ~ have the purpose of making aspects of the primary literature (→Primärliteratur) accessible to a large circle of researchers, for example if there is only one specimen of the original.

Quereinstieg (lateral entry, change of major) Switch from one subject to another after several semesters (→Semester) have already been completed and some of the credits from the old subject can be recognized for the new one so that the student (Quereinsteiger) can be enrolled in a higher subject-related semester in the new subject.

Querverweis (cross-reference) In dictionaries often appearing as an arrow to refer to another entry (→Lemmata) or text. In the internet, ~ are called hyperlinks.

Quorum (quorum) Lat. *quorum vos ... unum esse volumus* = "Of whom we wish that you be one." Expression from the Middle Latin administrative language. Today: minimum number of participants needed to pass decisions in a committee or body. If the number of members in attendance at a committee meeting (→Gremiensitzung) is enough for a vote to be taken according to the bylaws (→Satzung), then the ~ is considered met.

R

Ranking (ranking) Not generally recognized list of educational institutions according to standardized criteria based on statistical data or surveys, often carried out by serious journals such as DER SPIEGEL (since 1989), the British TIMES, and other non-university organizations. The current trend of ~ moves away from ranking lists but groups universities in fields.

Ranking in Deutschland (ranking in Germany) A ~ carried out by the →CHE in cooperation with the Bertelsmann Foundation and the German Rectors' Conference (→HRK) reached the following results according to state: ranked first were universities in Baden-Württemberg, and there the University of Heidelberg, followed by Bavaria, Mecklenburg-Western Pomerania, Thuringia, and Saxony. In the middle were Hesse, Saxony-Anhalt, Bremen, Rhineland-Palatinate, Berlin, and Brandenburg; at the end of the scale were North Rhine-Westphalia, Lower Saxony, Saarland, Schleswig-Holstein, and, finally, Hamburg.

Parameters for the study were: evaluations of the students, reputation of the university, average length of studies, and research performance.

Additional rankings are carried out by the news magazine FOCUS and DER SPIEGEL and the weekly newspaper DIE ZEIT.

Ranking weltweit (global ranking) Especially American and British rankings from large daily newspapers, but also the studies from the University of Shanghai get a great deal of attention. The rankings are not always based on the same study parameters (e.g. number of foreign students), but English-language universities regularly achieve top positions, in many cases Harvard is first. In most international lists, German universities have not achieved top positions in recent years, that is, among the first 30 spots.

R<u>a</u>ra (rare books) Lat. *rara* = rare. Collective term for old or seldom literature (individual works, first editions, etc.) from the time before 1850 that are usually kept in special areas in libraries. As with incunable (→Inkunabeln) or really all books, proper archiving of ~ in the stacks (→Magazin) requires a constant room temperature and humidity.

Raubdruck (pirated edition) Unauthorized copy of a copyright-protected work by a competing publisher whose identity is usually not clear. With the typically commercial distribution, the rightholders (author, heirs, and publisher) suffer damage. Trademark counterfeiting and pirated copies are related.

Rausprüfen (weeding out with tests) University slang for the more or less arbitrary measure in some degree programs of reducing the number of students by harsh examination requirements as only a small percentage of candidates (→Kandidat) have a chance of passing the examination.

Realität (reality) Lat. *res* = thing. True life as it exists independently of the observer and his perceptions and actions; it is thus the object of measurements, etc. However, even the assumption that there is a ~ that is completely independent of observers is problematic (→Objektivität).

Rechenzentrum (computing center) Central department for a university's IT with many tasks, for example providing students with e-mail accounts or creating database systems. Organizationally, a ~ is often divided into: hardware, software (e.g. databases), and operating units.

Recherche (research) Planned and iterative search for scientifically useful contents and thus the working technique of the targeted accumulation of information on a particular subject while filtering out aspects that are not relevant.

Rechtsaufsicht, staatliche (state legal supervision) The control of the legality of actions of public institutions such as schools or universities by state authorities can contradict the autonomy (→Autonomie) of the universities and is therefore a possible object of negotiations between representatives of universities and ministries (→HRK).

Rechts- und Strafgewalt (legal and penal power) Until the modern era, most universities had their own legal systems due to their autonomous charters (→Grundordnung), and they were regularly used. In addition to the notorious disciplinary measures against students (→Karzer; →Fidibus; →Pedell; →Kleiderordnung), in particular the autonomy of personnel policies should be mentioned that allowed the universities to select their students and instructors at their own discretion. Additional areas of application for a university's ~ were: purchasing property, construction, contact with other universities, and financial matters. The state-like sovereignty of the old universities gave rise to the expression "republic of scholars" (→Burse). Today one refers to the charter (→Grundordnung).

Redlichkeit, wissenschaftliche (scientific integrity, probity) Requirement that academics hold to the ethical principles of scientific publication, in particular in regards to intellectual property of other researchers, and thus also correct citation (→Zitieren) and documentation of results or preventing plagiarism (→Plagiat).

The document published by the German Research Foundation (→Deutsche Forschungsgesellschaft) "Safeguarding Good

Scientific Practice" focuses on the following aspects of "good practice": Control of leadership responsibilities in working groups; regulated supervision of young scientists; excluding honorary authorships; and regulations for dealing with accusations of scientific misconduct. In addition, the quality and originality should be the standard of evaluating publications and should always have priority over the number of publications. That leads to a strong devaluation of the impact factor (→Impact-Faktor).

Reduktion (reduction) Lat. *reducere* = lead back. One form of decreasing the scope or complexity of phenomena being observed in order to better understand them. ~ often takes place by using metaphors whose evocative contents are meant to better express the basic ideas. The problem of ~ lies in the degree of simplification allowed. While mathematical equations can be simplified according to rules, in many other disciplines simplification is linked to the question of whether what is simplified is comparable to the original, complex idea or not.

In the words of the mathematician Benoit Mandelbrot: *The goal of science has always been to reduce the complexity of the world to simple rules.*

Referat Lat. *referre* = report, assign, report (on).

1. (oral presentation) Short presentation of up to 20 minutes, usually a requirement for getting credit in seminars. ~ have several purposes: They serve as a basis for giving credit, as a basis for discussion in the seminars, and as a medium for informing the scientific community: ~ are usually closer to research than printed publications (→Publikation), which need more time until they reach the public. Presentations are structured as follows: greeting the audience and especially the chair of the meeting, introduction of the topic, placing the research question into the larger context of the event, presentation of important positions in the research, followed by the presenter's own interpretations, emphases, and structures, then the presentation of theses. The presentation can be supported by →handouts, slides, or other media.

2. (department, unit) A unit within the university administration. →Stabstelle

Referendariat (required internship, clerkship, student teacher period) A required element in the education of lawyers and teachers lasting around two years following the state examination (→Examen) in which they spend time at different legal stations (courts, law offices) or schools as a transition from studies to their career.

Referent 1. (speaker) Term for the person presenting in a presentation (→Referat), speech (→Vortrag), or lecture (→Vorlesung).

2. (officer, expert) Staff member responsible for a particular topic at a

university, e.g. ministries, contact to the *Landtag*, or advising services.

Reformdebatte (reform debate) Discussion about the necessity of university reforms (→Hochschulreform). The debate usually includes questions such as: tuition fees, university structure, relationship between universities and the state, and the position of lecturers within the university.

Regelstudienzeit (standard period of study) The number of semesters set down in the examination regulations (→Prüfungsordnung) in which a degree program should be completed (→Abschluss) in order to avoid being considered a long-term student (→Langzeitstudent) or losing the right to take examinations or receive financial support. The ~ are usually 3-4 years for Bachelor's degrees and 1-2 years for Master's degrees.

Regest (register, archival summary of document) In archives (→Archiv) and libraries (→Bibliothek), the ~ is a summary that is as concise a description of the contents of a document or file as possible with formal information on the location and date of issuance as well as the names of locations and people included.

Register (index) Academic annex to a work with a list of alphabetically ordered names, terms, or locations as an aid for systematic reading or researching within a book (→Anhang).

Reiter (shelf dummy) →Stellvertreter. Slang expression for a card that is placed where a book has been taken off the shelf in a library (→Bibliothek).

Rektor (rector, president) Lat. *regere* = guide, rule. The head of a university elected from among the professors with the traditional form of address "Magnificence" (→Magnifizenz) from the Latin *rector magnificus*. As managing director, the ~ is the chairperson of the senate (→Senat) and always a scientist with a post-doctoral lecturing qualification (→Habilitation). The ~ represents the university externally.

Rektor designatus (designated rector) Term for a rector who has been elected but has not yet started her term of office.

Rektorat (rectorate, rector's office, president's office) Head of the university at universities with a rector constitution. Members of the ~ are the rector (→Rektor), chancellor (→Kanzler), and vice-rectors (→Prorektor).

Rektoratsverfassung (rector constitution) The traditional charter of a university according to the principle that a regular professor (→Ordinarius) takes on the leadership of the university for a certain period of time, whereby he must continue to fulfill tasks of research and teaching. The ~ is one of two alternative types of administration that are typical at German universities. In contrast, the executive committee constitution (→Präsidialverfassung) often frees the head of the university from other tasks.

Rektorbecher (rector's chalice) Traditional symbol of office for a university rector in the form of a cup, but no longer officially in use at modern universities. However, it may be part of the university collection (→Hochschulsammlung) and thus an exhibition piece.

Rektorenkonferenz (rectors' conference) →Hochschulrektorenkonferenz

Rektorkette (rector's chain) Ancient chain of office for a university rector in the form of a heavy necklace or shoulder strap made of gold and silver, only worn at important academic ceremonies.

Rektorsiegel (rector's seal) Seal of the rector's office to certify documents. At early universities, also an emblem (→Siegel).

Rektorstab (rector's staff) Traditional symbol of office for a university rector in the form of a staff as tall as a person, analogous to a scepter. Symbol of the legal and penal power (→Rechts- und Strafgewalt) of the university in the Middle Ages and Early Modern age. As many other insignia (→Insignien), the ~ is likely also borrowed from the Byzantine court ceremony that was brought to the universities via the Catholic Church.

Rektortruhe (rector's chest) At old universities, especially in Great Britain, and in some cases even today a common place to store official insignia or documents, but usually a museum exhibit in the university collection (→Hochschulsammlung).

Repertorium (finding aid) Antiquated expression for →Findbuch.

Repetitorium (revision course) Lat. *repetitorium* = repetition exercise. Form of preparing for examinations, sometimes by simulating the examination conditions. The term is used particularly often in law.

Residenzpflicht (residency requirement) Traditional requirement for academic instructors to live close to the location of the university (→Fernuniversität).

Ressource (resource) Term for all tools and aids to carry out a course in a general sense. This can also include: whiteboard, projector, rooms.

Revolution, wissenschaftliche (scientific revolution) Chain of innovations with far-reaching consequences on the basis of ideas or technology that radically questions the previous construct of explanations on the issue and usually offers new, powerful explanations. A textbook example of ~ in the literature (→Literatur) is the innovation of Nicolaus Copernicus (1473-1543), whose work *Commentariolus* provided the basis for the modern idea of the solar system. Often many decades pass before the insights of a ~ receive general recognition or are disseminated, for example in the case of Darwin's theory of evolution.

Rezension (review) Lat. *censere* = assess. Discussion of a book according to standard guidelines. Writing a ~ is often part of the requirements to obtain credit for a course, or it is an important medium for academic authors to communicate with the expert community.

Rhetorik (rhetoric) Element of the liberal arts (→*artes liberales*). Art of speech. In today's usage, often a negatively connoted term for the technique of manipulating listeners with linguistic means. In academic usage, due to the requirement to moderation, not all possible rhetorical figures (→rhetorischen Figuren) are used equally.

Rhetorische Figuren (rhetorical figures) The following word constructions can often be found in academic texts or lectures:

euphemism: more positive expression instead of a more realistic one (e.g. "to pass away" = die); irony: use of an opposite term from that which is meant (e.g. "a masterpiece"); synonymia: repetition of the same meaning with different words, so that minimal differences in meaning are purposely used (e.g. from Shakespeare's Julius Caesar: "You blocks, you stones, you worse than senseless things!"); litotes: negation of the opposite, lesser degree for higher degree (e.g. "argued not unconvincingly" = (almost) convincingly); oxymoron: combination of contradictions (e.g. "try to square the circle"); permission: giving permission to others or an opponent (e.g. "For now, that is up to further research to determine"); apophasis: mentioning an important matter in passing (e.g. "...which, by the way, earned him the Noble Prize"); rhetorical question: emphasis of a statement by using a question (e.g. "Who could doubt that?")

Rigorosum (viva, viva voce) Lat. *rigor* = inflexibility, stiffness. Oral examination for the doctoral degree (→Promotion). In addition to discussing the dissertation (→Dissertation), in a ~ often other aspects of the discipline are tested, e.g. in political science, political theory and comparative politics may be tested although the dissertation was in the area of international relations. At some universities, this is in contrast to the defense (→Disputation), where the focus is solely on the subject of the dissertation.

Ringtausch (exchange of university places) Exchange involving more than two university places. At the end of the process, each student participating has a new university place (in a different degree program or at a different university).

Ringvorlesung (public lecture series) Interdisciplinary event series for a large audience with several lectures (→Vorlesung) on a topic carried out by various lecturers (→Dozent). Also called →Studium Generale.

Rite (pass, sufficient) Lat. *rite* = sufficient. Fourth grade for an academic work, corresponding to the grade 4 and the lowest passing grade (→summa cum laude).

RV (RV) Abbreviation for: →Ringvorlesung

Rückmeldung (re-registration) A renewal of enrollment (→Immatrikulation), usually done by simply transferring the required semester fee (→Semesterbeitrag) to the university for the coming semester. The ~ is subject to deadlines; typically if the first deadline is missed ~ can still be done with a late fee, but if the second deadline is missed then the student is automatically deregistered (→Exmatrikulation).

Ruf (appointment) Hiring (→Berufung) a suitable scientist for a professorship (→Lehrstuhl).

S

Sachbuch (non-fiction book) In contrast to fiction. Representation of facts that does not automatically have to have a scientific character. A ~ usually does not lead the reader through a plot in the sense of a drama but introduces existing, objective conditions. All scientific works are therefore non-fiction, but not all non-fiction books have a scientific structure, for example cookbooks.

Sabbatical (sabbatical) Sabbatical year according to the Biblical command Lev. 25:1 to keep one free or fallow year in every seven. Often a synonym for a research semester: time for a scientist to work on private studies, often in connection with a stay abroad, during which she is freed from teaching and administrative duties at the universities.

Sachregister (subject index) Part of an annex (→Anhang) in which all technical terms in a work are listed alphabetically with the pages in the work where they appear.

Samisdat (samizdat) Russian = self-publishing. The term originally comes from the countries of the Warsaw Pact. There, dissidents were often forced to publish their texts through non-official channels due to the publishing bans with consequences for the typographical appearance and the print run (→Auflage). The student movement (→Studentenbewegung) used the term for flyers, pamphlets, and other university political publications.

Sammlung, wissenschaftliche (academic collection) In addition to the collection of information media in libraries (→Bibliothek), ~ are key elements of research and teaching institutions. Depending on the subject area, interesting individual pieces (e.g. fossils, manuscripts, or medical compounds) are sorted according to topic, conserved, cataloged, and stored in the stacks (→Magazin), usually in connection with a temporary or permanent exhibition of the most important pieces, often together with the university library (→Universitätsbibliothek). That is why they help not only with scientific works, but also can themselves be the object of research.

Schein (course certificate) Student slang for a certificate of credit for a course (→Leistungsnachweis).

Schlagwort (keyword) A term that describes the contents of a text as precisely as possible without the term necessarily appearing in the title. Keywords are an important search criterion when researching titles. For each title, keywords are entered into the database for which one would search even if one doesn't know the exact wording of the title. That corresponds to the entry of a website in a search engine directory (→Stichwort).

Schmiss (dueling scar) Student expression for the scar of a wound in the face. In contrast to the widespread belief, however, it is not only an expression from fraternity members but comes from general 19th century student language.

Schnupperstudium (taster courses) Offer from universities for secondary school students to get to know academic methods. The ~ usually consists of individuals attending lectures without registering. A ~ is usually not possible for all subjects at a university (→Studium Generale).

Scholar **(scholar)** In the Anglo-American tradition, a term for a graduated university member below the level of a professor.

Scholarenmigration, mittelalterliche (scholar migration in the Middle Ages) Compared to the state of transportation in the Middle Ages, the European academics were highly mobile. Aided by the *lingua franca*, Latin, and by the equivalency of the degrees (→Philosophicum; →artes liberales), there was a never before seen exchange of personnel and knowledge. The ~ was hindered by the religious schism, transportation problems, and epidemics such as the plague in 1348, the year in which the University of Prague was founded. The ~ was the basis for a European-wide, highly international →scientific community.

Scholastik (Scholasticism) Lat. *schola* = school. Prevailing academic way of thinking and working in the high Middle Ages, in contrast to empirics (→Empirie), that was limited to the study of a few classic authors (usually Aristotle), church fathers, and the Bible (→Wegestreit). With the rise of humanism, new techniques, and the return to a concentration on antiquity, ~ became the epitome of unproductive and static science.

Schreibhemmungen (writer's block) Commonly seen syndrome in students that can be traced back to various causes and can manifest itself as a block when looking at a blank piece of paper or monitor. The most common reasons for ~ include: a lack of clarity in thoughts, being overwhelmed in terms of organization or content, reluctance, insufficient knowledge, or a false self-assessment. At most universities, there are now writing schools or psychological counselling to help with ~.

Schutzfrist (period of protection) Also: Sperrfrist. Usually lasts 30 years starting with the creation of the archival material during which third parties only have limited access. For special archive material that contains personal data, the ~ is 10 years starting with the person's date of death or 100 years starting with the birth date if the time of death is unknown (e.g. in the case of missing persons in catastrophes or wars). To regulate these deadlines and any exceptions, the respective archival laws and user regulations must be consulted.

Schutzheilige (patron saint) Patron saints of individual scientific disciplines according to the traditions of the Middle Ages and Early Modern era are: St. Michael – pharmacists; St. Barbara – architects; St. Lukas – physicians; St. Hieronymus – scientists and scholars in general; St. Ivo – lawyers; St. Aloysius – students; St. Johannes – booksellers.

Schwarzes Brett (bulletin board) Important forum for information between the university management (→Universitätsleitung), institute management, or chairs (→Lehrstuhl) on the one hand and the students on the other regarding news, dates, announcements, and opportunities in the teaching program but also for private information, for example the search for a student apartment. Each university body (→Gremium) has a special, reserved bulletin board to communicate its information. In areas often frequented by students such as the canteen or library, there is often a ~ for students to communicate with one another about anything from exchanging university places to apartments to extracurricular activities.

Scientific Community **(scientific community)** Collective term for the community of experts in a subject who are linked, for example, by reading certain publications and who attempt to develop their discipline (→Disziplin). Sometimes also used as a term for all scientifically working academics (→Weltbild).

SDS (SDS) Also: Sozialistischer Deutscher Studentenbund. In 1968, the organization grew to be the core of the student protests but had already existed before. At one point it had up to 2,500 members but self-dissolved in 1970. Famous members in the final phase were: Rudi Dutschke, Ulrike Meinhof, Bernd Rabehl, Dieter Kunzelmann, and Horst Mahler (→Studentenbewegung; →Achtundsechziger-Revolte).

Sekretär (secretary) Administrative position. Staff members at a university directly associated with a department (→Lehrstuhl), dean's office (→Dekanat), or another unit or committee (→Gremium). (→Personal)

Sekundärliteratur (secondary literature) Term for the entirety of texts that have been written for purposes of research (→Forschung) in contrast to primary literature (→Primärliteratur). Examples of ~ include: Essays (→Aufsätze), articles (→Artikel), monographs (→Monographien), commemorative publications (→Festschriften), miscellaneous sections of journals (→Miszellen), and textbooks (→Lehrbücher).

Selbststudium (self-study) Working on one's own initiative and independently to prepare for courses (→Lehrveranstaltung) or examinations (→Prüfung) as well as follow-up work for these. Key tools for ~

are: time plan, structure of content, reading list, excerpts (→Exzerpte), memorizing, comparing research approaches, and following debates currently ongoing in research, for example at conferences. In the context of courses, essentially only the results of the ~ are evaluated.

Semester (semester) Lat. *sex* = six and Lat. *mensis* = month. Half-year for students from April to September (summer semester) and October to February (winter semester), although some universities, e.g. the University of Mannheim, have shifted their schedules to more closely mirror the Anglo-Saxon semesters, thus making exchange programs easier. Courses usually take place between April-July and October-February. In the time in between there is a lecture-free period during which students write papers or take exams. The end of the semester therefore does not correspond to the end of the courses (→Vorlesungszeit).

Semesterabschlussfeier (end-of-semester celebration) Festively celebrated end of the semester in the form of a →party, a ball, or another ceremonial act. It is held by an institute, the entire university, or individual parts of a university, also by university congregations (→Hochschulgemeinde), student societies (→Studentenverbindung), and university groups (→Hochschulgruppe) or private persons.

Semesterbeitrag (semester fee) →Semestergebühr

Semesterferien (semester break) →Semester

Semestergebühr (semester fee) Small fee to be paid for enrollment and re-registration at the university. In contrast to the much higher tuition fees (→Studiengebühr), which are primarily for the purpose of supporting the costs of the university, the ~ are not sufficient to cover the costs a university pays for a student to study (→Studienkosten).

Semesterticket (semester ticket) Ticket for public transportation in connection with enrollment at a university; at some universities, it is an obligatory part of the semester fee (→Semestergebühr).

Semesterwochenstunden (contact hours per week) Also: SWS. Time unit lasting 45 minutes for academic instruction, used to calculating study performance as required by the examination regulations (→Prüfungsordnung). Also used to calculate the instructors' teaching load.

Seminar (seminar) Lat. *seminarium* = seminary. Academic form of teaching with the direction of one or more instructors (→Dozent) on a clearly defined topic (→Thema) and with the participation of those attending the course. Often participants must hold short presentations (→Referat) on individual topics. Participation in a ~ is a requirement for receiving credit (→Leistungsnachweis). The first ~ of a semester therefore usually serves to discuss organizational questions, for example the distribution of presentation topics. Later sessions then have a similar structure. After the instructor greets the participants, a presentation is held by one or more students, and the other students then discuss the topic of the presentation. Presentations with similar contents are typically held in sessions close together. The different types of seminars include: →Proseminar, →Hauptseminar, and →Oberseminar.

Seminarapparat (seminar binder) The collection of literature (→Fachliteratur) for a course (→Lehrveranstaltung) put together by the instructor or an assistant and made up of monographs, journals, reading lists, and compilations (→Kompilation) that is put out in the library for students to copy.

Seminararbeit (seminar paper) →Hausarbeit

Seminarbibliothek (seminar library, institute library) The collection of subject-area literature of an institute in its own building in contrast to the general university library (→Universitätsbibliothek), often concentrated very heavily on the research areas that are the focus of the professors in the institute.

Seminarraum (seminar room) In contrast to a lecture hall (→Hörsaal), usually a relatively small room without tiers, usually with tables and chairs arranged in a horseshoe form open to the board.

Seminarvortrag (seminar presentation) →Referat

Senat (senate) Lat. *senatus* = senate. Committee, comparable to a parliament, regulated by a university's charter (→Grundordnung) in which the various curiae (→Kurie) of the university are represented, whereby the professors always have the majority. The president or rector is the chairperson depending on the university charter. The tasks of the ~ are usually in the area of academic matters such as teaching, studies, continuing education, and research.

Senator (senator) Lat. *senex* = aged, old man. Member of the academic senate (→Senat).

Seniorstudent (senior citizen student) Student enrolled at a university as a senior citizen. At German universities, around 6,500 students are older than 60, making up less than 1% of the students. They are usually retirees. It should not be confused with the English term "senior student" at universities in the United States (→Freshman), which refers to students in their fourth year of studies.

Seniorenstudium (studies as a senior citizen) →Seniorstudent

Seriennummer (issue number, serial number) Exact numbering of a journal issue. The journal receives a call number (→Signatur) and each issue receives a number for unique identification, usually according to the year, quarter, month, or week as well as another number (→ISSN).

SFB (SFB) →Sonderforschungsbereich

Siegel (seal) The formal, usually decorative stamp of a university or university official, usually modeled after an earlier historical form, often a round stamp with the coat of arms of the country, state, or university. Older ~ often show patrons of the university's founding or ornamentation from the Middle Ages. While a university's logo can be freely available (→Uni-Shop), the ~ is an emblem that may only be used by authorized persons. Sphragistics and sigillography deal with the development of the historical seal (→Insignien).

Siegelführung (keeping of the seal) Lat. *sigillum* = seal. Right of a university to have its own seal for its documents as an expression of the legal independence and autonomy of a university in the Middle Ages and Early Modern era.

Siegelstempel (official seal) Sign of certification, stamp on official documents of a faculty or university, often taken from the graphic design of an old university seal (→Siegel). In the Middle Ages, it was an important element in the symbols of power of the always jealously guarded independent jurisdiction of the University especially vis-à-vis the sovereign prince but also vis-à-vis the non-academic citizens of the university cities.

Signatur 1. (call number) Book number or location number to find a volume in a library. It is marked on the cover, spine, and title pages of a book.

2. (signature) Signature on official documents

sine tempore (on the dot) Lat. *sine tempore* = without time. Punctual start to an event (→Veranstaltung) not 15 minutes later than the time given (→akademisches Viertel) as is often the case for university courses. Courses at technical universities often start sine tempore. The abbreviation is s.t.

Sitzung (session) Term for the actual meeting in the context of a course or committee (→Gremium).

Skript (lecture notes) Content summary of a course (→Lehrveranstaltung) in writing, usually for lectures (→Vorlesung), that can be completed by the listeners or one of the instructors. In the latter case, it is often the basis for an examination. The ~ for the current semester can usually be purchased at a local copy center (→Copyshop) or special university office for a small fee.

Sokal-**Affäre (Sokal affair, Sokal hoax)** A controversy provoked by the US physicist Alan Sokal in 1996 on the quality standards for publications. Alan Sokal submitted a →paper with the title: *Transgressing the Boundaries: Toward a Transformative Hermeneutics of Quantum Gravity* to the US cultural studies journal *Social Text* that was known for its post-modern orientation. Shortly after its publication, Sokal made it known in another journal that the paper was only made up of mismatched pieces from various postmodern theoreticians that he had exaggerated. The content of the text was nonsense, but it had still been accepted for publication (→Veröffentlichung). (→Wissenschaftsparodie; →Elfenbeinturm).

SOKRATES (Socrates Program) Program from the European Union to promote international cooperation in various areas of general education. Succeeded by the Lifelong Learning Program (LLP) in 2007, which in turn was succeeded by the →Erasmus+ program in 2014.

Sommeruniversität (summer university) Educational program from a university during the summer months of the lecture-free period for non-students or guest students (→Gaststudent), usually in the form of language courses for foreigners and prospective students.

Sonderbeauftragter (special representative) University employee for a specialized task. One differentiates between academic and institutional special tasks, for example gender equality and ensuring the corresponding directives are implemented at the university.

Sonderforschungsbereich (collaborative research center) Specially funded, narrowly defined subject at a university that typically takes a highly interdisciplinary approach to one topic.

Sondersammelgebietsplan (special collection plan) A national initiative funded by the German Research Foundation (→Deutsche Forschungsgesellschaft) to coordinate the collections of German libraries, whereby rare topics received targeted funding.

***Sophomore* (sophomore)** →*Freshman*.

***Sorority* (sorority)** Lat. *soror* = sister. Pronounced as in English. Term at universities modeled after those in the United States for women's societies analogous to the historically older and sometimes mixed gender →fraternities. The names of these student societies (→Studentenverbindung) are usually made up of three Greek letters according to the model of the Ur-sorority Kappa Alpha Theta from 1870.

Sozialbeitrag (social contribution) A fee included in the semester fees used to support the Student Services and thus the maintenance of the canteen (→Mensa), cafeteria, residence halls (→Wohnheim), and other institutions.

***Spectabilis* (literally: "noteworthy")** Lat. *spectabilis* = noteworthy, outstanding. Old-fashioned form of address for a dean (→Dekan), but only to be used in the Latin form by professors (→Professor). Other university members use the German word →Spektabilität.

Spektabilität (literally: "noteworthy") Lat. *spectabilis* = noteworthy, outstanding. Form of address for a dean (→Dekan).

Sperrfrist (blocking period) →Schutzfrist

Spickzettel (cheat sheet) Prohibited aid for examinations (→Klausur) in the form of a written note in order to be able to look up key information. Although completing a ~ while preparing for exam may make didactic sense, its use during an exam has consequences set out in the examination regulations.

Sponsion (sponsion) Lat. *sponsio* = solemn promise. In Austria, a common term for a ceremonial awarding of the title Magister (→Magistertitel) to the successful candidates (→Kandidat) by the dean (→Dekan).

Sprachlabor (language lab) →Sprachenzentrum

Sprachenzentrum (language center) Internal language school with diverse opportunities for learning foreign languages not only when studying languages but for all students regardless of their subject. Sometimes with very long waiting lists to participate in the desired courses or for mandatory certificates such as proof of mastery of the German language for foreign students.

Sprechstunde (office hours) Advising offer from professors for students each week. Students often need to sign up for a time slot and can get general advising (→Studienberatung) or discuss questions about obtaining credit (→Scheinerwerb), examination procedures, or content questions when preparing seminar papers (→Hausarbeit).

Sprengel (area) →Archivsprengel

SS (SS) Abbreviation for: →Sommersemester

Staatsexamen (state examination) →Staatsprüfung

Staatsprüfung (state examination) Final examination for university degree programs (→Studiengang) that lead to professions that fulfill a special public interest, including medical subjects, food chemistry, legal sciences, and teacher programs. The ~ is usually an academic degree that qualifies for a profession. For future teachers and jurists, in addition to the first ~, a preparatory period is required that concludes with the second ~.

Stabstelle (staff unit, department) Term for a central unit at a university on a lower level than the central university administration (→Hochschulverwaltung). The University of Stuttgart, for example, has the following structure:

Alumni, Campus Physician Service, Occupational Health and Safety, Data Protection, IT-Coordination, Women's Unit, Women's Representative, Internal Auditing, International Affairs, Marketing, Quality Development, Security, Environmental Protection, Academic Further Education, Central Data Protection Office.

Standardisierung (standardization) Unification of measuring units, types, forms, procedures, and rules in order to optimize the comparability of results, unify the flow of information, and more easily communicate methodological difficulties. The ~ is a technical task within an academic discipline but also an aspect of European university policy (→ECTS; →DIN).

Standeskleidung, studentische (student dress) Just as was the case with *magister* in the Middle Ages, the students as a group were required (or privileged) to wear certain insignia (→Insignien) in order to be recognized as members of their group (→Bursenzwang; →Kleiderordnung). The Middle Age ~ included the robe (→Talar) with wide sleeves and hood or hat. Later, more fashionable aspects were added such as poulaines or feathers in the hat that were no longer specifically for students, and wearing them was often a punishable offense. The following centuries show an ever increasing alignment between student and common clothing.

Statistik, angewandte (applied statistics) For almost all academic disciplines, but especially for the empirical, ~ is an indispensible ancillary science (→Hilfswissenschaft) to create overviews of large data amounts, usually with the assistance of modern IT. The application of statistical methods to scientific questions is part of the fundamental academic education in many disciplines.

Statutenbuch (book of statutes) Antiquated term for the written charter (→Grundordnung) of a university in the Middle Ages and Early Modern age. The ~ was considered proof of academic privileges vis-à-vis the sovereign and was also an insignia (→Insignie). At many universities, students had to swear an oath of loyalty on the ~ at their enrollment ceremony (→Immatrikulation).

Stellenausschreibung (job advertisement, job posting) A notification of an open position at a university that is usually first published internally then publicly on bulletin boards (→schwarzer Brett), employee information newsletters (→Mitarbeiterinformation), via the press office, and especially online.

Stellvertreter (shelf dummy) Usually a colored DIN A4 card placed on the shelf where a book was borrowed from a non-lending library (→Präsenzbibliothek) with a note about the current location, e.g. a professor's office (→Dienstzimmer).

Stereotypen (stereotypes) Prejudices that exist not only in regards to the perception of universities in the outside world (ivory tower (→Elfenbeinturm) and crazy scientist) but also within the university aided by the faculty structure – especially among the three large subject groups of the natural sciences (→Naturwissenschaften), social sciences (→Gesellschaftswissenschaften), and humanities (→Geisteswissenschaftler). Even if there is no standard ~, certain basic features of the prejudices can often be seen. In particular, in regard to the natural scientists these include ignorance of cultural matters, lack of understanding of anything that cannot be expressed in numbers, and a lack of elegance and style. Regarding the humanities, they include: ignorance of technological matters, tendency to be somewhat of a ninny, being overwhelmed by technology, and being bad at mental calculations. In regard to the social scientists: Exaggerated use of theories and data collections, incomprehensible jargon, research findings' lack of relevance.

Stichwort (keyword) A main term that appears in the title of a work. The ~ serves especially as a search criterion when researching (→Recherche) in databases and catalogs. The longer the title is, the more keywords it can include (→Schlagwort).

Stiftung 1. (endowment) Old term for founding a university usually by a sovereign or the citizens as with the University of Cologne. For younger universities, one speaks instead of founding documents.

2. (foundation) Organization to support a certain purpose on the basis of the interest from assets, for example to support gifted students, regulated in Secs. 80 ff. of the Civil Code (BGB) and in the provisions of the *Länder*'s foundation laws.
www.stiftungsindex.de

Stiftung für Hochschulzulassung (Foundation for University Admissions) Since 2008, responsible for allocating university places in all degree programs that have nationwide admission restrictions, including medicine, pharmacy, veterinary medicine, and dentistry.

Stiftungsurkunde (document of endowment) Historical document on the endowment (→Stiftung) of a university and usually part of the collection (→Sammlung).

Stipendiat (scholarship recipient, scholarship holder) A student supported by a scholarship (→Stipendium).

Stipendiendatenbank des DAAD (DAAD scholarship database) Overview of various offers of support for students (also for foreign students) searchable by criteria such as country of origin or subject.

Stipendium (scholarship) Lat. *stips* = small offering, and Lat. *pendere* = to pay. Financial, material, or other support for a student based on completed or expected achievements in a particular subject, often from public or private institutions, usually foundations (→Stiftung), after successful application. Scholarships are time-limited and often tied to a specific purpose.

StO (StO) Abbreviation for: →Studienordnung

Streik (strike) Form of action in collective bargaining disagreements from the side of the employees or protest action (→Protestaktion) by students at a university, e.g. to draw public attention to poor conditions for students.

Student (student) Lat. *studere* = strive. Person enrolled at a university (→Hochschule) for an academic education for a certain period of time. In a broader sense, someone who occupies themselves with obtaining knowledge.

Student, ewiger (eternal student) →Langzeitstudent

Studentenausweis (student identification card, student ID) Identification card for enrolled students valid for the length of a semester including the lecture-free period. The ~ must be regularly renewed by re-registering (→Rückmeldung) and serves to prove one's membership at the university or to take advantage of student discounts (→Leporello).

Studentenausweis, internationaler (international student ID) A document that can be obtained from the →AstA to prove enrollment at a foreign university. National student IDs are not recognized everywhere.

Studentenbewegung (student movement) Term for the protests held since the middle of the 1960s, especially among students, starting in Berkeley, Paris, Frankfurt am Main, and Berlin. Here Rudi Dutschke and the →SDS should be mentioned. A noteworthy, independent ~ did not exist in the GDR (→Achtundsechziger-Revolte). Ten years earlier there had been precursors of the ~, especially in the context of German re-armament (→Göttinger Achtzehn).

Studentenfutter (trail mix, literally "student fodder") Joking name for mix of dry cereal made up of various nuts, almonds, and raisins, often used for silent snacking during lectures. The first documented instance of ~ was in 1744.

Studentengemeinde (student congregation) Ecumenical or confessional association of students and other university members, usually with a large cultural program.

Studentenlied (student song) Term for a literary-musical genre with typical themes from student life such as: joy, love, camaraderie, mockery of professors, wine, and freedom. The internationally most well-known and often sung ~ is →*gaudeamus igitur*.

Studentenorden (student order) Predecessor or old form of student societies (→Studentenverbindung), organized according to the model of the Freemason lodges. ~ had their golden age in the 18th century and were primarily characterized by secret symbols and rites as well as esoteric doctrines of salvation.

Studentenparlament (student parliament) Annually elected body of a university to choose the →AstA representatives and pass guidelines (→Leitlinien). In Austria, the corresponding institutions are often called "student representation," in German university jargon also: Stupa.

Studentenportal (student portal) Internet-based offer for students with access to relevant topics of student life: studies, examinations, qualifications, applications, career, stays abroad, part-time jobs, accommodations, internships, seminar paper marketplace, language trips, and leisure time.

Studentenproteste (student protests) →Protestaktionen

Studentenschaft (student body) The entirety of all students enrolled at a university who are represented at various levels of the administration: departmental student representatives (→Fachschaft), student representative council (→Fachschaftsrat), student parliament (→Studentenparlament), and →AstA.

Studentensekretariat (registrar's office, student secretary's office) →Immatrikulationsbüro

Studentensprache (student language) Slang or special form of language that has always existed among students. Today, for example, it is characterized by rhyming abbreviations such as "Hiwi," "Uni," or "Ersti." Many terms of the older ~ are now in general use, for example the expression "jemandem eine Abfuhr erteilen" (to reject someone). The ~ has been systematically researched in terms of linguistics since around 1900: The early ~ was highly interfused with Latin expressions or used an ironic-false form of Latin (for example the expression *ex Ärmulo* = improvised). Only since the time after World War I can a sharp decline in Latin be seen. (→ankreiden; →Wörterbuch, studentisches)

Studentenverbindung (student society, fraternity/sorority) Also: Korporation. Voluntary association of (usually male) students in the form of an organized community with more or less inclusion of the former students (→Philister). Societies are organizationally located around a residence hall (→Wohnheim). The principle of a lifelong alliance of the members applies, and they recognize each other with certain symbols, coats of arms, colors, etc. Former members support the active ones with financial contributions. The grassroots structure of a ~ allows for quick election and voting out of officers; new members are only accepted as full members after a probationary period; individual societies can unite into overarching organizations. A further differentiation is made by the terms color-wearing/non-color-wearing or hitting/non-hitting.

However, one differentiates primarily among Corps, Burschenschaften, Landsmannschaften, Turnerschaften, Jagdschaften, and musical and confessional ~ (in Europe and the US usually Christian but also Jewish and Muslim). In Germany, there are currently around 1,000 ~. Around 3% of the students enrolled at German universities are members of a ~ (→Burse).

Studentenverbindungen, Diskussion über (discussion about student societies) The German debate on the topic of societies can be summarized as follows: the critique focuses on the under-representation of women in the membership; the function of the society as an old boy network or clique; antiquated definition of honor and reactionary political attitudes of the members; alcohol abuse and isolation from the outside world; and a lack of clarity about the differences among the individual societies. This criticism comes up against references to the grassroots democracy of the student societies; the ideal of equality; the cosmopolitan attitude; and the principle of tolerance that most societies hold to, as well as the persecution they experienced in the Third Reich and the GDR, the historical role of the societies in various battles for freedom and revolutions, and the normality of student societies in other countries.

The colors of the Federal Republic of Germany set down in Art. 22 of the Basic Law (GG) originated in the colors of the society in Jena. Due to its commitment in the revolution of 1848 for a democratic constitution, the tricolor was made to a symbol of the democratic tradition in Germany.

Studentenwerk (Student Services)
→Deutsches Studentenwerk

Studentenwohnheim (student residence hall, dormitory) A building for long-term housing of students operated by state, quasi-state, or private institutions, usually with moderate rent and relatively simple furnishings, thus also a suitable location for regular parties (→Party) and a key element of →networking within the student body. (→Gästehaus)

Studentenzahlen (number of students) In 2014, there were around 2.7 million students enrolled at German universities. The number of female students continues to rise, but the proportion of women decreases the higher the level of qualification (→Dissertation; →Habilitation).

Studentenzeitung (student newspaper) In contrast to the university newspaper (→Universitätszeitung), the ~ is an unofficial publication that can be affiliated with an individual university or be regionally oriented. ~ can also be online publications with no printed version. In terms of topics, ~ are primarily oriented on questions of student life such as jobs, internships, and the search for a place to live.

Studie (study) The investigation of a question with surveys, individual interviews, or tests and measurements is a key element of all empirical sciences. With a ~, first data is collected that is then interpreted iteratively in the next phases. The original research hypothesis can be problematic because – depending on the question – the results might already be predetermined. (→Versuch; →Empirie)

Studienabbruch (dropping out) Leaving the university before finishing (→Abschluss) and thus without a degree (→Grad). In decreasing order, the number of drop-outs according to subject are: humanities, art history, business and economic sciences, social sciences, law, engineering, and medicine.

Studienabbrecherquote (drop-out ratio) The number of students who do not finish their degree in relation to the number of students enrolled at a university. The higher the ~ of a university, the fewer the number of students who actually achieve a degree. This number is relevant for the →rankings.

Studienanfänger (new students, first-semester students) Term for all students newly enrolled in their first university semester (→Hochschulsemester) even before the start of the lecture period (→Vorlesungszeit) and thus not identical with the term →Erstsemester.

Studienanfängerquote (new student ratio) Term for the portion of a secondary school year that starts studying at a university (→Hochschule) instead of starting an apprenticeship, for example. In Germany, the quota of 32% is relatively low compared to other OECD countries, where it is over 40% in some.

Studienbeginn, durchschnittlicher (average age for starting studies) In international comparison, German first-semester students are relatively old, although the average age has gradually decreased from 22.5 in 1991 to 21.7 in 2013.

Studienberatung, fachspezifische (subject area advising) Advising service offered at the faculty level (→Fakultätsebene) by instructors for students on basic questions dealing with their studies (→Studium), examinations (→Prüfungs), scheduling, and selection of courses.

Studienberatung, zentrale (central student advising) Institution at a university to advise students on matters of general organization of their studies, the organization of the university, possibilities for studying, requirements of degree programs, and possibilities for changing degree programs, and also includes so-called "career centers" and in some cases the international office (→AAA). Specific contents of ~ are: first-semester introduction and tutorials, managing schedules, study and examination regulations, advising secondary school students on deciding to study at a university, organizing university informational days, →dies academicus, help with problems studying, and advising beyond graduation: choosing a profession. All advising services of the ~ must be confidential, neutral, and in the interest of the person seeking advice.

Studienberechtigte (students with the qualification to enter university) The proportion of a secondary school year from which the new students of the following years can be drawn. This number has increased by almost 25% in Germany in recent years. The number of women with a university entrance qualification has increased sharply, as well.

Studienbuch (course record book) Booklet handed out by the enrollment office (→Immatrikulationsbüro) to document the credits (→Leistungsnachweise) and courses that must be shown to the examinations office (→Prüfungsamt) before registering for examinations. At some universities, it is only a collection of certificates of enrollment (→Immatrikulationsnachweis) and does not look like a book or folder. Increasingly, the credits are recorded electronically and students at some universities no longer have to keep paper documents of the credits they have received.

Studienbüro (office of student affairs, studies office) →Immatrikulationsbüro

Studiendauer (length of studies) Criterion for university evaluations (→Hochschulevaluation). Average number of semesters students need to complete their degree.

Studiendekan (dean of studies) Instructor of a department (→Fachbereich) responsible for teaching and examinations.

Studienführer (student guide) Self-help literature for students to better tackle difficulties in their studies and for questions on preparing for exams, assistance in getting rid of writing blocks, and optimizing working techniques.

Studiengang (degree program, course of study) Term for the chosen combination of subjects as allowed by the examination regulations from the first subject-related semester to the conclusion of studies.

Studiengang, internationaler (international degree program) Usually a degree program that includes 2 semesters at a foreign university with the goal of obtaining a degree from that university as well as the home university.

Studiengebühr (tuition fee) Financial contribution from students to maintain the quality of research and teaching at the universities that was not collected between the 1970s and 2005. In 2005, the Federal Constitutional Court overturned the legislation prohibiting tuition fees, and many *Länder* introduced them, in many cases the tuition was 500€ per semester with several exceptions, e.g. for students with children, foreigners from partner universities, or disabled students. As of the WS 2014/2015, however, all *Länder* had once again revoked the tuition fees. ~ is a very controversial topic in Germany even though they are normal in many other countries. Opponents of ~ use arguments of equality while the supporters compare the costs of apprenticeships and the costs of university places (→Studienplätze).

Studienjahr (academic year) →akademisches Jahr

Studienkolleg (preparatory course) Course for preparing foreign students who would like to study at a university and need to take an intensive language course in order to understand the language of instruction (→Unterrichtssprache).

Studienkosten (costs of studying) Amount of money needed to pay for a student over the course of studies until obtaining a degree. On average, in 2001 each student was subsidized with 7,170 euros. The average graduate cost 78,250 euros.

Studienleistung (non-graded coursework, non-assessed coursework) Work that is done to obtain credit for a course but is not counted toward the final grade. ~ could include presentations, lab reports, written literature summaries, art projects, or other smaller assignments and are usually graded as pass/fail.

Studienordnung (study regulations) Entirety of all provisions that regulate the administrative process of studying. Typical contents of a ~ include: general remarks on studying, degree programs, degree, objectives of the program, requirements for studying, duration and start of studies, structure of studies, types of courses, courses in the basic study period, courses in the advanced study period, and the final thesis.

Studienplan (study plan, curriculum) Fixed goals for an individual degree program (→Studiengang) or group of degree programs as set by the faculty. This primarily includes a list of prerequisites, credits to be obtained (→Leistungsnachweis), examinations to be completed, the general progression of studies, possible degrees, and in some cases the possible professions. Depending on how structured the degree program is, a ~ can be more or less flexible and allow the students more or less freedom.

Studienplatz (university place, study place) Unit of capacity at universities. In Germany, the number of students is around twice as high as the official number of university places available (→Massenuniversität).

Studienplatzbörse (marketplace for exchanging university places) Institution to exchange university places while circumventing the central office for allocating university places insofar as the admission restrictions are not regulated by the individual university. This is done, for example, if two students studying medicine in their third semester – one in Berlin and one in Tübingen – would like to switch spots.

Studienstiftung des deutschen Volkes e.V. (German National Academic Foundation) Largest German foundation to support gifted students under the patronage of the Federal President for students and doctoral candidates at comprehensive universities, scientific and technical universities, art academies, music academies, and universities of applied sciences in the form of scholarships (→Stipendium) and open programs.
www.studienstiftung.de

Studienverlauf (progression of studies) General term for all processes associated with achievements completed: taking courses, credits, examinations, degrees, and diplomas.

Studienversagen (failing) Term for an enrolled student failing to fulfill the requirements set down by the examination regulations (→Prüfungsordnung), to procure funding for studies, or to overcome psychological difficulties such as writing blocks or test anxiety, or failing simply because the subject matter is too much for them.

Studierender (student) In "politically correct" language, this is the common, gender-neutral synonym for →"Student."

Studierende, ausländische (international student, foreign student) Due to the unfamiliarity with German degrees abroad, German universities have been at a disadvantage in international comparison, particularly when looking at universities in the United States and Britain. However, this has been changing due to the phasing out of the German degrees and the introduction of the →Bachelor's and →Master's degrees. The average percentage of international students at German universities is around 12%, whereby the majority come from European countries, but an increasing number come from Africa and the countries of the former Eastern bloc. Among the international students, 28% are foreigners with a German education, whereby students with Turkish heritage make up the largest group.

Studierende im Ausland (students abroad) In 2012, 135,960 German students studied at international universities. In comparison to 2002 (64,249), the number more than doubled. The most popular countries for studying abroad were: Austria, the Netherlands, Switzerland, the United Kingdom, the United States, France, China, Sweden, Denmark, and Hungary.

Studierendenschaft, verfasste (constituted student body, elected student body) Also: verfasste Studentenschaft. The elected student representation at a university as set down by law in some *Länder* or in a university's by-laws. ~ is often incorrectly used as a synonym for the entire student body.

Studierendenzahlen (number of students) →Studentenzahlen

Studium (studying, studies) Lat. *studium* = pursuit, enthusiasm, zeal. The education at a university (→Hochschule) is organized into selected subject combinations and various degrees (→Abschluss). The ~ begins with enrollment (→Immatrikulation) and ends with deregistration (→Exmatrikulation) after graduation (→Graduierung), possibly at another university after changing universities (→Hochschulwechsel). The duration of ~ (→Studiendauer) varies according to the subject.

Studium Generale (studium generale, general studies) General education offer with events, usually lectures, that are of interest beyond the boundaries of a single discipline. The ~ also serves the university as a platform for public relations work and interdisciplinary dialogue, for example with lecture series (→Ringvorlesungen). (→Gasthörer)

Stundenplan (schedule) Arrangement of courses in a semester according to time in a weekly overview. In less structured (→verschulte) subjects, the individual students have the possibility to freely choose the number and topics of courses to attend while other degree programs are highly structured and the schedule is almost completely set by the →curriculum.

Stupa (student parliament) Slang for student parliament (→Studentenparlament)

Style Sheet **(style sheet)** Instructions or template for the graphic design of manuscripts to be submitted as they are determined by publishers or instructors. They are usually freely available online.

Summa cum laude (summa cum laude) Lat. *summa cum laude* = with the highest distinction. Highest level of evaluation for an academic work (especially for doctorates) corresponding to the grade (→Note) "very good." In slang, often abbreviated: "*summa.*"

SWS (SWS) Abbreviation for: →Semesterwochenstunden

Symposion/Symposium (symposium) Greek *symposion* = drinking party. Subject-oriented gathering to exchange ideas in the framework of a more or less social round. The term ~ is derived from the work of the same name by the Greek philosopher Plato. A ~ can also be used to refer to a gathering of academics at which the discussion of scientific subject matter is neglected entirely in favor of a convivial social event (→Bacchus).

Synopse (synopsis) Greek *synopsis* = view with. Short summary or abstract of a publication or contribution (→Abstract).

Systematik (systematics) The entirety of the planned, methodologically ordered attempts to fit the scope or terminology (→Terminologie) of a subject into certain structures in order to be able to optimize the clarity, make didactics (→Didaktik) easier, and better coordinate research (→Forschung).

T

Tabakverbot (prohibition of tobacco) →Fidibus

Tabellenteil (table section) Part of the annex (→Anhang) in which data material in table form is sorted according to certain criteria so that the main text of the academic narrative does not have to be interrupted by too many tables.

Tag der offenen Tür (open house day, open day) Aspect of a university's public relations work in which the institutions and buildings are open to the broader public.

Tagung, wissenschaftliche (academic conference) →Kongress

Tagungsbericht (conference report, conference proceedings) Publication of the results of an expert meeting in the form of a book or in a journal (→Periodikum). ~ are communications closely associated with research that report on important news in the scientific community and have both a content and social function.

Talar (robe) Lat. *talaris* = reaching to the ankles. Ancient festive clothing in the form of a dark robe for judges, spiritual leaders, and university professors. Today they are typical primarily at Anglo-Saxon universities during graduation ceremonies. Originally, as today in the USA, the color, cut, and emblems of the ~ show the rank and faculty membership (→Insignie; →Kleiderordnung).

Talarrecht (right to wear robes) Today a seldom exercised privilege in Germany for university members to wear robes (→Talar). In other countries, the ~ is more common. For example at the University of Helsinki, a dagger may even be worn with the robe. In Germany, robes have been widely viewed as antiquated since 1968 and are seldom worn. A mocking verse of the student movement (→Studentenbewegung) was: "Unter den Talaren, Muff von tausend Jahren!" (Under the robes is the musty smell of a thousand years!) In fact, the academic and church dress can be largely traced back to Byzantine ceremonial clothing and is thus older than "a thousand years."

Tantiemen (royalties) Result-dependent share, for example of an author, on the sale of his work (→Werk) according to the number of books sold or other regulations of the publishing contract. ~ can be paid for book publications and for contributions in scientific journals.

Tanzmeister (dance master) At universities in the Middle Ages and Early Modern era, the ~ was the instructor responsible for the courtly education of the students, a kind of etiquette instructor for the obligatory lessons in socially proper behavior.

Technische Hochschule (technical university) Originally a university with a focus on natural sciences and engineering subjects, but today equal to comprehensive universities whereby some smaller differences, primarily in traditions, have been consciously kept (→akademisches Viertel).

Tektonik (arrangement, structure of the collection) Arrangement of a collection, library, or archive (→Archiv) in groups or archival departments, e.g. according to the principle of provenance (→Provenienz).

Tempus-Tacis (Tempus Tacis) EU cooperation program with the successor states of the Soviet Union. www.etf.eu.int

Term **(term)** →Semester

Terminalraum (computer room) Also: PC-Pool. Location of a large number of computers in a computing center (→Rechenzentrum).

Terminologie (terminology) The entirety of technical terms in a subject or topic that are necessary in order to be able to describe subject-specific questions adequately, professionally, and in a way that saves time. The mastery of correct ~ in a discipline is a primary learning objective for students in the basic study period (→Grundstudium).

Termpaper **(term paper)** Refers to a short seminar paper (→Hausarbeit) to be written in a short period of time at English-language universities that is not entirely comparable with a German seminar paper, as several ~ usually have to be written per semester.

terra incognita **(terra incognita)** lat. *terra incognita* = unknown territory. Metaphorical term for a new, unresearched topic, whereby it can be general new territory that has never been touched by humans or new territory in relation to the experience of an individual. The search for ~ and its exploration is one of the most important tasks of a researcher, and he does not even necessarily have to leave his library to do so (→Forschung; →Expedition).

Test Old-French *teste* = earthen vessel.
1. (pop quiz) Short and usually unannounced exam with or without a formal character or grades.
2. (test) Type of scientific experiment (→Versuch) but with a less strict experimental set up with the purpose of seeing whether an arrangement works. Tests are "experiments with a small scale" and therefore are only rarely considered true proof (→Beweis). (→Versuch und Irrtum)

Testat (credit certificate) Written confirmation of (successful) attendance of a lecture or seminar (→Leistungsnachweis).

Th__e__ma (topic) Greek *thema* = topic, proposed. Object of an academic study or seminar paper (→Hausarbeit). Often incorrectly used as a synonym for title (→Titel).

Theoretikum (building for theory) Traditional name for a building, especially in connection with a university clinic, that is only for teaching purposes and made up of lecture halls, seminar rooms, and libraries in contrast to the administrative buildings or the treatment rooms.

Theorie (theory) Greek *theoria* = contemplation. Intellectual complex of statements and hypotheses to explain facts. A ~ is often in competition with other ~. Decisive for the value of a ~ is the possibility to derive tenets from it or to also be able to explain newly observed phenomenon with it, and ~ are thus the foundation of scientific work.

Theorie, obsolete (obsolete theory) Once valid but in the meantime falsified theory that can still be applied for certain purposes. Theories can therefore be obsolete to different degrees.

Theoriebildung (theory-building) Process of developing theories on the basis of progress in general research, special studies, or isolated questions and expert communication. The ~ is of fundamental importance for progress within a subject.

Thesaurus (thesaurus) Greek *thesauros* = stored treasure. Term for an organized list of words within a subject or language, often with references and sorted according to generic terms and subordinate terms.

These Greek *thesis* = proposition. A scientific claim that is supported by arguments in conjunction with a speech (→Vortrag) or examination (→Prüfung). Characteristics and functions: Important findings of the work are described in a concentrated form. The speaker's chain of thought becomes clear through this. The participants are thus to be informed about the topic's critical points; catchy wording can serve as a basis for the debate following the presentation (→Referat).

In newer usage according to the English-American model, it is also sometimes used as a synonym for a final thesis (→Abschlussarbeit).

Thesenblatt (handout) →*Handout*

Thesis e.V. (Thesis e.V.) Interdisciplinary, Germany-wide network for doctoral candidates and those with completed doctorates for the purpose of professional exchange. The registered association has around 600 members. Topics are: effects of university reform, funding the work, networking.
www.thesis.de

Titel (title) 1. Lat. *titulus* = label, heading. Form of address under consideration of the academic degree, for example Doctor or Master, or the position of the office holder. In Austria, it is typical to use nearly all academic titles in forms of address.

2. The name of a book as it is shown in lists. Often incorrectly used as a synonym for book (→Buch).

Titelblatt (title page) The first page, e.g. of a seminar paper, with important information on the text, author, and course for which it is being written. Key elements are: name of the university and course, name of the instructor including title, semester, date, name, address, e-mail, and semester of the author, title and subtitle of the work.

The ~ is numbered but the page number is not shown, thus the next page has the number 2.

Titelei (prelims, front matter) The first 5 pages of a book or in another position in a different medium (→Medium) in which the relevant publisher's bibliographical information (→bibliographische Information) is noted. This includes: name of the author or editor; year of publication; title and subtitle; place of publication/publisher; edition; and often a copyright notice.

Titularprofessor (titular professor) Term for a person who has the title of professor but does not have a regular professorship, that is, the person holds the title but does not have the rights and obligations of a professor

TOEFL **(TOEFL)** Abbreviation for: *Test of English as a Foreign Language.* For international students, obligatory proof of English language proficiency before starting studies at a university in the United States or one possibility for proving English proficiency for English-language degree programs in Germany, carried out under the supervision of the *Educational Testing Services*.
www.ets.org

Trainee **(trainee)** Many organizations now offer trainee programs in which recent graduates spend a set amount of time working in many of the company's departments on a rotation with the goal of getting to know the entire company and thus being suited for future management roles.

Transkription (transcription) 1. Term for writing down content that has not yet been put into writing, for example tape recordings or audio files.

2. Changing one script into another, for example Greek to Latin.

Trimester (trimester) Division of academic year into three parts instead of two semesters (→Semester). Trimesters are each around 15 weeks long but are not typical in Germany.

Trivialität (triviality) →artes liberales; →Philosophicum. Term for information that everyone knows or that does not offer anything new because it is part of general knowledge. Usually used in a pejorative sense.

Tutor (tutor) Lat. *tutor* = guardian, protector. Supervisor of students, at universities in the United States or Britain usually a very intensive cooperation through long parts of the studies (→Studium).

Tutorium (tutorial) Accompanying, introductory course usually during the basic study period (→Grundstudium) to learn or deepen knowledge of practical abilities, e.g. using a microscope or how to manage bibliographies within a subject. It is usually led by an advanced student and in parallel to another course (→Lehrveranstaltung) such as a lecture (→Vorlesung).

TVÖD-L or TV-L (TVÖD-L, collective bargaining agreement of the *Länder*) Abbreviation for: Tarifvertrag für den öffentlichen Dienst der Länder. Insofar as they are not civil servants (→Beamte), university employees are typically hired under the conditions of ~.

U

Ü (Ü) Abbreviation for: Übung, →Tutorium

UB (UB) Abbreviation for: →Universitätsbibliothek

Überprüfbarkeit (controllability, reproducability) Key requirement for academic work. The findings presented must be able to be controlled and replicated using proof from the literature and material used at any time in order to ensure the scientific integrity of a statement (→Sokal-Affäre).

Überqualifikation (over-qualification) Term for a possible discrepancy between the education received and the profession practiced if the education was directed at a higher professional goal that could not be reached for various reasons. The proverbial example of ~ is the humanities scholar as a taxi driver.

Übung (exercise course) →Tutorium

Unfallversicherung (accident insurance) Protection for students automatically included in the semester fee (→Semesterbeitrag) for all activities related to studying in the context of being at a university.

Uni-assist (uni-assist) An organization founded in 2004 with the support of 170 German universities, the German Academic Exchange Service (→DAAD), and the German Rectors' Conference (→Hochschulrektorenkonferenz) to check the applications of international prospective students before forwarding them to the respective universities. Depending on the agreement with the individual university, ~ can check the degree certificates as well as other application requirements. Separate applications must be sent to ~ for each university to which the international prospective student would like to apply. In 2015, the first application each semester checked by ~ cost 75€, applications for additional universities cost 15€ each, although some universities cover these costs for the applicants.
http://www.uni-assist.de/

Unikat (unique specimen) Term for a valuable individual piece, usually referring to a manuscript, book (→Rara), or other information media. An important task of libraries is to digitalize such documents, thereby making them available for research without damaging the originals with use. Famous ~ include the Codex Manesse, the Gutenberg Bibles, and the Dead Sea Scrolls.

Uni-Laden (university shop) →Uni-Shop

Uni-*Rankings* (university rankings) →Hochschulranking

Uni-*Shop* (university shop) Commercial provider of a university's memorabilia, particularly using the university logo or seal (→Siegel) on mugs, sweatshirts, and pens. At some universities the ~ is run by a private provider (→Alumni).

***United Nations University* (United Nations University)** University network of the United Nations with its headquarters in Tokyo and German seat in Bonn. The "Institute for Environment and Human Security" is located there.

Universalgelehrter (university scholar) →Gelehrter

Universität (university) Lat. *universitas* = entirety. Historically oldest type of higher education institution (→Hochschultyp) set up according to the principle of research and teaching (→Forschung und Lehre) for education in subjects that usually include the humanities (→Geisteswissenschaften), law, business and economic sciences, social sciences (→Gesellschaftswissenschaften), natural sciences (→Naturwissenschaften), medicine, agricultural sciences, forestry, nutritional sciences, and engineering. The tasks of the ~ are to preserve the entirety of the sciences in research and teaching. Originally, the term *universitas magistrorum et scholarium* referred to the sum of all teachers and students, later to the institution itself. An important administrative structural unit at a ~ is the department/chair (→Lehrstühle). (→Universitätsgeschichte)

Universität-Gesamthochschule (university – comprehensive higher education institution) A type of higher education institution (→Hochschultyp) created in the 1970s to link the tasks of comprehensive universities (→Universität), art academies (→Kunsthochschule), and universities of applied science (→Fachhochschule).

Universitätsball (university ball) Festive evening event at a university with a dress code, a program, and dancing.

Universitätsbibliothek (university library) Central library (→Bibliothek) of a university (→Hochschule) in contrast to institute or seminar libraries, without a subject orientation but with a focus on academic literature. In ~ you can often find valuable manuscripts, unique specimens, and other rare items (→Rara).

Universitätsbibliothek, international berühmte (internationally renowned university library) Examples of ~ are especially the Bodleian Library at the University of Oxford, the Cambridge University Library, and the Fisher Library at the University of Sydney, the largest house in the southern hemisphere. Other world-famous libraries are: *Tushuguan* in Beijing; *Biblioteca Nacional Madrid*; *Biblioteca Nazionale Centrale* in Florence; Harvard University Library; *Kokuritsa Kokkai Toshukan* in Tokyo; *Koninklijke Bibliotheek* Den Haag; *Österreichische Nationalbibliothek* in Vienna; *Rossiiskaya Gosudarstuennaya* in Moscow; and *Schweizerische Landesbibliothek* in Bern.

Universitätsbibliothek, Schwächen der (weaknesses of the university library) Despite in part large subsidies, libraries have structural weaknesses. The most common critique points are: long waiting times, not enough borrowable copies, problems in the reservation system, loss due to theft, not enough digitalization, and thus not enough content online.

Universitätsbuchhandlung (university bookstore) Term for a bookstore that works in close cooperation and is geographically close to a university and provides literature according to the topics in the current course catalog.

Universitäts-Chor (university choir) Musical association of university members for vocal music.

Universitätsgeschichte (university history) Academic discipline to research the development of the modern university (→Universität) from the Middle Age Latin and cathedral schools (→Domschule). In the 12th century, set forms of →*studium generale* first developed in Paris under the protection of the popes. There, the hierarchy (→Hierarchie) of academic degrees (→Grad) that was later accepted as standard in Europe began as well as the structure of the faculties (→Fakultät). With the Great Western Schism between 1378 and 1417, the German sovereigns were forced to turn away from Paris and set up their own universities, as German students were no longer allowed to study in Paris. In the order of their creation or founding, the German universities were Prague 1348; Heidelberg 1386; Cologne 1389; Erfurt 1392; and Leipzig 1409 (→Grundordnung).

Universitätsgesetz (state higher education act) Respective implementation of the German Higher Education Framework Act (→Hochschulrahmengesetz) at the level of the *Länder*.

Universitätsklinik (university clinic) A hospital belonging to a medical faculty (→Fakultät) with the task of linking research, teaching, administration, and hospital operations. Often the only area of a university that makes a financial profit or that brings in the highest amount of external funding (→Drittmittel). Made up of: outpatient clinics and treatment rooms, inpatient rooms, a building for theory (→Theoretikum), areas for administration, supplies, and waste management as well as residence halls and services such as chapels or cafeterias.

Universitätskultur (university culture) Collective term for all activities and traditions that are connected to university operations and the history of the individual university.

Universitätsorchester (university orchestra) Musical association of university members for instrumental music.

Universitätsradio (university radio) Radio station belonging to a university, often with rotating student editors for purposes of public relations or information for the university public.

Universitäts*ranking* (university ranking) →Ranking

Universitätssammlung (university collection) →Hochschulsammlung

Universitätssport (university sports) →Hochschulsport

Universitätsstadt (university city) In a general sense, a term for a city with one or more universities. In a more specific sense, however, used for a city whose appearance is significantly characterized by the university and its social environment. German examples of this use could include Heidelberg, Freiburg, and Tübingen.

Universitätsverlag (university press) Term for a publishing house that publishes academic works in cooperation with a university or under the direction of a university or as an independent company. ~ are commercial companies that in part bring in good profits particularly at universities in the United States and Britain.

Universitätsverwaltung, zentrale (central university administration) Administration of a university (→Hochschule) at the level above the faculties (→Fakultät). (→Gremium; →Rektorat)

Universitätsgründung (university founding) Act of officially establishing a university. Middle Age ~ were often done under the patronage of feudal lords to enhance their own area, for example after the Reformation or to make up for lost territory. Modern ~ are often supported by organizations from business and society.

Unterrichtssprache (language of instruction) Term for the language in which a course is taught. Besides German, in Germany English is recognized as a ~ because it is the most important academic language internationally. Increasingly, entire degree programs are being offered in English in order to improve the attractiveness of the university for international students. Other languages also appear as ~, however, e.g. Polish (Europa-Universität Frankfurt/Oder) or French (Saarland University). The classic ~ at universities, however, was Latin (→Latein). Many technical academic terms therefore have Greco-Roman roots.

Urlaubssemester (semester leave of absence) Time counted as a university semester (→Hochschulsemester) but not as a subject-related semester (→Fachsemester) in the context of studies during which students can do internships, spend time abroad outside of the context of organized exchanges, or take time off for personal reasons. During this time, examinations may be taken but there is no right to financial assistance (→Bafög).

Urheber (creator, author) Also: Autor. Creator of a work as an individual or together with others. This work is protected by the Copyright

Act (→Urheberrechtsgesetz) from intellectual theft and plagiarism (→Plagiat).

Urheberrechtsgesetz (Copyright Act) The law on the protection of intellectual property in literature, science, and art regulates the appropriate remuneration of copyright holders for their work or for the use of their work by third parties. The ~ also regulates the reproduction, distribution, and exhibition of works as well as the transfer of rights (→Verlagsvertrag).

V

Vademecum (handbook) Lat. *vade mecum* = go with me! Guide for important information about a university (→Hochschule), usually with brief biographies of the instructors (→Dozent).

Venia docendi (authorization to teach) →Venia Legendi

Venia Legendi (authorization to teach) Lat. *venia legendi* = authorization to read, seldom also: Lat. *venia docendi* = authorization to teach. Authorization to hold lectures (→Vorlesung) in a certain subject, obtained by successful completion of a post-doctoral lecturing qualification (→Habilitation).

Veranstaltung (course, event) Also: Lehrveranstaltung. Term for all forms of academic teaching and instruction. The most common types are seminars (→Seminar); lectures (→Vorlesung); labs (→Praktikum); and exercise courses (→Übung and →Tutorium).

Verbindung (association, society) →Studentenverbindung

Verbundkatalog (union catalog, joint catalog) Common catalog (→Katalog) of several libraries (→Bibliothek) to improve possibilities for researching. The books requested are then usually made available with inter-library loan (→Fernleihe). (→Bibliotheksverbundsystem)

Verbundsystem (network, joint system) →Bibliothekverbundsystem

Verifikation (verification) →Falsifikation

Verlag, wissenschaftlicher (academic publisher) Term for a commercial publishing house that has specialized in the publication of academic writings. In contrast to a university press (→Hochschulverlag), however, it is usually administratively and commercially independent from a university.

Veröffentlichung (publication) Also: Publikation. The term can describe both information that is made public as well as the medium with which this information was published. Media include books, online articles, or journals. The term "public" can be understood in various degrees as a specific academic audience or the broader public. The number of publications is a key aspect of an academic biography. Formally, ~ must fulfill certain structural criteria:

Information on the title, author information with contact addresses, abstract (→Abstract), introduction, description of the state of research, hypotheses (→Hypothese), existing sources (→Quellenlage), methods (→Methode) to be used, findings, discussion of the findings, summary, and literature references (→Literaturangaben). (→*Peer Review*)

Veröffentlichung, *offline* (offline publication) Publication on digitally readable media not necessarily connected to the internet, for example CD-ROMs, DVDs, or files.

Veröffentlichung, *online* (online publication) Publications that can only be viewed online, for example on a website or in the form of a newsletter.

Verschult (structured, literally "school-like") University slang term with a slightly negative connotation to describe degree programs or courses that are based less on the participants' self-initiative and more on frontal teaching methods by an instructor. Typical examples are examinations in medicine or the basic study period in business and economic sciences. Characteristics of this kind of structure are: →multiple-choice tests, more written exams than papers, more lectures than seminars, short presentations and not much time for discussion by participants, detailed and almost complete notes on lectures, and in general less freedom in terms of content and choice of topics for students.

Versorgungszentrum (supply center) Logistical center of a clinic or other institution that needs a great deal of materials for storing and distributing elements for use and wear and tear, or for transporting material in the broadest sense.

Versuch 1. (experiment, trial) Scientifically (→wissenschaftlich) organized experiment in which a previously precisely defined situation is constructed. Used in most subjects in one way or another. With the controlled observation and measurement of the processes, insights are gained. ~ must fulfill certain criteria in order to produce scientifically significant findings: replicability, quantifiability, and objectivity (→Objektivität). ~ can investigate causality (→Kausalität) or be oriented on ends. A third type of experiment is purely intellectual in nature, the thought experiment (→Gedankenexperiment). Famous examples are Galileo's experiments on the free fall and Pavlov's experiments on conditioning dogs.

2. (essay) Loan translation of the French-English *essay* = special type of essay (→Aufsatz).

Versuch und Irrtum (trial and error) Most important approach in all disciplines (→Wissenschaft) to find theories on the basis of iteratively improved tests, whereby the explanations are continually improved by ~ on the research question. Both the results of trial and error as well as the observation of this process can be evaluated scientifically.

Verteiler (mailing list) University address list for distributing news via e-mail or post, especially for invitations and announcements of special events, usually operated by the university's own press office (→Pressestelle).

Verwaltung (administration) Besides research and teaching (→Forschung und Lehre), the third key area of work for a professor, e.g. creating schedules, planning excursions, making purchases, and obtaining external funding (→Drittmitteleinwerbung).

Verwaltungsfachhochschule (university of public administration) University of applied sciences supported by the federal government or the government of one of the *Länder* that is responsible for educating people in a certain sector of public administration for a career in higher service (gehobener Dienst). Students at a ~ have the status of civil servant candidates (→Beamte).

Verwertungsgesellschaften (copyright collectives) Association of authors and publishers to look after copyrights vis-à-vis third parties, particularly regarding the copying of texts, which harms both authors and the publisher. On the basis of legally set fees, the ~ collect contributions that are then distributed to the authors and publishers. Academic texts can also be included insofar as the text is registered with the ~ as having been published.
www.vgwort.de/

Verzeichnis lieferbarer Bücher (directory of deliverable books) Entire catalog in the form of a book and online for all books currently on the market in the Federal Republic of Germany as the basis for ordering via a commercial book store but only conditionally suitable as a tool for academic research.
www.vlb.de

Vita (CV, résumé) Lat. *vita* = life.
→Biographie

VL (VL) Abbreviation for: →Vorlesung

VLB (VLB) Abbreviation for: →Verzeichnis lieferbarer Bücher.

Volkshochschule (adult education center) Despite its name, not a true university (→Hochschule). The ~ is a non-profit institution for adult education supported by communities or associations. The instructors usually have an academic education, and courses range from practical skills (sewing, cooking) to languages to sports or cultural topics.

Volkswirtschaftslehre (economics) Area of business and economic sciences (→Wirtschaftswissenschaften) with a high number of students (→Studentenzahlen) that examines national and/or global markets. According to the Nobel Prize winner Paul A. Samuelson, ~ "is the study of how men and society choose, with or without the use of money, to employ scarce productive resources which could have alternative uses, to produce various commodities over time and distribute them for consumption now and in the future amongst various people and groups of society." With its high degree of relevance for society, it has points of contact with almost all other academic disciplines (→Nexialistik).

Vollversammlung (general meeting, plenary) Highest decision-making gathering of students at a university. A ~ is only called together rarely, for example when preparing a strike (→Streik).

Vollzeitstudium (full-time studies) Regular studies in contrast to evening studies (→Abendstudium) or →studium generale.

Volontär (trainee) Person who voluntarily completes a certain type of internship (→Praktikum), usually in the context of journalistic professions or publishing in general (→Volontariat).

Volontariat (traineeship) Internship (→Praktikum) for a small or no salary at a company (usually a publisher or journalistic company) that is to ease later career entry in this field.

Vorabdruck (preprint) Draft of an academic text immediately before it is published or given out for →peer review but is still to be made available to broad parts of the scientific community in order to lessen the effects of publication delays. ~ are rarely cited as they are more difficult to find than regular publications, usually only online.

Vordiplom (intermediate diploma) When Diplom degree programs were common, this was obtained when the basic study period (→Grundstudium) was completed successfully.

Vorklinik (pre-clinic) First stage of medical education with basic subjects, career introduction, and labs (→Praktika). With the reforms of medical education, the ~ has in some cases been replaced by problem-based learning from the beginning of studies.

Vorlesung (lecture) Specific form of academic instruction as a weekly or regular event in a lecture hall (→Hörsaal) under the direction of an instructor (→Dozent) on a set topic each semester or over the course of several semesters, usually without a chance for dialogue.

Vorlesungsfreie Zeit (lecture-free period) →Vorlesungszeit

Vorlesungsverzeichnis (course catalog) Catalog (→Katalog) in the form of a book for the courses (→Lehrveranstaltung) offered by a university for a particular →semester with an extensive informational part for general understanding about how the university works, deadlines, and contacts. Now often only available online.

Vorlesungsverzeichnis, kommentiertes (commented course catalog) Extensive description of the courses (→Lehrveranstaltung) for a semester according to subject, usually published by the individual faculties (→Fakultät). Here the first literature references (→Literaturangaben) can usually be found.

Vorlesungszeit (lecture period) Time period within a →semester during which the courses (→Lehrveranstaltung) take place. An academic year (→akademisches Jahr) has two ~, interrupted by the lecture-free periods. In academic discussions, ~ and "semester" are often used as synonyms, although this is not completely correct.

Vortrag (speech, lecture) A one-time event to present a topic to a larger audience, often by a guest, and lasting between 30-90 minutes, whereby there are no set limits. It should not be confused with the much shorter presentations (→Referat) or the regularly occurring lecture courses (→Vorlesung). After a ~, there is often a discussion or academic social gathering.

Vorwort (foreword) Accompanying text for longer academic texts such as monographs or edited volumes with the purpose of presenting acknowledgements, personal notes, and technical information about the edition in a prominent position. In contrast to an introduction (→Einleitung), however, nothing is written about the content. That is why seminar papers (→Hausarbeit) have introductions but no ~.

VroniPlag (VroniPlag) Controversial wiki for the critical control of academic plagiarism (→Plagiat) of dissertations (→Dissertation). Especially the works of politicians and prominent persons are evaluated. What is innovative on the site is especially the precise graphic representation of the percentage of plagiarism on each page.

Vulgariter (vulgarism) Lat. *vulgaris* = belonging to the people. Term for an everyday expression used in the context of academic diction. The term is used to avoid the impression that the author had a break in style. ~ include slang expressions and dialect words that are usually avoided in the academic writing style. The difference between ~ and standard language is particularly strict in German, much more so than in Anglo-American academic texts, for example.

W

Wahlen (elections) Democratic procedure to select representatives of a group, whereby university ~ favor the group of professors, who usually have a guaranteed majority in all relevant committees (→Ordinarienverfassung).

Wahlfach (elective subject) Subject that a student may choose to take. Instead of an ~, another subject may be chosen without this having negative consequences for the degree program.

Wahlmodul (elective module) →Wahlfach

Wahlpflichtfach (semi-elective subject) Some examination regulations allow for a limited selection from several subjects, of which one or more must be chosen in a degree program. A ~ is thus in some respects between elective subjects (→Wahlfach) and compulsory subjects (→Pflichtfach).

Wahlpflichtmodul (semi-elective module) →Wahlpflichtfach

Wahlspruch (motto) A university's ~ is usually used in both Latin and German. The ~ of the oldest university in the Federal Republic, Heidelberg, is: *semper apertus* and calls for studying the "always opened" book of wisdom, while the German ~ is: "the living spirit."

Wartburgfest (Wartburg Festival) A political demonstration held in 1817 at the Wartburg near Eisenach that is controversial regarding its importance for the development of modern German democracy (→Bücherverbrennung). Around 10% of German students at the time participated.

Wartesemester (waiting semester) Number of semesters that have passed since obtaining the university entrance qualification without being enrolled at a university (→Hochschule) or enrolling in a certain subject. ~ can be counted in order to circumvent a →numerus clausus.

Wegestreit (*Wegestreit*, literally argument about the paths) Reform debate at universities in the 15th century, named after the two "paths," the *via moderna* und *via antiqua*, whereby the modernists followed the empirical methods of Wilhelm von Ockham and the traditionalists followed the scholastic (→Scholastik) teachings according to Thomas Aquinas and thus the primacy of deductive methods over inductive ones (→Universitätsgeschichte).

Welcome Center (Welcome Center) Institution at many German universities to offer assistance for international visiting scholars or newly hired international researching staff and professors.

Weltbild, wissenschaftliches (scientific world view) The total of all ideas, terms, values, prejudices, hopes, convictions, and fears that serve as a basis for academic work and are related to the researcher's world and social environment. The ~ is based in particular on the conviction that the processes of the world "out there" can be recognized and described, and by doing so it is possible to improve the position of people. It is thus a linear, dynamic world view. Important aspects are also: trust in technological progress, optimism, the iterative search for explanations, readiness to intervene in processes or even to want to improve nature. But even the ~ itself can be the object of research and is therefore not a →dogma but is in part subject to harsh criticism from academics. On the negative side of ~ are aspects such as: relative or absolute lack of feeling about the object of research, cynicism about other approaches, presumptuousness, lack of responsibility, ivory tower thinking (→Elfenbeinturm), elite behavior, and intellectual arrogance vis-à-vis non-academics.

Weltuniversität (world university)
→ *United Nations University*

Werk (work) Term for the result of an intellectual or artistic effort that enjoys copyright protection. The Copyright Act (→Urheberrechtsgesetz) defines a work as a "specific intellectual creation in the areas of literature, musical art, or visual arts." That is why academic papers and publications are also ~ and have legal protection from plagiarism (→Plagiaten). Important in this context is also the work of copyright collectives (→Verwertungsgesellschaft).

Who-is-Who (Who's Who) Reference work with biographical basis for a specific topic, for example the history of a university, a department, or an era with biographical information, focuses, and other essential details.

Wichs (formal uniform for student societies) Term from the language of student societies (→Studentenverbindung): Parade uniform or student riding uniform in the style of the early 19th century with gloves, sash, top boots, and cap (→Mütze).

Wiederholungsprüfung (retest, repeat examination) Second (or third) attempt to pass an examination. If an examination is failed, then most examination regulations state that a ~ must be attempted; there is therefore a participation requirement. The number of ~ is usually limited to one or in some cases two.

Wirtschaftswissenschaften (business and economic sciences) Group of academic disciplines to investigate economic issues that have traditionally been a part of the humanities and social sciences but have their own characteristics regarding methods and applications. The most important division is between business administration and economic sciences (→Volkswirtschaftslehre), whereby only the second group is relevant for the Nobel Prize (→Nobelpreis).

At universities, ~ have a special role due to the large number of students enrolled in these degree programs.

Wissenschaft (science, academics) The entirety of efforts to systematically and methodically research objects of knowledge in order to discover or describe hypothesized regularities. A typical division is between natural sciences and the humanities, but a clear and coherent division is difficult to define. Processes in ~ are characterized by iteration of observation, sorting, and describing, whereby a key fourth step is in the evaluation of the individual aspects and the entirety. There are various theories about the motivation of working in ~ from natural human curiosity to acquisitiveness and the desire for prestige. The Greek philosopher Aristotle expressed it as follows: *The start of all sciences is wondering that things are as they are.*

Wissenschaft, exakte (exact science) →Logik, deduktive; →Logik induktive

Wissenschaft als Beruf (science as a vocation) Title of a famous speech by the sociologist Max Weber in 1917 on the question of the link between political and scientific activity. Well-known and oft-criticized is especially the sentence: *Politics does not belong in the lecture hall.*

Wissenschaft im Nationalsozialismus (science in National Socialism) The situation of the universities during the Third Reich was characterized from the beginning by: harassment, employment bans, restrictions, the revocation of university autonomy, the end of the freedom of research and teaching (→Forschung und Lehre), forced retirements, eviction, arbitrary judicial decisions, judicial murders, indoctrination, enforced conformity, and the prohibition of student societies, whereby these interventions in no way all came from outside. In part they received active and voluntary support, approval, or tolerance from university members (→Bücherverbrennung). Numerous German academics became victims of the regime, and many emigrated, especially to the USA.

The quality of teaching was profoundly damaged not only by personnel losses, however, but also by the ideologization of the sciences, in particular with the introduction of the so-called "nationalist sciences" ("völkische Wissenschaften"), which differentiated, for example, between Jewish and German nuclear physics.

Wissenschaft in der DDR (science in the GDR) The entire university of life in the GDR was largely paralyzed by the dictatorship, the lack of personnel and resources, ideology, and a lack of funding. Within the Warsaw Pact it had a certain respectable size, but in international comparison especially with Western Europe and the United States, it was without a chance for the most part. Today, publications from the former GDR are hardly recognized in general, also due to their now advanced age of at least 20 years, and are themselves the object of research. The university landscape in the GDR was characterized by paternalism by the state and party, which also negatively affected the quality of the research findings, for example by the mandatory citation of Marx, Engels, and Lenin in all subjects.

Wissenschaft in den Vereinigten Staaten (science in the United States) On the points of social acceptance, personnel, output of publications, and financial support, US academic life is among the most powerful in the world. Almost 3% of the US gross domestic product is invested in research, and this does not include in part enormous sums from the private sector such as AT&T's funding of the Bell Laboratories or many other university spin-offs. The largest contractor of US research projects is the Pentagon, especially in regards to aerospace technology. Due to the comparatively good working conditions, excellent reputation, high salaries, often clearer legal regulations, and solid project funding, international researchers often find the USA more attractive than their own country.

Wissenschaften, "pathologische" ("pathological science") The expression, which is controversial because it is discriminatory, comes from the Nobel Prize winner Irving Langmuir and refers to ideas or theories that do not die out despite being falsified. The philosopher of science Thomas S. Kuhn represented the opposing opinion, according to which every research approach remains current in one way or another and can still contribute to knowledge. Within the humanities, the term ~ makes less sense than in the natural sciences due to the differing concepts of progress.

Wissenschaftler, der verrückte (the crazy scientist) Motif in literature and movies, in part influenced by real, important scientists with unusual personal habits or an eccentric appearance, style of clothing, and behavior, for example Friedrich Nietzsche, Theodor Mommsen, and Albert Einstein or John (János) von Neumann. Important examples that have influenced the literary image of the scientist as a threat to safety in general or at least to their direct environment include Prof. Moriarty; Dr. Frankenstein; Dr. Strangelove; Dr. Jekyll; Dr. Mabuse; Dr. No; and Dr. Bunsen Honeydew.

Wissenschaftlichkeit (scientific nature, scientific character) The following criteria must be fulfilled if a study is to be carried out in a scientific manner: objectivity: separation from the object and the person; reliability: dependability and replicability of studies; validity: correct proof of sources and findings; impartiality; openness regarding results; consideration of the state of research and sources; proper han dling of sources and measurement results; documentation: correct fixation of the results in writing according to the rules of academic writing. In addition, studies should be free of tautologies or paradoxes (→Paradox) and have a certain explanatory value.

Wissenschaftsgeschichte (history of science) Each subject area can be examined according to its specific development, which is why the ~ is part of every discipline. Typical topics are: biographies of important representatives of the subject, history of innovations, history of the relation of the subject to its historical or social environment, and history of publications and didactic methods (→Universitätsgeschichte).

Wissenschaftsjournalismus (science journalism) Reports about scientific projects, experiments, and findings in the media that turn to a broader public without being able to include the sometimes important details of the topic. The value of even the most serious ~ therefore lies in the external effects for the experts, as the contents are usually only second hand, which greatly increases the danger of errors in the report (→Populärwissenschaft).

Wissenschaftsparodie (science parody) Literary genre that focuses mockingly on the weaknesses of the customs of academic publications, especially the linguistic weaknesses of writing using many nouns (→Nominalstil) or the circumstances of academic work in order to draw attention to structural problems (→Elfenbeinturm). Examples are the so-called Sokal Affair (→Sokal-Affäre) or the "stone louse" as an entry in Willibald Pschyrembel's clinical dictionary, and in particular also Gary Larson's cartoons. The "Schofel-Archive" of the Göttingen German professor Christian Wagenknecht is another example.
wwwuser.gwdg.de/~cwagenk

Wissenschaftspreise (science prize) Recognition for important achievements in the area of science, usually awarded by foundations together with a university. Many prizes are named after the person who endowed them, for example the Nobel Prize (→Nobelpreis). The EU awards three important prizes: The Descartes Prize for scientific collaborative research, the EU contest for young scientists, and the Prize for Scientific Communication.

Wissenschaftsrat (German Council of Science and the Humanities) Initiative founded in 1957 by the federal and *Länder* governments to advise them in questions of university policies and development. The ~ is the oldest organization of its kind in Europe.
www.wissenschaftsrat.de

Wissenschaftssatire (science satire) →Wissenschaftsparodie

Wissenschaftsstandort (scientific location) The geographical area of a *Land* or region under consideration

of the existing educational and research institutions, usually used in the context of questions of the job market or state subsidies. Criteria for the strengths of a ~ are: the number of patent registrations, number of researchers and amount of sums invested, number of students, →rankings, amount of external funding (→Drittmitteln), growth of the institutions, publications (→Publikation), and prizes received.

Wissenschaftstheorie (philosophy of science) Philosophical discipline to describe scientific processes and the overall development and thus never completely separable from the history of science (→Wissenschaftsgeschichte). One can describe ~ as a research discipline that focuses on science (→Wissenschaft). Important contributions were made by Paul Feyerabend and Karl Popper, among others (→Weltbild).

Wissensexplosion (explosion of knowledge) The problem of the exponential increase in the number of available publications due to the possibilities of modern publication techniques. The term ~ also describes the increase in the number of academics (→Wissenschaftler) and research activities as a whole. Currently there are around 200,000 regularly published journals (→Zeitschrift) worldwide. In natural sciences and technology, around 4 million publications currently appear annually.

Wissensgebäude (body of knowledge) The entirety of all theories on a question or the entirety of all theories. This term is used to describe the general state of knowledge in a discipline (→Disziplin) or a civilization.

Wissenstransfer (knowledge transfer) Communication of usually technical or commercially relevant information between the universities on the one hand and institutions, organizations, and states on the other or also within or between various research institutions, whereby the question of intellectual property is always a sensitive subject.

There are numerous programs from the EU or UN for ~ in developing countries in the context of the state development policies.

Wohnheim (residence hall, dormitory) →Studentenwohnheim; →Gästehaus; →Burse

W*o*rkshop (workshop) Organizational form of learning and working, usually lasting multiple days during which the participants, often with differing study backgrounds, collect and exchange ideas on a topic and then apply them practically, for example in university theater groups.

Wörterbuch, studentisches (student dictionary) Already in the 18th century, the century of the encyclopedias, attempts were made to document and scientifically describe student slang, e.g. 1781 by Christian Friedrich Augustin. As is the case with every specialist language, today's student language (→Studentensprache) is constantly evolving so that no ~ can be valid for a long period of time (→ankreiden).

WS (WS) Abbreviation for: Winter→semester

Z

Zeitschrift (journal) More or less regularly appearing, research-oriented publication organ that can be subscribed for distributing news from the scientific community. A subscription is usually very expensive and is rarely held by private persons.

Zeitschriftenabkürzungen (journal abbreviations) The titles of most periodicals (→Periodika) are usually shortened to a few letters in bibliographies (→Bibliographie). To decipher unknown abbreviations, you can use university library catalogs (→Katalog), databases, or special publications such as →ISSN compact (→Wissensexplosion).

Zeitschriftenauslage (journal racks) Area of a non-lending library (→Bibliothek) in which current journals (→Periodika) on a subject are displayed before they are sorted into the closed stacks (→Magazin). Normally, the journals are stored in a kind of drawer construction that includes the most recent issues of the journal.

Zeremonie (ceremony) Lat. *caerimonia* = ceremony. A festive event or part of a festive event at a university, for example at the beginning of the semester or during →*dies acacemicus* in the context of an inaugural lecture, honoring scientists, or other events that are celebrated such as an →inauguration.

Zertifikat (certificate) Lat. *certificare* = certify, register. Official or private declaration of an achievement, for example successfully attending a language school or →workshop in contrast to official transcripts (→Zeugnis).

Zeugnis (transcript of records, degree certificate) Official summary of all grades at the end of an academic year, usually together with grades from the *Gymnasium* or examinations, for example an intermediate examination ~. The documents for the final ~ are called official documents (→Urkunde) or diplomas (→Diplom) at universities.

Zeugnis der allgemeinen Hochschulreife (certificate of qualification for general university entrance) Document on the successfully completed *Abitur* examination, that is, the completion of general secondary education. The ~ gives the holder the right to study at a university without restrictions as to the subject (→Abitur).

Zeugnisabschrift (copy of degree certificate, copy of transcript of records) Certified copy of a degree certificate or transcript of records (→Zeugniss), for example to submit to an examinations office so that the original of the document can remain with the owner.

Zirkelschluss (circular reasoning) Term from logic (→Logik) to refer to an invalid conclusion. The statement is its own condition. In its most consistent form, this type of statement is easily recognized, but they are often to be found in differing degrees so that the circular character is more difficult to recognize. In everyday speech, arguments such as "I don't want to because I don't feel like it!" are often accepted, but not in academic studies.

Zitat (citation) Lat. *citare* = summon. The exactly reproduced wording of another's statement in oral or written form. ~ must always be marked in academic literature, that is, it must be made clear which part of a text are from the author and which parts are from others. Citations are usually commented with footnotes (→Fußnote) and listed in the literature references. The cited contents are put in quotation marks. In terms of contents, ~ are not to replace the author's own statements but to complement and prove them.

Zitationsindex (citation index) Criterion for evaluating universities (→Hochschulevaluation): A statement based on the evaluation of scientific journals about which journals produce the best response from the scientific community. The higher the ~, the "more important" the journal or researcher is. An important study on this is carried out annually by Thomson Scientific Inc. in Philadelphia. The index shows how often a publication is cited in scientific journals. Scale: In the ranking for 2004, 882,500 keywords from German institutes in the TSI databases provided the basis for the data.

Zitierweise (citation style) There are several methods of correct citation. The parenthetical style, also called the American ~, does not use footnotes and instead shows the reference directly in the text, whereby the name of the author, year of publication, and page number are given in parentheses. The so-called "long citation" is noted with a footnote (→Fußnote) or →endnote outside of the text and includes the authors' last name, authors' first name, title of the publication, location of the publisher, and the year as well as the page numbers of the reference (→Bibliographie).

Zitierweise, einheitliche (uniform citation style) The decisive rule for creating literature references is consistency. Mixed forms are not permissible.

Zitierweise nach Internetquellen (citation style for internet sources) As with printed sources, the point of correct citation of online sources is also to make it possible for the reader to definitively find the quote and thus ensure the controllability of the sources used. The following must therefore be included:
Title of the document (possibly with explanatory commentary), URL, name of the institution, date accessed, and type of document if it's not apparent from the URL (pdf, doc).

ZP (ZP) Abbreviation for: →Zwischenprüfung

Zulassung 1. (admission) The process of evaluating an applicant for a university place according to their school grades and other criteria to determine whether to accept them as an enrolled student.

2. (license) The certification for someone who has passed a state examination (→Staatsexamen), e.g. a lawyer, to start work.

Zulassungsamt (admissions office) University institution that decides on the admission of an applicant to a certain degree program (→Studiengang), also taking into consideration any waiting semesters (→Wartesemester).

Zulassungsarbeit (thesis) Final thesis (→Abschlussarbeit) at a pedagogical university and requirement for being admitted (→Zulassung) to the state examination (→Staatsprüfung).

Zulassungsbescheid (notification of admission) Notification sent to applicants for a university place (→Studienplatz) stating that they can start studies at the university to which they applied.

Zulassungsbeschränkung (admission restrictions) Set number limit for the university places in a subject. Which applicants are admitted used to be regulated almost entirely based on their school grades (→Numerus Clausus) but now include other criteria such as volunteer work or grades in a specific subject relevant to the degree program.

Zürcher Rede (Zurich speech) Speech by Winston Churchill in the Aula at the University of Zurich on 19 September 1946 to the academic youth of the world. His call became famous:

France and Germany must take the lead together. Great Britain, the British Commonwealth of Nations, mighty America and I trust Soviet Russia - for then indeed all would be well - must be the friends and sponsors of the new Europe and must champion its right to live and shine. Therefore I say to you: let Europe arise!

ZVS (ZVS) Abbreviation for: Zentralstelle für die Vergabe von →Studienplätzen, which was formerly responsible for allocating university places for subjects with central admissions restrictions such as medicine, pedagogics, information systems, etc., until 2008, when it was replaced by the →Stiftung für Hochschulzulassung.

Zwangsberatung (forced counselling) Administrative method of the examinations office to encourage students whose studies are delayed to accelerate them and hold to the →curriculum (→Langzeitstudenten). A ~ is used, for example, if a student does not register for a mandatory examination or cannot register because the required credits are lacking. The ~ is thus a step before expulsion (→Zwangsexmatrikulation) in order to make the student aware of the risks of the delays.

Zwangsexmatrikulation (forced deregistration, expulsion) Deregistering a student due to missed deadlines or failed examinations (→Prüfung). However, the ~ is in general always an emergency option at the end of a longer process of escalation.

Zweithörer (no direct translation) A student enrolled at a university who also attends courses (→Lehrveranstaltungen) at a second university.

Zweitstudium (second degree program) When a student who has completed a degree program chooses to start another degree in a different subject. The ~ does not include an advanced degree program (→Aufbaustudium, →Master), which builds on the first degree. Fees are usually assessed for a ~.

Zwischenprüfung (intermediate examination) Combination of examinations (→Klausur, →Prüfung) and showing proof (→Vorlage) of credits to complete the basic study period (→Grundstudium), usually in the humanities and comparable with the preliminary Diplom (→Vordiplom).

Zwischenprüfungsordnung (intermediate examination regulations) University-specific regulations for carrying out the intermediate examination according to requirements and deadlines.

Annex

List of Abbreviations in Academic Publications (German and English)

a.a.O.	am angeführten Ort (in the location listed)
Abb.	Abbildung (picture, image)
Abs.	Absatz (paragraph)
Anh.	Anhang (attachment, annex)
Anm.	Anmerkung (comment)
Art.	Artikel (article)
Aufl.	Auflage (edition)
bearb.	bearbeitet (edited)
Bd.	Band (volume)
Bde	Bände (volumes)
cf.	confer, compare
comp.	compiled by, compiler, compilation
Diss.	Dissertation
Dok.	Dokument (document)
ebd.	ebenda (ibid)
Ed. (in a German text)	Edition
ed. (in an English text)	edited by, editor, edition
et. al.	et alii
f.	folgende
ff.	fortfolgende
Fn.	Fußnote (footnote)
gem.	gemäß (according to)
ggf.	gegebenenfalls (possibly)
Habil.	Habilitationsschrift (post-doctoral lecturing qualification thesis)
Hg	Herausgeber (editor)
ibid.	ibidem

Kap.	Kapitel (chapter)
n.d.	no date
n.p.	no place
n.pag	no pagination
narr.	narrated by, narrator, narration
ns	new series
o.J.	ohne Jahr (no year)
o.O.	ohne Ort (no location)
o.O.u.J.	ohne Ort und Jahr (no location or year)
qtd.	quoted
rpt.	reprint, reprinted
S.	Seite (page)
s.	siehe (see)
trans.	translated by, translator, translation
übers.	übersetzt (translated)
unver.	unverändert (unchanged)
u.U.	unter Umständen (possibly)
veränd.	verändert (changed)
verb.	verbessert (corrected)
vgl.	vergleiche (cf.)
vollst.	vollständig (complete)
Vorw.	Vorwort (forward)
z.B.	zum Beispiel (for example, e.g.)
Ziff.	Ziffer (number)

List of Abbreviations in and around the university (including apartment ads)

AAA	→Akademisches Auslandsamt (office of international affairs)
AG	→Arbeitsgruppe (working group)
AiP	→Arzt im Praktikum (first-year resident doctor)
AK	Arbeitskreis (working group)
App	Appartement (apartment)
→AStA	Allgemeiner Studierenden Ausschuss (student steering committee)
BA	→Bachelor; →Berufsakademie (university of cooperative education); Business Administration
→BaföG	Bundesausbildungsförderungsgesetz (federal financial assistance for education)
Bd. (apartment ad)	Bad (bathroom)
Bes. (apartment ad)	Besichtigung (viewing)
Bj (apartment ad)	Baujahr (year built)
BK (apartment ad)	Betriebskosten (maintenance costs)
BLK (apartment ad)	Balkon (balcony)
BW/BaWa (apartment ad)	Badewanne (bathtub)
c.t.	cum tempore, 15 Minuten später als die volle Stunde, →akademisches Viertel (academic quarter-hour)
CBT	→computer-based training
→CHE	Centrum für Hochschulentwicklung (Center for University Development)
CO (in course catalog)	→Kolloquium (colloquium)
DAAD	→Deutscher Akademischer Austauschdienst (German Academic Exchange Service)
DFG	→Deutsche Forschungsgemeinschaft (German Research Foundation)
DG (apartment ad)	Dachgeschoss (attic floor, top floor)
→DSH	Deutsche Sprachprüfung für den Hochschulzugang (German language test for university admission)

DSW	→Deutsches Studentenwerk (German National Association of Student Affairs)
Du. (apartment ad)	Dusche (shower)
EBK (apartment ad)	Einbauküche (kitchen included)
ECTS	→European Credit Transfer System
EG (apartment ad)	Erdgeschoss (ground floor)
ELW (apartment ad)	Einliegerwohnung (in-law suite)
EX (in course catalog)	→Exkursion (excursion)
Fak.	→Fakultät (faculty)
GATE	→Guide to Academic Training and Education
GEW	→Gewerkschaft Erziehung und Wissenschaft (German Union for Education and Science)
GS	→Grundstudium (basic study period)
HFG	→Hochschulfreiheitsgesetz (Freedom of Institutes of Higher Education Act)
HIS	→Hochschul-Informationssystem (university information system)
Hiwi	wissenschaftliche Hilfskraft (student assistant)
HK (apartment ad)	Heizkosten (heating costs)
HRK	→Hochschulrektorenkonferenz (German Rectors' Conference)
HRG	→Hochschulrahmengesetz (German Higher Education Framework Act)
HS (in course catalog)	→Hauptseminar (advanced seminar)
→ILIAS	Integriertes Lern-, Information- und Arbeitskooperations-System (Integrated learning, information, and working cooperation system)
KDB (apartment ad)	Küche, Dusche und Bad (kitchen, shower, and toilet)
Kel. (apartment ad)	Keller (cellar)
KM (apartment ad)	Kaltmiete (rent without utilities)
KMK	→Kultusministerkonferenz (Conference of the Ministers of Education)
KT (apartment ad)	Kaution (deposit)

KVV	→kommentiertes Vorlesungsverzeichnis (commented course catalog)
LA	→Lehramt (teaching profession)
MA	→Magister Artium (German Master's degree) or →Master
Möbl. (apartment ad)	möbliert (furnished)
Mtl. (apartment ad)	monatlich (monthly)
n.A. (apartment ad)	nach Absprache (by arrangement)
NC	Numerus Clausus (admission restrictions);
NK (apartment ad)	Nebenkosten (utilities, usually does not include electricity)
N.N.	→Nomen Nominandum (yet to be named)
NR (apartment ad)	Nichtraucher (non-smoker)
n.V.	nach Vereinbarung (by appointment, by arrangement)
OG (apartment ad)	Obergeschoss (upper level)
→OPAC	Online Public Access Catalogue
PA	→Prüfungsamt (examinations office)
PO	→Prüfungsordnung (examination regulations)
Prof.	→Professor
PS (in course catalog)	→Proseminar (introductory seminar)
RV	→Ringvorlesung (lecture series)
SFB	→Sonderforschungsbereich (collaborative research center)
SS	Sommersemester (→Semester) (summer semester)
SWS	→Semesterwochenstunden (contact hours per week)
SZ (apartment ad)	Schlafzimmer (bedroom)
→TOEFL	Test of English as a Foreign Language
→TVÖD-L	Tarifvertrag für den öffentlichen Dienst der Länder (collective bargaining agreement of the *Länder*)
→Ü	Übung (exercise course)
UB	→Universitätsbibliothek (university library)
UG (apartment ad)	Untergeschoss (basement, lower level)

Univ.	→Universität (university)
VL (in course catalog)	→Vorlesung (lecture)
VO	Verordnung (ordinance)
Wfl./Wohnfl. (apartment ad)	Wohnfläche (floor space)
Whg (apartment ad)	Wohnung (apartment)
wiss. MA	wissenschaftlicher Mitarbeiter (research associate)
WM (apartment ad)	Warmmiete (rent including utilities, often without electricity)
WZ (apartment ad)	Wohnzimmer (living room)
ZB (apartment ad)	Zimmer mit Bad (room with bathroom)
Zi (apartment ad)	Zimmer (room)
ZuLa	→Zulassung (admission)
Zzgl./zgl. (apartment ad)	zuzüglich (not including)

Oral forms of address

Degree/Status

Baccalaureus
(secondary school diploma)

Dekan
(Dean)

Diplom
(Diplom degree)

Doktor
(doctorate)

Doktor h.c.
(honorary doctorate)

Doctor habil.
(post-doctoral lecturing qualification)

Honorarprofessor
(honorary professor)

Lizentiat
(licentiate)

Magister Artium/Master

Präsident
(president)

Professor

Rektor
(rector/president)

Address

Herr *Last Name*
Frau *Last Name*

Herr Professor/Herr Dekan/
Spektabilität (formal)
Frau Professorin/
Frau Dekanin/
Spektabilität (formal)

Herr *Last Name*
Frau *Last Name*

Herr Doktor *Last Name*
Frau Doktor *Last Name*

Herr Doktor *Last Name*
Frau Doktor *Last Name*

Herr Doktor *Last Name*
Frau Doktor *Last Name*

Herr Professor *Last Name*
Frau Professorin *Last Name*

Herr *Last Name*
Frau *Last Name*

Herr *Last Name*
Frau *Last Name*

Herr Professor *Last Name*
Frau Professorin *Last Name*

Herr Professor *Last Name*
Frau Professorin *Last Name*

Herr Professor *Last Name*
Frau Professorin *Last Name*

Written forms of address for postal addresses on letters

Degree/Status	Address
Baccalaureus (secondary school diploma)	Herr *Last Name* B.A. Frau *Last Name* B.A.
Dekan (Dean)	An den Dekan der Fakultät x der Universität y, Herrn Prof. *First and Last Name* An die Dekanin der Fakultät x der Universität y, Frau Prof. *First and Last Name*
Diplom (Diplom degree)	Herrn Dipl.-Subject Abbreviation *First and Last Name* Frau Dipl. Subject Abbreviation *First and Last Name*
Doktor (doctorate)	Herrn Dr.-Subject Abbreviation *First and Last Name* Frau Dr.-Subject Abbreviation *First and Last Name*
Doktor h.c. (honorary doctorate)	Herrn Dr.-Subject Abbreviation *First and Last Name* Frau Dr.-Subject Abbreviation *First and Last Name*
Doctor habil. (post-doctoral lecturing qualification)	Herrn Dr.-Subject Abbreviation *First and Last Name* Frau Dr.-Subject Abbreviation *First and Last Name*
Honorarprofessor (honorary professor)	Herrn Prof. Dr. *First and Last Name* Frau Prof. Dr. *First and Last Name*
Lizentiat (licentiate)	Herrn Lic. theol *First and Last Name* Frau Lic. theol *First and Last Name*
Magister Artium/Master	Herrn *First and Last Name* M.A./MBA/M.Sc. Frau *First and Last Name* M.A./MBA/M.Sc.
Präsident (president)	An den Präsident der Universität x Herrn Prof. Dr. *First and Last Name* An die Präsidentin der Universität x Frau Prof. Dr. *First and Last Name*

Professor	Herrn Prof. Dr. *First and Last Name*
	Frau Prof. Dr. *First and Last Name*
Rektor	An den Rektor der Universität x
(rector/president)	Herr Prof. Dr. *First and Last Name*
	An die Rektorin der Universität x
	Frau Prof. Dr. *First and Last Name*

Written forms of address for e-mails and letters
(Note: If a person holds multiple titles, only the highest is used)

Degree/Status	Address
Baccalaureus (secondary school diploma)	Herr *Last Name* Frau *Last Name*
Dekan (Dean)	Herr Professor/Herr Dekan/ Spektabilität (formal) Frau Professorin/Frau Dekanin/ Spektabilität (formal)
Diplom (Diplom degree)	Herr *Last Name* Frau *Last Name*
Doktor (doctorate)	Herr Dr. *Last Name* Frau Dr. *Last Name*
Doktor h.c. (honorary doctorate)	Herr Dr. *Last Name* Frau Dr. *Last Name*
Doctor habil. (post-doctoral lecturing qualification)	Herr Dr. *Last Name* Frau Dr. *Last Name*
Honorarprofessor (honorary professor)	Herr Professor *Last Name* Frau Professorin *Last Name*
Lizentiat (licentiate)	Herr *Last Name* Frau *Last Name*
Magister Artium/Master	Herr *Last Name* Frau *Last Name*
Präsident (president)	Herr Professor *Last Name* Frau Professorin *Last Name*
Professor	Herr Professor *Last Name* Frau Professorin *Last Name*
Rektor (rector/president)	Herr Professor *Last Name*/ Magnifizenz (formal) Frau Professorin *Last Name*/ Magnifizenz (formal)

Lists of Universities

German Universities according to Size

Source: Statistisches Bundesamt (2014/15)

1. Fernuniversität in Hagen:	77,395 students
2. Universität München:	52,006 students
3. Universität zu Köln:	49,772 students
4. Universität Frankfurt am Main:	46,613 students
5. Ruhr-Universität Bochum:	42,718 students
6. Westfälische Wilhelms-Universität:	42,592 students
7. RWTH Aachen:	42,300 students
8. Universität Hamburg:	42,106 students
9. Universität Duisburg-Essen:	41,065 students
10. Universität Erlangen-Nürnberg:	39,414 students

European Universities according to Founding Year

1. University of Bologna, founded 1088
2. University of Oxford, founded 1096
3. University of Paris, founded 1150
4. University of Modena, founded 1175
5. University of Cambridge, founded ca. 1208
6. University of Salamanca, founded 1218
7. University of Padua, founded 1222
8. University of Naples, founded 1224
9. University of Siena, founded 1240
10. University of Coimbra, Lisbon, founded 1290
11. Complutense University of Madrid, founded 1293
12. University of Rome, founded 1303
13. University of Pisa, founded 1343
14. University of Prague, founded 1348
15. University of Pavia, founded 1361
16. University of Krakow, founded 1364
17. University of Vienna founded 1365
18. University of Pécs, founded 1367
19. University of Heidelberg, founded 1386
20. University of Ferrara, founded 1391
21. University of Leipzig, founded 1409

Universities in Germany

Akademie der Bildenden Künste Stuttgart

Albert-Ludwigs-Universität Freiburg, Freiburg im Breisgau

Alice-Salomon-Fachhochschule für Sozialarbeit und Sozialpädagogik, Berlin

Bauhaus-Universität Weimar

Bayerische Julius-Maximilians-Universität Würzburg

Bergische Universität Wuppertal

Berufsakademie Heidenheim

Berufsakademie Karlsruhe

Berufsakademie Lörrach

Berufsakademie Mannheim

Berufsakademie Mosbach

Berufsakademie Ravensburg

Berufsakademie Stuttgart

Brandenburgische Technische Universität Cottbus

Bundesakademie für Wehrverwaltung und Wehrtechnik Mannheim

Burg Giebichenstein Hochschule für Kunst und Design, Halle

Carl-von-Ossietzky-Universität Oldenburg

Christian-Albrechts-Universität, Kiel

Deutsche Sporthochschule Köln

E.A.P. Europäische Wirtschaftshochschule, Berlin

Eberhard-Karls-Universität Tübingen

ehemalige Universität Fulda

ehemalige Universität Herborn

Ernst-Moritz-Arndt-Universität Greifswald

Europa Fachhochschule Fresenius Köln

Europa-Universität Viadrina, Frankfurt (Oder)

Evangelische Fachhochschule Darmstadt

Evangelische Fachhochschule Freiburg im Breisgau

Evangelische Fachhochschule für Sozialarbeit und Sozialpädagogik, Berlin

Evangelische Fachhochschule Hannover

Evangelische Fachhochschule Reutlingen-Ludwigsburg

Evangelische Fachhochschule Rheinland-Westfalen-Lippe, Bochum

Evangelische Hochschule für Kirchenmusik Halle

Evangelische Hochschule für soziale Arbeit Dresden

Fachhochschule Aachen

Fachhochschule Aalen

Fachhochschule Albstadt-Sigmaringen

Fachhochschule Ansbach

Fachhochschule Aschaffenburg

Fachhochschule Augsburg

Fachhochschule Biberach, an der Riß

Fachhochschule Bielefeld

Fachhochschule Bochum

Fachhochschule Bonn-Rhein-Sieg

Fachhochschule Brandenburg

Fachhochschule Braunschweig/Wolfenbüttel

Fachhochschule Buxtehude

Fachhochschule Coburg

Fachhochschule Darmstadt

Fachhochschule Deggendorf,

Fachhochschule des Bundes für öffentliche Verwaltung Mannheim

Fachhochschule Dortmund

Fachhochschule Erfurt

Fachhochschule Frankfurt am Main

Fachhochschule Fulda, Fulda

Fachhochschule für Kunsttherapie Nürtingen, Nürtingen

Fachhochschule für öffentliche Verwaltung Kehl

Fachhochschule für öffentliche Verwaltung Ludwigsburg

Fachhochschule für Rechtspflege Nordrhein-Westfalen, Bad Münstereifel

Fachhochschule für Sozialwesen Esslingen

Fachhochschule für Sozialwesen Mannheim

Fachhochschule für Technik und Gestaltung Mannheim

Fachhochschule für Technik und Wirtschaft, Berlin

Fachhochschule für Verwaltung und Rechtspflege Berlin

Fachhochschule für Verwaltungswissenschaften, Speyer
Fachhochschule für Wirtschaft, Berlin
Fachhochschule Furtwangen
Fachhochschule Gelsenkirchen
Fachhochschule Gießen-Friedberg, Friedberg
Fachhochschule Gießen-Friedberg, Gießen
Fachhochschule Hamburg
Fachhochschule Hannover
Fachhochschule Heidelberg
Fachhochschule Heilbronn
Fachhochschule Hof
Fachhochschule Ingolstadt
Fachhochschule Jena
Fachhochschule Kaiserslautern
Fachhochschule Kaiserslautern, Pirmasens
Fachhochschule Kaiserslautern, Zweibrücken
Fachhochschule Karlsruhe
Fachhochschule Kempten
Fachhochschule Kiel
Fachhochschule Köln
Fachhochschule Konstanz
Fachhochschule Landshut
Fachhochschule Lippe und Höxter, Detmold
Fachhochschule Lippe und Höxter, Höxter
Fachhochschule Lippe und Höxter, Lemgo
Fachhochschule Magdeburg-Stendal
Fachhochschule Merseburg
Fachhochschule Minden
Fachhochschule München
Fachhochschule Münster
Fachhochschule Neubrandenburg
Fachhochschule Neu-Ulm
Fachhochschule NORDAKADEMIE, Elmshorn

Fachhochschule Nordhausen

Fachhochschule Nordostniedersachsen, Lüneburg, Suderburg, Buxtehude

Fachhochschule Nürtingen

Fachhochschule Offenburg

Fachhochschule Oldenburg/Ostfriesland/Wilhelmshaven

Fachhochschule Osnabrück

Fachhochschule Pforzheim

Fachhochschule Ravensburg-Weingarten

Fachhochschule Regensburg

Fachhochschule Rosenheim

Fachhochschule Rottenburg

Fachhochschule Schmalkalden

Fachhochschule Schwäbisch Gmünd

Fachhochschule Senftenberg

Fachhochschule Stralsund

Fachhochschule Stuttgart - Hochschule der Medien

Fachhochschule Stuttgart - Hochschule für Technik

Fachhochschule Telekom, Leipzig

Fachhochschule Theologisches Seminar des Bundes Evangelisch-Freikirchlicher Gemeinden, Wustermark-Elstal

Fachhochschule Ulm

Fachhochschule Weihenstephan, Freising und Triesdorf

Fachhochschule Westküste, Heide

Fachhochschule Würzburg-Schweinfurt

Fern-Universität in Hagen

FHT Esslingen

Filmakademie Baden-Württemberg, Ludwigsburg

Folkwang Hochschule, Essen

Freie Universität Berlin

Friedrich-Alexander-Universität Erlangen-Nürnberg

Friedrich-Schiller-Universität Jena

FU-School of Personal Relations, Berlin

Georg-August-Universität Göttingen

Georg-Simon-Ohm-Fachhochschule Nürnberg

Hamburger Universität für Wirtschaft und Politik

Heinrich-Heine-Universität Düsseldorf

Helmut-Schmidt-Universität - Universität der Bundeswehr Hamburg

Hochschule Bremen

Hochschule Bremerhaven

Hochschule für Bankwirtschaft, Frankfurt am Main

Hochschule für Bildende Künste Braunschweig

Hochschule für Bildende Künste Dresden

Hochschule für Bildende Künste Hamburg

Hochschule für Gestaltung Karlsruhe

Hochschule für Grafik und Buchkunst, Leipzig

Hochschule für Jüdische Studien, Heidelberg

Hochschule für Kirchenmusik Dresden

Hochschule für Kirchenmusik, Herford

Hochschule für Musik Dresden

Hochschule für Musik Franz Liszt Weimar

Hochschule für Musik Freiburg im Breisgau

Hochschule für Musik *Hanns Eisler*, Berlin

Hochschule für Musik Karlsruhe, Karlsruhe

Hochschule für Musik und Darstellende Kunst, Frankfurt am Main

Hochschule für Musik und Kunst Hannover

Hochschule für Musik und Theater Hamburg

Hochschule für Musik und Theater Rostock

Hochschule für Musik und Theater, Leipzig

Hochschule für Musik, Köln

Hochschule für Schauspielkunst *Ernst Busch*, Berlin

Hochschule für Technik und Wirtschaft Dresden

Hochschule für Technik, Wirtschaft und Kultur, Leipzig

Hochschule Harz - Hochschule für angewandte Wissenschaften

Hochschule Mittweida

Hochschule Reutlingen

Hochschule Vechta

Hochschule Wismar

Hochschule Zittau

Humboldt-Universität zu Berlin

International School of Management, Dortmund

Johannes Gutenberg-Universität Mainz

Johann-Wolfgang-Goethe-Universität Frankfurt am Main

Justus-Liebig-Universität Gießen

Katholische Fachhochschule Freiburg im Breisgau

Katholische Fachhochschule Münster

Katholische Fachhochschule Nordrhein-Westfalen, Köln

Katholische Fachhochschule, Berlin

Katholische Universität Eichstätt-Ingolstadt

Kunsthochschule Berlin-Weißensee Hochschule für Gestaltung, Berlin

Kunsthochschule für Medien Köln

Ludwig-Maximilians-Universität München

Martin-Luther-Universität Halle-Wittenberg

Medizinische Hochschule Hannover

Merz Akademie, Stuttgart

Multimedia Campus Kiel

Munich Business School, München

Musikhochschule Lübeck

Muthesius Hochschule Kiel

Naturwissenschaftlich-Technische Akademie Isny

Otto-Friedrich-Universität, Bamberg

Otto-von-Guericke-Universität Magdeburg

Pädagogische Hochschule Freiburg im Breisgau

Pädagogische Hochschule Heidelberg

Pädagogische Hochschule Ludwigsburg

Pädagogische Hochschule Schwäbisch Gmünd

Pädagogische Hochschule Weingarten

Palucca Schule Dresden

Philipps-Universität Marburg, Marburg

Philosophisch-theologische Hochschule St. Georgen der Jesuiten, Frankfurt (Main)

Rheinische Fachhochschule Köln

Rheinische Friedrich-Wilhelms-Universität, Bonn

Rheinisch-Westfälische Technische Hochschule Aachen

Ruhr-Universität, Bochum

Ruprecht-Karls-Universität Heidelberg

Staatliche Hochschule für bildende Künste, Frankfurt am Main

Staatliche Hochschule für Musik Trossingen

Staatliche Hochschule für Musik und Darstellende Kunst Mannheim

Staatliche Studienakademie, Gera

Technische Fachhochschule Berlin

Technische Fachhochschule Georg Agricola Bochum

Technische Fachhochschule Wildau

Technische Universität Bergakademie Freiberg

Technische Universität Berlin

Technische Universität Braunschweig

Technische Universität Chemnitz

Technische Universität Clausthal

Technische Universität Darmstadt

Technische Universität Dresden

Technische Universität Garching

Technische Universität Hamburg-Harburg

Technische Universität Ilmenau

Technische Universität Kaiserslautern

Technische Universität München

Technische Universität Weihenstephan, Freising

Thüringer Fachhochschule für öffentliche Verwaltung Gotha

Tierärztliche Hochschule, Hannover

Ukrainische Freie Universität, München

Universität Augsburg

Universität Bayreuth

Universität Bielefeld

Universität Bremen,
Universität der Künste Berlin, (ehemals Hochschule der Künste Berlin)
Universität des Saarlandes, Homburg
Universität des Saarlandes, Saarbrücken
Universität Dortmund
Universität Duisburg-Essen
Universität Duisburg-Essen
Universität Erfurt
Universität Hamburg
Universität Hannover
Universität Hildesheim
Universität Hohenheim
Universität Karlsruhe
Universität Kassel
Universität Koblenz-Landau
Universität Konstanz
Universität Leipzig
Universität Lüneburg
Universität Mannheim
Universität Osnabrück
Universität Paderborn
Universität Passau
Universität Potsdam,
Universität Regensburg
Universität Rostock
Universität Siegen
Universität Stuttgart
Universität Trier
Universität Ulm
Universität Witten/Herdecke
Universität zu Köln
Universität zu Lübeck
Westfälische Wilhelms-Universität Münster
Zeppelin University Friedrichshafen

Universities in Austria

Akademie der bildenden Künste, Wien
Donau-Universität Krems, Krems
Fachhochschul-Campus Wien
Fachhochschule der Wirtschaft Wien
Fachhochschule des Berufsförderungsinstituts Wien
Fachhochschule für Biotechnische Verfahren, Tulln
Fachhochschule Hagenberg
Fachhochschule Holztechnikum Kuchl
Fachhochschule Salzburg
Fachhochschule St. Pölten
Fachhochschule Steyr
Fachhochschule Technikum Kärnten, Feldkirchen/Spittal an der Drau/Villach
Fachhochschule Technikum Wien
Fachhochschule Tirol, Innsbruck
Fachhochschule Vorarlberg, Dornbirn
Fachhochschule Wels
Fachhochschule Wiener Neustadt
Fachhochschul-Studiengänge Kufstein
FH Burgenland, Eisenstadt/Pinkafeld
FH Joanneum, Graz/Kapfenberg/Bad Gleichenberg
IMC Fachhochschule Krems, Krems
Johannes-Kepler-Universität Linz
Karl-Franzens-Universität Graz
Katholisch-Theologische Privatuniversität Linz
Leopold-Franzens-Universität Innsbruck
Management Center Innsbruck
Medizinische Universität Graz
Medizinische Universität Innsbruck
Medizinische Universität Wien
Montanuniversität Leoben
Paracelsus Medizinische Privatuniversität Salzburg

Paris-Lodron-Universität Salzburg
Philosophisch-Theologische Hochschule, Stift Heiligenkreuz
Private Universität für Medizinische Informatik und Technik Tirol, Innsbruck
Technische Universität Graz
Technische Universität Wien
Theresianische Militärakademie, Wiener Neustadt
Universität für angewandte Kunst Wien
Universität für Bodenkultur Wien
Universität für künstlerische und industrielle Gestaltung Linz
Universität für Musik und Darstellende Kunst Graz
Universität für Musik und darstellende Kunst Wien
Universität Klagenfurt, Klagenfurt
Universität Mozarteum Salzburg
Universität Wien
Veterinärmedizinische Universität Wien
Wirtschaftsuniversität Wien

Universities in Switzerland

AKAD Hochschule für Berufstätige

Berner Fachhochschule (BFH)

École Polytechnique Fédérale de Lausanne

Eidgenössische Fachhochschule für Sport in Magglingen

Eidgenössische Fachhochschule für Sport Magglingen

Eidgenössische Technische Hochschule Zürich

Fachhochschule Aargau Nordwestschweiz

Fachhochschule beider Basel (FHBB)

Fachhochschule Solothurn in Olten Fachhochschule

Fachhochschule Wallis in Sierre

Fachhochschule Zentralschweiz in Luzern

Fernfachhochschule Schweiz

Hochschule für Angewandte Psychologie in Zürich

Hochschule für Gestaltung und Kunst Luzern

Hochschule für Gestaltung und Kunst Zürich

Hochschule für Musik und Theater

Hochschule für Musik und Theater in Zürich und Winterthur

Hochschule für Pädagogik und Soziale Arbeit beider Basel

Hochschule für Soziale Arbeit Zürich

Hochschule für Technik in Buchs

Hochschule für Technik Rapperswil

Hochschule für Technik und Architektur in Horw bei Luzern

Hochschule für Technik und Wirtschaft in Chur

Hochschule für Technik Zürich

Hochschule für Wirtschaft Luzern

Hochschule Wädenswil in Wädenswil

Höhere Fachschule für Drogistinnen und Drogisten in Neuenburg

Hotelfachschule Lausanne

Institut für Finanz und Management (IFM) in Genf

Lemania College in Lausanne

Musikhochschule der Musik-Akademie in Basel

Musikhochschule Luzern
Pädagogische Fachhochschule Graubünden in Chur
Pädagogische Hochschule Zentralschweiz
Pädagogische Hochschule Zürich
Private Hochschule Wirtschaft
Schweizerische Hochschule für Landwirtschaft, Zollikofen
Schweizerische Tourismusfachschule in Sierre
Universität Basel
Universität Bern
Universität Freiburg in Freiburg
Universität Genf in Genf
Universität Lausanne
Universität Lugano
Universität Luzern
Universität Neuenburg in Neuenburg
Universität St. Gallen
Zürcher Hochschule Winterthur

List of common subjects

Aerodynamik (Aerodynamics)

Afrikanistik (African Studies)

Agrarwissenschaft (Agricultural Sciences)

Ägyptologie (Egyptology)

Akustik (Acoustics)

Albanologie (Albanology)

Alchemie (Alchemy)

Allgemeinchirurgie (General Surgery)

Allgemeine Chemie (General Chemistry)

Allgemeine Relativitätstheorie (General Theory of Relativity)

Allgemeinmedizin (General Medicine)

Altertumswissenschaft (Classical Studies)

Amerikanistik (American Studies)

Analytische Chemie (Analytical Chemistry)

Anästhesiologie (Anesthesiology)

Angewandte Physik (Applied Physics)

Angiologie (Angiology)

Anglistik (English Studies)

Anorganische Chemie (Inorganic Chemistry)

Anthropologie (Anthropology)

Arbeitswissenschaft (Occupational Science)

Archäologie (Archaeology)

Architektur (Architecture)

Asphalttechnologie (Asphalt Technology)

Assyriologie (Assyriology)

Astronomie (Astronomy)

Astrophysik (Astrophysics), Astronomie (Astronomy)

Atomphysik (Nuclear Physics)

Bakteriologie (Bacteriology)

Baltistik (Baltic Studies)

Bauchchirurgie (Abdominal Surgery)

Bauingenieurwesen (Civil Engineering)
Berechenbarkeitstheorie (Computability Theory)
Berufswissenschaft (Vocational Science)
Betriebswirtschaftslehre (Business Administration)
Bibliothekswissenschaft (Library Science)
Biochemie (Biochemistry)
Bioinformatik (Bioinformatics)
Biologie (Biology)
Biophysik (Biophysics)
Biotechnologie (Biotechnology)
Bohemistik (Czech Studies)
Botanik (Botony)
Brennstoffchemie (Fuel Chemistry)
Buddhismusforschung (Buddhist Studies)
Bulgaristik (Bulgarian Studies)
Chemie (Chemistry)
Chemieingenieurwesen (Chemical Engineering)
Chirurgie (Surgery)
Chronologie (Chronology)
Computerlinguistik (Computational Linguistics)
Computervisualistik (Computational Visualistics)
Demografie (Demography)
Dermatologie (Dermatology)
Design (Design)
Dialektologie (Dialectology)
Diplomatik (Diplomacy)
Elektrodynamik (Electrodynamics)
Elektrotechnik (Electrical Engineering)
Elementarteilchenphysik (Elementary Particle Physics)
Endokrinologie (Endrocrinology)
Epidemiologie (Epidemology)
Ernährungswissenschaft (Nutritional Science)
Erziehungswissenschaft (Electrical Engineering)

Ethnobotanik (Ethnobotany)

Ethnologie (Ethnology)

Ethnomedizin (Ethnomedicine)

Etymologie (Etymology)

Evangelische Theologie (Protestant Theology)

Evolutionslehre (Evolutionary Science)

Experimentalphysik (Experimental Physics)

Fennistik (Finnish Studies)

Festkörperphysik (Solid State Physics)

Filmwissenschaft (Film Science)

Finanzmathematik (Financial Mathematics)

Finanzwirtschaft (Finance)

Finnougristik (Finno-Ugrian Studies)

Forstwissenschaften (Forestry Science)

Galloromanistik (Gallo-Roman Studies)

Gartenbau (Horticulture)

Gastroenterologie (Gastroenterology)

Genealogie (Geneology)

Genetik (Genetics)

Gentechnik (Genetic Engineering)

Geodäsie (Geodesy)

Geografie (Geography)

Geologie (Geology)

Geophysik (Geophysics)

Geowissenschaften (Earth Sciences)

Geriatrie (Geriatrics)

Gerichtsmedizin (Forensic Medicine)

Germanistik (German)

Geschichte (History)

Graphentheorie (Graph Theory)

Gräzistik (Ancient Greek)

Gynäkologie und Geburtshilfe (Obstetrics and Gynecology)

Hals-, Nasen-, Ohrenheilkunde (Otorhinolaryngology)

Hämatologie (Hemotology)
Hepatologie (Hepatology)
Heraldik (Heraldry)
Hermeneutik (Hermeneutics)
Hispanistik (Spanish Studies)
Histologie (Histology)
Hungarologie (Hungarian Studies)
Hydromechanik (Hydromechanics)
Hygiene (Hygiene)
Immunologie (Immunology)
Indologie (Indology)
Industrial Design (Industrial Design)
Informatik (Informatics)
Informationswissenschaft (Information Science)
Ingenieurwissenschaften (Engineering)
Innere Medizin (Internal Medicine)
Intensivmedizin (Intensive Medicine)
Islamwissenschaft (Islamic Studies)
Italianistik (Italian Studies)
Japanologie (Japanese Studies)
Judaistik (Jewish Studies)
Jura (Law)
Kardiologie (Cardiology)
Katholische Theologie (Catholic Theology)
Kaukasiologie (Caucasology)
Keltistik (Celtic Studies)
Kernphysik (Nuclear Physics)
Kinderchirurgie (Pediatric Surgery)
Klassische Mechanik (Classical Mechanics)
Klassische Philologie (Classical Philology)
Klimawandel (Climate Change)
Kombinatorik (Combinatorics)
Kommunikationswissenschaft (Communication Science)

Komplexitätstheorie (Complexity Theory)
Kontinuumsmechanik (Continuum Mechanics)
Koreanistik (Korean Studies)
Kosmologie (Cosmology)
Kroatistik (Croatian Studies)
Kryptografie (Cryptography)
Kulturtechnik (Cultural Technology)
Kunstgeschichte (Art History)
Labormedizin (Laboratory Medicine)
Laserphysik (Laser Physics)
Lateinamerikanistik (Latin American Studies)
Lateinische Philologie (Latin)
Linguistik (Linguistics)
Literaturwissenschaft (Literature)
Logik (Logic)
Logistik (Logistics)
Ludologie (Game Studies)
Lusitanistik (Portuguese Studies)
Marketing (Marketing)
Maschinenbau (Mechanical Engineering)
Mathematik (Mathematics)
Medieninformatik (Media Informatics)
Medienpädagogik (Media Education)
Medienwissenschaft (Media Studies)
Medizin (Medicine)
Medizininformatik (Medical Computing)
Meereskunde (Oceanography)
Metaphysik (Metaphysics)
Meteorologie (Meteorology)
Metrologie (Metrology)
Mikrobiologie (Microbiology)
Molekularphysik (Molecular Physics)
Mongolistik (Mongolian Studies)

Musikwissenschaft (Musicology)
Mythologie (Mythology)
Nautik (Nautical Science)
Neonatologie (Neonatology)
Nephrologie (Nephrology)
Neurochirurgie (Neurosurgery)
Neurologie (Neurology)
Niederlandistik (Dutch Philology)
Notfallmedizin (Emergency Medicine)
Nuklearmedizin (Nuclear Medicine)
Numismatik (Numismatics)
Oberflächenphysik (Surface Physics)
Öffentliches Recht (Public Law)
Ökologie (Ecology)
Ökotrophologie (Home Economics)
Onkologie (Oncology)
Ontologie (Ontology)
Ophthalmologie (Ophthalmology)
Optik (Optics)
Organisationswissenschaften (Organizational Sciences)
Organische Chemie (Organic Chemistry)
Orientalistik (Orientalism)
Orthopädie (Orthopedics)
Ozeanografie (Oceanography)
Pädagogik (Pedagogics)
Pädiatrie (Pediatrics)
Paläobiologie (Paleobiology)
Paläografie (Paleography)
Paläontologie (Paleontology)
Papyrologie (Papyrology)
Parasitologie (Parasitology)
Pathologie (Pathology)
Personalwirtschaft (Human Resources)

Pflegemanagement (Nursing Management)
Pflegewissenschaft (Nursing Science)
Pharmakologie (Pharmacology)
Pharmazie (Pharmaceutics)
Philatelie (Philately)
Philosophie (Philosophy)
Photogrammetrie (Photogrammetry)
Physik (Physics)
Physik der Flüssigkeiten (Fluid Physics)
Physik der Flüssigkristalle (Liquid Crystal Physics)
Physikalische Chemie (Physical Chemistry)
Physiologie (Physiology)
Plastische Chirurgie (Plastic Surgery)
Pneumologie (Pneumology)
Politikwissenschaft (Political Science)
Polonistik (Polish Studies)
Produktdesign (Product Design)
Produktionsmanagement (Production Management)
Projektmanagement (Project Management)
Psychiatrie (Psychiatry)
Psychologie (Psychology)
Psychoonkologie (Psycho-oncology)
Publizistik (Journalism)
Qualitätsmanagement (Quality Management)
Quantenchromodynamik (Quantum Chromodynamics)
Quantenelektrodynamik (Quantum Electrodynamics)
Quantenelektronik (Quantum Electronics)
Quantenphysik (Quantum Physics)
Radiologie (Radiology)
Radioonkologie (Radiation Oncology)
Raumplanung (Spatial Planning)
Rechnungswesen (Accounting)
Rechtswissenschaft (Law)

Relativitätstheorie (Theory of Relativity)

Rhetorik (Rhetoric)

Rheumatologie (Rheumatology)

Romanistik (Romance Studies)

Rumänistik (Romanian Studies)

Russistik (Russian Studies)

Semiotik (Semiotics)

Serbistik (Serbian Studies)

Serbokroatistik (Serbo-Croatian Studies)

Sinologie (Sinology)

Skandinavistik (Scandanavian Studies)

Slawistik (Slavic Studies)

Slowakistik (Slovakian Studies)

Sorabistik (Sorbian Studies)

Sozialpädagogik (Social Education)

Soziologie (Sociology)

Spezielle Relativitätstheorie (Special Theory of Relativity)

Sphragistik (Sphragistics)

Sportwissenschaft (Sports Science)

Sprachwissenschaft (Linguistics)

Standardmodell (Standard Model)

Statistik (Statistics)

Strafrecht (Criminal Law)

Systemtheorie (Systems Theory)

Technische Chemie (Technical Chemistry)

Technische Optik (Technical Optics)

Theaterwissenschaft (Theater Studies)

Theologie (Theology)

Theoretische Chemie (Theoretical Chemistry)

Theoretische Physik (Theoretical Physics)

Thermodynamik (Thermodynamics)

Thoraxchirurgie (Thoracic Surgery)

Tibetologie (Tibetan Studies)

Tourismus (Tourism Studies)
Toxikologie (Toxicology)
Transplantationsmedizin (Transplantation Medicine)
Turkologie (Turkology)
Typografie (Typography)
Ukrainistik (Ukrainian Studies)
Umweltingenieurwesen (Environmental Engineering)
Unfallchirurgie (Trauma Surgery)
Urologie (Urology)
Venerologie (Venereology)
Verfahrenstechnik (Process Engineering)
Verfassungsrecht (Constitutional Law)
Vermessungswesen (Surveying)
Versicherungsmathematik (Insurance Mathematics)
Verwaltungsrecht (Administrative Law)
Verwaltungswissenschaft (Administrative Science)
Veterinärmedizin (Veterinary Medicine)
Vexillologie (Vexillology)
Virologie (Virology)
Völkerkunde (Ethnology)
Volkskunde (Folklore)
Volkswirtschaftslehre (Economics)
Vorsorgemedizin (Preventive Medicine)
Wahrscheinlichkeitstheorie (Probability Theory)
Wasserwirtschaft (Water Management)
Werkstoffwissenschaften (Materials Science)
Wirtschaftsinformatik (Information Systems)
Wirtschaftsingenieurwesen (Industrial Engineering)
Wirtschaftsmathematik (Business Mathematics)
Wirtschaftspolitik (Economic Policy)
Wirtschaftswissenschaften (Business and Economic Sciences)
Wissenschaftshistoriographie (Historiographs of Science)
Zahnmedizin (Dentistry)

Zivilrecht (Civil Law)
Zoologie (Zoology)
Zytologie (Cytology)

Further Literature

ALESI, BETTINA. *Lebenslanges Lernen und Hochschulen in Deutschland. Literaturbericht und annotierte Bibliographie (1990-1999) zur Entwicklung und aktuellen Situation.* Wittenberg 1999.

AMMON, ULRICH. *Ist Deutsch noch internationale Wissenschaftssprache? Englisch auch für die Lehre an den deutschsprachigen Hochschulen.* Berlin 1998.

AVENARIUS, HERMANN. *Hochschulen und Reformgesetzgebung. Zur Anpassung der Länderhochschulgesetze an das Hochschulrahmengesetz.* Berlin 1979.

BRETSCHNEIDER, FALK. PASTERNACK, PEER (Ed.). *Akademische Rituale. Symbolische Praxis an Hochschulen.* Leipzig 1999.

BURCHARDT, ANJA. *Blaustrumpf - Modestudentin – Anarchistin? Deutsche und russische Medizinstudentinnen in Berlin 1896 – 1918.* Stuttgart 1997.

COBBAN, ALAN B. *English University Life in the Middle Ages.* London 1999.

CZESCHLIK, DIETER. (Ed.). *Irrtümer in der Wissenschaft.* Berlin 1987.

DAHRENDORF, RALF. *Universities after Communism.* Hamburg 2000.

DEMANDT, ALEXANDER. *Stätten des Geistes: große Universitäten Europas von der Antike bis zur Gegenwart.* Cologne 1999.

DEWEDNEY, A. D. *200 Prozent von Nichts. Die geheimen Tricks der Statistik und andere Schwindeleien mit Zahlen.* Basel 1994.

FÜSSEL, STEPHAN. *Im Zentrum: das Buch.* Mainz 1997.

GOLÜCKE, FRIEDHELM. *Studentenwörterbuch.* Würzburg 1987.

GRENDLER, PAUL F. *The Universities of the Italian Renaissance.* Baltimore 2002.

HAMMERSTEIN, NOTKER. (Ed.). *Universitäten und Aufklärung.* Göttingen 1995.

HAMMERSTEIN, NOTKER. *Antisemitismus und deutsche Universitäten: 1871 – 1933.* Frankfurt/Main. 1995.

KOCKA, JÜRGEN. (Hg.). *Universitäten und Eliten im Osten nach 1945.* Göttingen 1998.

MIETHGE, JÜRGEN. *Studieren an mittelalterlichen Universitäten.* Leiden 2004.

MÜHLBERGER, KURT. *Aspekte der Bildungs- und Universitätsgeschichte: 16. bis 19. Jahrhundert.* Wien 1993.

MÜLLER-BÖLING, DETLEF (Ed.). *Qualitätssicherung in Hochschulen, Forschung, Lehre, Management.* Gütersloh 1995.

NOAM CHOMSKY. *The Cold War & the University: Toward an Intellectual History of the Postwar Years.* New York 1997.

RENATE HEUER. SIEGBERT WOLF (Ed.). *Die Juden der Frankfurter Universität.* New York 1997.

ROGGER, FRANZISKA. *Der Doktorhut im Besenschrank. Das abenteuerliche Leben der ersten Studentinnen - am Beispiel der Universität Bern.* Bern 1999.

RÖSLER, ALBRECHT. BOECKMANN, KLAUS B. SLIVENSKY, SUSANNA. (Ed.). *An japanischen Hochschulen lehren. Zur Vermittlung von Sprache und Kultur der deutschsprachigen Länder - ein Handbuch.* Munich 2000.

SAGER, PETER. *Oxford & Cambridge: eine Kulturgeschichte.* Frankfurt/Main 2003.

SEIDENSPINNER, GUNDOLF. *Hochschul-Lexikon.*1991.

THIESSEN, FRIEDRICH. (Ed.). *Aufbruch an deutschen Hochschulen. Beiträge zur Reform des deutschen Hochschulwesens.* Berlin 2000.

TURNER, GEORG. *Hochschule zwischen Vorstellung und Wirklichkeit. Zur Geschichte der Hochschulreform im letzten Drittel des 20. Jahrhunderts.* Berlin 2001.

TURNER, GEORG/WEBER, JOACHIM D. *Das Fischer Hochschullexikon. Begriffe Studienfächer Anschriften*, Frankfurt /M 1998.

VERWEYEN, THEODOR. *Bücherverbrennungen.* Heidelberg 2000.

WEBER, WOLFGANG E.J. *Geschichte der europäischen Universität.* Stuttgart 2002.

WETTMANN, ANDREA. *Heimatfront Universität: preußische Hochschulpolitik und die Universität Marburg im Ersten Weltkrieg.* Cologne 2000.

WITT, ARMIN *Das Galilei Syndrom. Unterdrückte Entdeckungen und Erfindungen.* Munich 1992.

ibidem-Verlag

Melchiorstr. 15

D-70439 Stuttgart

info@ibidem-verlag.de

www.ibidem-verlag.de
www.ibidem.eu
www.edition-noema.de
www.autorenbetreuung.de